Also available at all good book stores

9781785317927

9781801500630

9781801500067

9781801500500

9781785318245

9781801500586

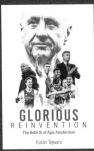

9781801500692

9781801501323

9781801501149

The
Nearly
Men

The Nearly Men

THE ETERNAL ALLURE OF THE GREATEST TEAMS THAT FAILED TO WIN THE WORLD CUP

AIDAN WILLIAMS

First published by Pitch Publishing, 2022

Pitch Publishing
9 Donnington Park,
85 Birdham Road,
Chichester,
West Sussex,
PO20 7AJ
www.pitchpublishing.co.uk
info@pitchpublishing.co.uk

A CIP catalogue record is available for this book
from the British Library.

ISBN 978 1 80150 093 7

Typesetting and origination by Pitch Publishing
Printed and bound in India by Replika Press Pvt. Ltd.

Contents

For Sarah, Elliot and Iris

Acknowledgements

THERE ARE, of course, a huge number of people to thank for helping me make this book a reality. My colleagues at *These Football Times* have been hugely inspirational, influential and helpful. In particular, my thanks goes to Omar Saleem for giving me the platform to develop and showcase my writing online and in magazines, enabling it to progress from an interest to a hobby to a passion. And to Stuart Horsfield, Steven Scragg and Gary Thacker for the hours spent chatting about subjects like this on podcasts, and for inspiring and encouraging this project. The simple advice to write the book you would like to read is the best guidance anyone could give. The rest of the *These Football Times* community have been equally supportive and encouraging throughout.

Many people have directly assisted in the research and development of the various subjects covered in the book, all taking the time and effort to share their knowledge. The Dutch football writer Elko Born was very helpful on several chapters, as was the Brazilian journalist Fernando Duarte, both providing an excellent local perspective. So too did Nebojša Marković on matters Yugoslav and Ricardo Serrado on Portugal, both with hugely valuable insight. David

Bailey helped add thoughts and detail to my Hungarian sections, as did Richard Hall about Italy and Tom Middler for Austria. Dean Lockyer assisted with some background on his specialism, the 1930 World Cup.

Dr Peter Watson, South American Studies Fellow at Leeds University, gave a huge amount of helpful insight into the wider implications discussed in all of the South American chapters. I'm grateful too to Chris Lee for providing some contacts, while others fell my way courtesy of the podcasts I'm lucky enough to be involved in at *These Football Times*.

Jane Camillin at Pitch Publishing must be thanked for giving me the chance to have my thoughts published, and for all the assistance throughout. As must Duncan Olner, whose artistic talents produced a wonderful cover design from little more than my vague suggestions.

And finally, to my wife, Sarah, for encouraging and supporting me throughout, and for reading the drafts on a subject she strangely doesn't share my passion for. And to my children Elliot and Iris who think it's all terribly exciting.

Introduction

*Maybe we were the real winners in the end. I
think the world remembers our team more.*

Johan Cruyff

CLOSE YOUR eyes and let your mind wander through the
images of World Cups past. Picture the decisive incidents,
the great teams, the magical moments. You may see Diego
Maradona surging through the England defence on his way
to delivering the 1986 World Cup. Maybe you see Pelé and
Carlos Alberto in 1970, or Geoff Hurst's hat-trick and
Bobby Moore lifting the trophy in 1966. Perhaps you see
Kylian Mbappé, Mario Götze, Andrés Iniesta or Zinedine
Zidane delivering glory.

Those are the images of victory. Decisive moments that
led to the claiming of what remains the most iconic and
sought-after trophy in football. But I'll wager you also saw
Zico, Sócrates and Falcão in 1982, slain by Paolo Rossi's
bolt from the blue.

Or perhaps you saw the beauty of the 1974 Netherlands,
the elegant cool of Johan Cruyff and the rhapsody in
orange. Maybe you saw Italians slumped in defeat in
their home tournament in 1990, or Eusébio cracking in a

blistering strike in 1966, or Dennis Bergkamp achieving perfection in 1998.

In every montage of the victorious moments, the images are interspersed with moments of magnificence achieved by those who did not walk off with the glory, those whose journeys gave us magical memories, but ultimate frustration. A World Cup contains many compelling stories and many iconic moments; some of the winners, some of the losers.

Many teams leave a World Cup with thoughts of what might have been. A twist of fate here and there and the outcome may have been different; perhaps a defeat avoided, a narrow win gained, or progression to a later round. For most, this is restricted to these more minor moments. For a select group of teams though, the thoughts of what might have been are focused on the final glory. There are a group of beaten teams through the World Cup's glorious history who left the tournament thinking that it could, and in some cases should, have been they who lifted the prize; they who the world feted as champions; they who left the World Cup confirmed as the world's finest.

Some of these teams are the most iconic in World Cup history, producing many of the most memorable moments – the images your mind may have pictured at the start of this introduction. They are memorable for what they did achieve as well as what they didn't. They left us with a lasting legacy, be that of unfulfilled potential, of crushed dreams, or of the magic they produced that could have seen them prevail.

Some such teams fell at the last, within agonising touching distance of that beautiful golden trophy. Others were defeated before reaching the final denouement, cut down before their time, denying both them and us of more moments to sate our appetite for aesthetic elegance or undisputed supremacy. But each lives on in our minds as some of the world's greatest.

We can all speculate about who might or should have won each World Cup. From the first event in 1930 through to the most recent tournament there will always be claims that the wrong team prevailed, that the real winners, the best team, fell short. Indeed, how often have the most lauded teams won the World Cup? Brazil in 1970, certainly. Argentina and Maradona in 1986 perhaps. Beyond that? Not many. So often, the most beautiful, those who thrilled us the most, producing art rather than simply football, seemed destined to fail.

It almost pains me to think of some of the teams whose destiny remained unfulfilled, leaving me wanting to replay the day their dreams were crushed and to be able to install the just result to take the place of the actual one. I see the pain of Puskás and Kocsis in 1954, the frustration of Cruyff and Van Hanegem in 1974, the bereft beauty of Zico and Sócrates in 1982, the tears of Baresi and Donadoni in 1990, and dream of what could have been, of a World Cup history where greatness was bestowed on those who were truly the greatest.

But alas, sport doesn't work this way. Part of the joy of football is the fact that the best team doesn't always win. It's all the greater for this, of course, as the sense of unpredictability gives it the intoxicating allure, the very essence of competition and daring to dream, that we love so much. As such, the history of the World Cup is replete with teams whose greatness remains despite not lifting that glorious golden trophy.

Greatness cannot be counted in trophies alone. I would argue that true greatness is found in the legacy of those whose memory lasts through the years. The victor is not always remembered as fondly as the vanquished. Even the greats can be beaten and this is particularly pronounced in knockout competitions such as the World Cup, where a single error or piece of misfortune can have devastating consequences. The result doesn't always reflect the performance, but this can leave us feeling denied what we feel was the deserved outcome. Others may not have produced groundbreaking artistry, but seemed destined for glory, swept on a wave of euphoria and certainty, only for it all to fall apart when destiny called.

This then feeds into the enduring allure of the question 'what if?' that appeals to so many. The appeal of the unknown and what might have been, where things turn out the way we wanted them to. This book is a tribute to those teams, some very familiar, others perhaps less so, who gave us so much but left without the glory of victory. I wrote it because it's a subject that fascinates me and because I wanted to know more about these teams, and what better way to do that than to research and write about them? But more than that, it was to celebrate the greatness that can be achieved not through victory, but through the inspiration and influence they bestowed and the enduring legacy they left behind.

What became clear in most of these stories was that, far from being a comfortable progression up until the point it went wrong, frequently in the final itself or the semi-final, most teams that we view as being vastly unfortunate not to win the World Cup had ridden their luck to some extent to get as far as they had. It's very rare that one side will dominate to such an extent that progression is seamless. Many champions, as well as those who ultimately fell short, require an element of fortune on the way to reaching their destiny. How many had to come through penalty shoot-outs, or close, nervy encounters? How many nearly didn't even qualify at all before claiming a place in sporting folklore?

What is also clear is that, so often, the fortunes of the nation in the World Cup are tied to the fortunes of the nation in other areas. When footballing failure is mirrored in a downturn in national fortunes or belief, it's hard to separate the two. Such is the significance to the national mood and the international perception of a country that footballing success can bring, so too the disappointment of unfulfilled dreams can impact negatively on the country as a whole. When the hands of fate decide on defeat rather than glory, the fallout can transcend the game, affecting national confidence, exposing societal issues, affecting the very sense of nationhood.

The weight of expectation can be heavy, and can stifle some of the greatest teams when it matters the most. When victory stands for more than simply sport, when the pressures of a nation's people, or indeed a nation's political regime, demand victory and can barely contemplate anything but victory, it can become a burden too heavy to bear. If the 11 footballers who carry this weight fail to overcome another set of 11 equally elite footballers, it can lead to repercussions and recriminations beyond reason. And even when not so linked to political nationhood, defeat, when within reach of glory, can still precipitate a huge sporting change, as barren years have often followed the destruction of a dream.

My interest in this subject perhaps comes from supporting a club and nation who have both obstinately failed to achieve anything of note in my entire life. My hopes of glory have repeatedly turned to dust. Failure has come in a variety of forms: frequently abject, often expected, but occasionally it has been beautifully, agonisingly glorious.

The most celebrated period in my club side's recent history, and the most fondly recalled era from my time following them, was a glorious failure. The Newcastle United team that could have, should have, won the Premier League in 1996 may have shattered my hopes and dreams but they grabbed my heart. They remain in the collective memory of many a football fan far more than the team who overcame them. The sheer joy of their play and the entertainment they provided captured the imagination of so many, but even more importantly, we remember them so well precisely because they failed. There is an enduring beauty to the sporting tragedy, one that tugs on the heartstrings and appeals on a deeper, subjective level than the more obvious virtues of simply celebrating victory.

This is a feeling that can be applied to many in this book; a theme which crops up time and again. For all the pain of the defeat, the enduring legacy of the vanquished required that defeat. We love them because their greatness did not require victory to define it. Victory is, of course, the aim, and is the ultimate achievement, but it is a transitory thing. Four years down the line, that victory will belong to someone else. That glory isn't taken away, of course not, but the world moves on, and unless your victory is of the ilk of Brazil in 1970, or of Argentina and Diego Maradona in 1986, then it simply isn't discussed as much as those great teams who didn't win. We are instinctively drawn to the unjust, wanting to right the wrongs, if only in our own minds, of those who we believed truly deserved it.

I don't claim this book to be definitive or impartial. The teams covered here are very much a personal choice, and some will no doubt disagree with those I have or haven't included. But in a way, that is the whole point. Objectively, it is easy to talk of the winners and hail them as the champions, the best in any given year. This subject, however, is inherently an exercise in subjectivity; of personal feelings and emotion, of the impact certain teams and their stories have had on me, and of how they could have prevailed, or, for some, how they really should have prevailed. These are the teams that have resonated the most with me. Some are familiar, in which case I hope to give a different perspective, while others may be less well told. For you it could be a different list, but that is no less than I would expect. We are all impacted differently by sporting greatness or perceived greatness.

It's about those who could or should have won, rather than simply those who dazzled briefly but didn't really come close. Some iconic greats are not in this book as a result, perhaps notably the only two sides to have lost a penalty shoot-out in a World Cup Final – as close as you can get to victory without achieving it. Others to miss the cut were those greats who were overshadowed by even greater teams in the same tournament; their stories are eclipsed by others in my mind such as with France in 1982. But even so, I've gone back and forth several times on both those I have included, and those I have excluded. This is no exact science. There is little foundation in logic, but there is a surfeit of emotion and idealism.

What I'm decidedly not trying to do is to answer the frequently discussed question of who is the greatest team not to win the World Cup. That is for you, dear reader, to make up your own mind if you want to. I can't answer for you, and don't want to attempt to. Ultimately, though, it matters little as all suffered the same fate. Do I have a personal answer for who I consider the greatest? Perhaps, but it is a personal choice and that is why I'm not going to impose my opinions on you. That is for each individual to judge on their own. But really what I hope this book shows is that it doesn't matter who was the best of these unfulfilled teams, but that many great teams and players have come so close and failed, while grabbing the world's attention nonetheless.

Equally, I'm hoping to argue that in many cases it ultimately doesn't matter who actually won. Can the more worthy prize be the lasting legacy and memory of true greatness; a greatness that can only be earned through a revolutionary approach, an artistic elegance, a sense of destiny, or captivating beauty? For some, such romantic ideals can simply be waved away as a loser's lament, of defeated teams claiming moral victory in the absence of actual victory. For others, like me, who can see that success can't be judged in trophies alone, those who are fans of football no matter which team produces it, the game opens up so much more. We can see that glory doesn't require victory, that a legacy can be won despite defeat. Simply, that there is more to the game than winning alone.

Most of all, this is a celebration of those who shot for the stars and narrowly missed, but whose exploits and accomplishments are frequently celebrated more than those of the winners. It is my homage to the kind of greatness that didn't need victory in order to define it.

1

Argentina 1930

*If there is one game I would not like to
remember, it's Uruguay–Argentina in the
World Cup Final. Yet it always comes back to
my mind. It's in my mind. I'd do anything to
go back there and play again.*

Francisco 'Pancho' Varallo

WHEN THE first World Cup was being planned for 1930,
Uruguay seemed the obvious choice of hosts. They were the
double Olympic champions from the 1920s, impressing all
observers with their brand of delightfully technical football,
as if from another world compared to the more prosaic
European approach. Uruguay were the clear lone symbol
of football excellence and progression, or so the common
perception would have you believe. But across the Rio de
la Plata, Argentina too were excelling in the world's game
through the late 1920s and into that first World Cup year.

For all the claims of British football primacy in the early
decades of the 20th century, the pompously self-imposed
isolation of the home associations means we can't fully judge

what might have happened in those three pre-war World Cups had the British nations taken part. A strong argument can be made, however, that the football being played by the national teams sitting either side of the Rio de la Plata by the early 1930s was at least as good as anywhere in the world.

Tales from the pioneering days of the World Cup never fail to pique my interest and resonate with my self-declared obsession, but until looking into the subject more, I had been fairly fixed in my view that Uruguay winning the inaugural World Cup was the correct result. They had, after all, dominated the two preceding Olympic tournaments, laying sufficient claim to being world champions before the World Cup existed as to be allowed to add a pair of stars to their national team shirts for those pre-World Cup titles.

And yet the more I looked into it, the more I was persuaded that their fellow *rioplatense* nation of Argentina could and perhaps should have prevailed on the day of the first official World Cup Final. It wasn't simply that they were ahead in the final at half-time, making victory a distinct possibility. It goes beyond that, to a team that were as much a part of the international supremacy of football from that part of the world as Uruguay. Argentina could equally point to various outside influences affecting their chances in that epic first final. That clash in Montevideo was the culmination of a decade of development and innovation by these South American giants.

When Uruguay dazzled the world at the 1924 Olympics, winning the gold medal in spectacular style, a new and unexpected shift in power was made clear to all willing to take notice. It wasn't simply the size of their victories, more often than not by a suitably hefty margin, but it was also the manner in which they achieved them which made Uruguay stand out. The slick, highly technical style of play was worlds away from the blood and thunder of the British game, but even when pitched against some of Europe's more forward-thinking nations, Uruguay's style had blown them away on the path to victory.

The South American *fútbol criollo*, a style built on individual flair and creativity, quick passes and rapid changes in rhythm, established itself in Argentina and Uruguay in the early development of the game in South America. It made these two nations not only the most advanced football nations on their continent but, as evidenced by the manner in which Uruguay stunned the old world in the 1924 Olympics, among the most advanced in the world.

In Argentina, news of Uruguay's newly elevated international status was greeted with a hint of Latin American pride but also with a sense of disbelief and no little envy. Equally, though, the prevailing attitude was simply that, had Argentina been there, it was they who would have won it. To Argentinian minds, there was nothing special about this Uruguay team. In what is the oldest international fixture outside of Britain, the regularity of their contests – sometimes up to five or six clashes a year in the 1920s – meant that Argentina had beaten this Uruguay team numerous times with overall honours fairly evenly shared between the two.

To now see Uruguay heralded around the football world stuck in the throat. No sooner had Uruguay returned from their Olympic triumph in Paris than Argentina were challenging the newly crowned champions to two matches, one in Buenos Aires and one in Montevideo. The challenge was accepted, perhaps unwisely, but it served a purpose for both. For Uruguay, it was a chance to confirm their status against their noisy neighbours, while to Argentina it was a chance to transport their local rivalry on to the global stage; to demonstrate to the world what they felt was the real truth: that the real master of the world's game was not Uruguay, but Argentina. As Dr Peter Watson, Latin American Studies Fellow at Leeds University, explained to me, 'For Argentina there was no sense of inferiority but, if anything, a frustration at the fact that they saw themselves as superior.'

This wasn't just in footballing terms either. Argentina was the economic power, the dominant force, with Buenos Aires the cultural capital of the region, and Argentinians knew it. Whereas for Uruguay, a created buffer state between Brazil and Argentina, the cultural closeness to Argentina had led them to seek ways of developing their national identity, of proving they weren't Argentinian. Excelling at football was a prime means, and against Argentina it meant trying that bit harder against those they perceived as always looking down their noses at Uruguay.

In Buenos Aires, while missiles rained down on the Uruguayan players from the stands, the teams played out an inconclusive goalless draw, before a 3-2 victory for Argentina in Uruguay three weeks later. Point proven? To Argentinians, absolutely yes: proof of their belief that they would have won gold given the opportunity.

As if to emphasise the relative parity between the two, however, they would face each other a further five times over the remainder of 1924, drawing three times. The other two games produced more Argentine solace with two more single-goal victories, one of which became famed for the goal scored directly from a corner by the winger Cesáreo Onzari. Given it was against the Olympic champions, the goal became known as a *Gol Olimpico*, taking a gleeful dig at the Uruguayans who may have been the toast of Europe's football intelligentsia but who Argentina were revelling in beating once again amid a raucous, rather hostile atmosphere. Of the seven clashes between the two sides in 1924 since Uruguay had been elevated to their lofty international status, Argentina had won three, drawn four and lost none against their bitter rivals. Just who was the greater team of the era again?

But if this meant that Argentina felt justified in their claims of supremacy, Uruguay could point to the fact that one of those drawn games helped Uruguay claim the title of South American champions in November that year, topping the four-team round robin held in Montevideo as a way of honouring the Olympic champions. This was an early indicator of a recurring theme which would become an intense source of frustration for Argentina. For all of their victories against Uruguay, when it came to dishing out the silverware, Argentina seemed perennially destined to miss out to their rivals.

Argentina may have claimed the 1925 Campeonato Sudamericano, but the behind-the-headline story was that Uruguay had withdrawn, meaning Argentina claimed their second continental title against decidedly weaker opposition, as the Brazil of the day would be classed in comparison to the *rioplatense* royalty. When Uruguay took part again in 1926, they won, claiming their sixth title, and so it was not until the 1927 edition when Argentina earned their most rewarding success to date.

Their 3-2 win in the pivotal clash in that year's tournament was a cathartic breakthrough for Argentina, not because they had beaten Uruguay – they were well used to doing that – but that they had beaten them to a trophy. What is more, it had served as the Olympic qualifiers with the predictable top two taking their place in the 1928 Games. Being champions of South America was all well and good, but becoming a global champion, replicating what Uruguay had done with such style in 1924, was the essential next step.

A very strong squad was assembled to make the trip to Amsterdam, with the boundaries of amateurism pushed beyond its limits. Argentina were hardly alone in this, however, with the issue of defining amateur status having caused increasing problems for several years already, leading to the withdrawal of the British football associations from FIFA over the matter. While this would ultimately result in the creation of the World Cup to be first held two years later, it also meant that the 1928 Olympics saw a particularly strong football tournament, with Italy, Spain and France also contenders for glory.

For most, though, a South American final was the expected outcome and Argentina began in overwhelming form, swatting aside the United States 11-2 in the first round and Belgium 6-3 in the quarter-final. The Boca Juniors forward Domingo Tarasconi scored four in both wins, and then a hat-trick in the semi-final – a 6-0 thrashing of Egypt. As the goals flew in with astonishing regularity in Amsterdam, back in Buenos Aires the fans were captivated by news of the games, listening to loudspeaker broadcasts outside the offices of the newspaper *La Prensa* reading out the stream of telegrams sent by journalists at the Games.

Uruguay had progressed rather less spectacularly, but arguably against stronger opposition in overcoming the Netherlands, Germany and then Italy in the semi-final after a replay, giving the tournament the expected final that most observers had wanted. The 40,000 tickets available for the final weren't enough to satisfy the demand in Amsterdam to see the two most intoxicating national teams of the day, while in Buenos Aires the crowds stretched for several blocks around the *La Prensa* offices as the throngs partied in between the intermittent loudspeaker broadcasts from thousands of miles away.

The 1928 final was another tight game between two well-matched sides, with Pedro Petrone giving Uruguay a first-half lead before Manuel Ferreira levelled five minutes after the break. A 1-1 finish in those days didn't lead to any sudden-death decider through the luck of a coin toss or a penalty shoot-out. Instead, the sides met again three days later, and again Uruguay took the lead in the first half, this time through Roberto Figueroa, while Argentina equalised more swiftly this time through the domineering midfielder Luis Monti.

Following Monti's goal, it was Argentina who had the better of the match, creating a succession of chances. Stern Uruguayan defence and an inspired goalkeeping performance kept them at bay, however. When the winning goal came, it was for Uruguay: Héctor Scarone securing their second successive gold medal, and sealing an intense sense of frustration in Argentina. Where 1924 could be brushed aside, this was a real shock to the system. 'A blow to the national confidence,' as Peter Watson described it.

This frustration led to the two sets of players, regular acquaintances, falling out in quite spectacular style. When the famous Argentine tango singer Carlos Gardel invited both teams to a cabaret show in Paris at the start of their long journey home, his attempt at enabling the players to reconcile backfired when fighting broke out mid-show between the arguing teams. As Argentina's Raimondo Orsi recalled, 'The *rioplatense* brotherhood went to hell,' adding that he smashed a violin on the head of Uruguayan star José Andrade in the melee.

It was of little solace at the time but the manner of Argentina's progression, and the *fútbol criollo* style of both of the finalists, meant that the world was at last paying attention to Argentina as much as to Uruguay. The downside of this success, though, was the attention paid to their players from European clubs seeking to add *rioplatense* talent to their squads. Italian clubs were chief among them, and with the implementation of new allowances in Italy defining the Italian diaspora abroad as true Italians, the earliest examples of what would become a theme of player migration from Argentina and Uruguay to Italy began.

Many of these lost players ultimately represented the Italian national team rather than the countries of their birth, but such was the strength of *rioplatense* football that the increasing loss of players wasn't yet enough to significantly weaken the national teams of Uruguay and Argentina. They remained among the best in the world for now at least, though the ongoing drain would eventually diminish them both. For Argentina, the loss of the aforementioned Orsi, a hugely impressive winger, was particularly painful, and he would later be a part of Italy's World Cup-winning team in 1934.

Further comfort came Argentina's way in winning the 1929 Campeonato Sudamericano, beating Uruguay 2-0 to seal the title. With no tournament having taken place in 1928 due to the Olympics, that meant Argentina had won two successive continental championships, but with Uruguay having won the clash that mattered most, the frustration lingered on. With the newly announced inaugural World Cup set to begin just eight months after Argentina's South American triumph, the opportunity for Argentina to get one over on their rivals on the global stage was there for the taking. What is more, with Uruguay hosting the World Cup in Montevideo as a reward for their Olympic successes, and coinciding as it did with Uruguay's centenary celebrations, the chance to rain on Uruguay's parade was one that all of Argentina desperately hoped their national team could take.

All of my talk of how good Argentina were in this era is not to denigrate Uruguay at all. They were an incredible team, gaining their historic victories through the perfection of a style of play that most simply could not match. The Uruguayan version of *fútbol criollo* was a more direct style than that developed in Argentina, more about using their speed of pass and movement to hit teams on the counter-attack than the more possession-based attack of the Argentine equivalent. In the earlier years of their rivalry this difference led to the coining of the phrase, 'Argentina attack, Uruguay score.' Through the years, the styles grew more robust, but increasingly technical, pacy and hugely effective.

History has given Uruguay a deserved place in the pantheon of great international teams, but the margins between them and Argentina were wafer-thin. They were so evenly matched, so familiar with each other, and both well used to winning, that the triumphs of one could so easily have belonged to the other. It is in this regard that I am seeking to highlight Argentina's successes in this era. While they had arguably trailed Uruguay at the start of the 1920s, by 1930 they were at least Uruguay's equal. World Cup history has a tendency to gloss over this fact, content with the apparently obvious narrative of the two-time Olympic champions going on to win the World Cup as the clear best team of the time. That wasn't the case in the 1928 Olympics, and neither was it true in the 1930 World Cup, with both going into the tournament with realistic hopes of victory.

It was a tournament taking place with a reduced field when compared to the 1928 Olympics, particularly when it came to the European contingent. There would be no Italy, Spain, Germany or the Netherlands. There would be no British representation either, resplendent in their isolation when either England or Scotland would have been realistic contenders.

Indeed, this inaugural World Cup took place virtually unnoticed back in Britain, with only a short Press Association report on the final itself making any reference to the tournament at all, while *The Times* opted to ignore it entirely. Only four European teams travelled to Uruguay, a protracted process in itself, leading to a weaker field than had been hoped for, but as noted by Jonathan Wilson in his Argentinian football history *Angels With Dirty Faces*, 'Few doubted anyway that Argentina and Uruguay were the two best teams in the world and their meeting in the final seemed pre-ordained almost from the moment of the draw.'

Argentina went into the 1930 tournament with a squad that had gained in experience and new talent since the 1928 Olympics. They may have lost Orsi in the forward line, but exciting new young talents had emerged in the form of 21-year-old Carlos Peucelle, Alejandro Scopelli, 22, and the 20-year-old Francisco Varallo. This all added to the experience through the spine of the team from Ángel Bossio in goal and defender Fernando Paternoster, to Luis Monti in the midfield and the captain Manuel Ferreira up front. If the Olympic squad had been the strongest to represent Argentina up to that point, the 1930 World Cup squad took that to another level.

Argentina's World Cup began amid controversy and seemingly stayed that way throughout, with any and every incident giving the local population all the excuse they needed to antagonise the Argentinian group. Their campaign began against France, who had already played their own opening match two days earlier, beating Mexico 4-1. The day before Argentina played France was Bastille Day and Montevideo's large French population duly celebrated with gusto, with many taking the opportunity to do so outside the Argentina team hotel, keeping the players up for much of the night.

The French players were no doubt tired after their opening match, but soon had injury concerns with Argentina making a very physical start to their World Cup in a fixture originally intended to be played in the huge, newly built Estadio Centenario. Construction delays meant the showpiece stadium was not ready for its opening day, so Argentina took on France in the more frugal and intimate confines of the Estadio Parque Central. Early in the match, Monti crashed into Lucien Laurent, the French forward famed for scoring the first-ever World Cup goal, injuring his ankle and leaving him limping for the rest of the game, a powerless bystander to much of the proceedings. Then the goalkeeper Alex Thépot, injured in France's opening match two days before, was hurt again, leaving his team battling on with a hobbling forward and a lame goalkeeper.

That they held on until the final ten minutes in the face of the tough Argentine attacks is impressive, but Argentina were not playing as fluidly as usual. In part, they were perhaps unused to facing the different approach of a European side, but they were lacking their usual zest in attack with Ferreira playing as a more orthodox centre-forward than he was usually required to do. Whatever the reasons, France held out until the 81st minute when Monti smashed home a free kick from just outside the box.

The French began to fight back though, and three minutes later had managed to set the winger Marcel Langiller clear through on goal. Only 84 minutes had elapsed at this point but the Brazilian referee bizarrely blew for full time as Langiller raced through. Despite the obvious protests this caused, it was only after the teams had retired to the dressing room that the referee saw fit to ask the teams to complete the match. All French momentum had gone by then though, leaving Argentina able to see out the win to the backdrop of a hostile reaction from the largely Uruguayan crowd.

Such was the unpopularity of the result and the manner in which it was secured that several French players were carried shoulder-high from the pitch by spectators, while the Argentinian players were jeered and pelted with stones and any other object to hand. In the furore, Argentina even threatened to withdraw from the tournament, apparently only agreeing to remain in Uruguay once the Argentinian president, no less, had been given a guarantee of his countrymen's safety.

Argentina's captain Ferreira may not have played to his usual high standards but that wasn't the reason he would miss the next game against Mexico. Far from being dropped from the line-up, instead he had returned to Buenos Aires to sit a law exam; not something that usually distracts a potential World Cup-winning captain mid-tournament. In his place was the diminutive striker, Guillermo Stábile, who was fabulously described by Jonathan Wilson as, 'A short goal-scorer from Huracán whose thin moustache and narrow-eyed gunslinger's stare gave the impression that he regarded the world with an air of amused and possibly lethal detachment.'

Stábile had never played for Argentina before and arguably only got his chance thanks to Ferreira's inconvenient exam schedule, but it was an opportunity he would seize, ultimately going on to become the first-ever top scorer at a World Cup. Against Mexico, played at the now-ready Centenario, he scored a hat-trick on his international debut in a 6-3 victory. The convincing win could easily have been more, with a missed penalty by Paternoster among the spurned opportunities.

Stábile was picked alongside the returning Ferreira, now in his more familiar inside-left position, for the final group game against Chile, scoring twice more in the first quarter of an hour. Argentina won this group decider 3-1, but aside from more Stábile strikes, it was best remembered for the mass brawl which broke out following an inevitably robust foul from Monti. His aggression provoked the Chilean right-back to punch him in return, sparking a rumpus with at least 30 officials from either side joining the melee on the pitch which had to be broken up by the police. Such was Argentina's unpopularity in Uruguay by now that the local law enforcement was also required to protect the team in their hotel.

Back home, the team's exploits in winning their group and securing a place in the semi-finals were far from unpopular. Such was the frenzy being built up by the news of their successes that thousands of fans made the trip across the Rio de la Plata to see their heroes take on the United States in the Estadio Centenario. The match, against a team Argentina had beaten 11-2 at the Olympics two years before, began relatively evenly with the USA twice going close through Ralph Tracey. But as soon as Monti had put Argentina ahead midway through the first half, there was only going to be one winner as their dominance grew.

Soon after his missed opportunities, Tracey was injured in a bone-crunching challenge from Alejandro Scopelli, but played on as best as he possibly could with what was later found to be a broken leg. With Tracey unable to return after the break, the USA were forced to continue with ten men. When their goalkeeper sustained a leg injury in the second half, any faint hopes of a fightback rapidly vanished as the already dominant Argentina cut loose. Stábile scored two more, as did the inside-forward Carlos Peucelle, following on from a goal by Scopelli as Argentina hit the USA for six.

A last-minute consolation for the beaten Americans, scored past the goalkeeper Juan Botasso who had come into the team for the semi-final and final, was little solace for a well-beaten opponent. The Americans had also suffered from a bizarre incident when their physio dropped a bottle of chloroform with the resultant spillage temporarily blinding the midfielder Andy Auld. For all the American setbacks though, Argentina had dominated the game to such an extent, their skill and technical ability simply overwhelming their opponents at will, that their place in the final was just reward.

They remained the arch-villains for the home fans, however, with the Uruguayan newspaper *El Diario* noting that the Americans had been truly sporting, 'Refusing to lose their temper in spite of the continued fouls of the Argentina players.' Argentina were undoubtedly a tough, rough team, but they were also technically excellent – both qualities equally attributable to their Uruguayan rivals.

The hosts played their own semi-final the next day in the same stadium, and anything Argentina could do Uruguay could match as the 6-1 score was repeated as Yugoslavia were eased past. Two spectacular performances from the two great national teams of the day ensured the final that all had expected.

Thousands more packed on to a fleet of ships crossing from Buenos Aires to be in Montevideo for this highly anticipated clash, sent off by a huge farewell party lining the docks with shouts of 'Argentina si! Uruguay no!' Many of those ships would be unable to reach Uruguay though, having to sit out some heavy fog before safely continuing and arriving too late for the match. Offices in the Argentinian capital closed for the afternoon to allow everyone to listen in, this final being played on a Wednesday afternoon rather than a weekend, many of whom congregated outside the newspaper offices again in what was becoming a tradition.

In Montevideo, the stadium gates were opened at eight in the morning and the stands were full to bursting by midday, well ahead of the kick-off at 2.15pm and well beyond the official 68,000 capacity. There is a magnificent aerial photograph taken of the swamped approaches to the stadium, full of fans making their way for the big occasion, taken during the morning, with the stands clearly almost full already.

As the atmosphere bristled, so too did various other factors. Amid fears of safety, all fans entering the stadium were checked for firearms and other weapons, as were all Argentinians who did make it across the Rio de la Plata by boat, with some reports citing a significant number of confiscated revolvers from those landing in the Uruguayan capital. The referee, Belgian John Langenus, was so rapt by what he termed a 'genuine fear' for his and his linesmen's safety that he only agreed to take charge on condition that all of the officials were escorted afterwards by mounted police straight to their ship, due to depart that evening.

Relationships between the two teams had been strained since that explosive 1928 Olympic final, and this rematch – the 111th *rioplatense* derby – would be no different. The first manifestation of this was slightly comical with both teams insistent on using their own ball for the final. Thankfully, a suitable compromise was reached, with the Argentinian ball used for the first half and the Uruguayan for the second. More sinister, and significantly more disruptive to Argentinian preparations, were the death threats directed at the hugely influential Luis Monti and his family in the event of a victory for his nation.

Monti was a forceful character, difficult to intimidate on the football field either physically or emotionally, but this was on another level altogether. At first, he understandably refused to play for fear of the consequences of winning. This caused huge dismay in the Argentina camp on a personal and a footballing level. Purely in football terms, the fact that the obvious replacement for Monti, the experienced Adolfo Zumelzu, was injured compounded matters. Plans were hatched to play the inexperienced defender Alberto Chividni in Monti's midfield role only for Monti to declare on the morning of the final, after a night of soul-searching, that he would play after all. Whether this was a personal decision, or one made under the duress of the Argentinian football authorities, is unclear. He took the field in body, but played in a manner that belied the fear he held within, one team-mate describing his performance as 'paralysed': an intimidating man playing under huge intimidation.

For their part, Uruguay were without one of their principal strikers, Peregrino Anselmo, who had scored three goals in the tournament up to then. A bout of illness for Anselmo brought a recall for Héctor Castro, who had played and scored in the opening game in Anselmo's place but had not been selected since. He is notable for having lost most of one arm in a childhood accident, but by the end of the day he would have his place in history for other reasons.

The game began in a hostile manner on and off the pitch, with no quarter being given in many brutally robust challenges. As the home side aimed to unsettle Argentina physically, so the crowd's hostility was also affecting the opposing players. 'The stadium was full and there was no barrier between the crowd and the players,' recalled the striker Francisco Varallo. 'We were afraid they would kill us.'

Uruguay took an early lead, with the Argentinian ball, when a blocked shot fell to Castro who set up Pablo Dorado to smash a ferocious shot under the body of Botasso in Argentina's goal. If Argentina had been unsettled up to this point, this seemed to sting them into action, an equaliser coming eight minutes later when Ferreira released Peucelle on the right, who flew past a startled defender and sent a fierce shot into the far corner of the goal.

Shortly before half-time, a long pass from Monti was uncharacteristically misjudged by the usually excellent Uruguayan defender José Nasazzi, allowing Stábile to score his eighth goal of the World Cup. From chaotic beginnings, Argentina had not only settled but become dominant, establishing the lead their play deserved and going into the break well in control despite their issues and the severely hampered performance of Monti in the heart of their midfield.

Argentina had suffered several injuries in a bruising first half, however, with Uruguay intent on intimidation of the more usual footballing variety with their physicality. Both Botasso and Juan Evaristo also had knocks, while Varallo would injure himself soon after the restart. In addition, such were the effects of the hostility from the stands that the defender José Della Torre told his team-mates at the interval, despite Argentina leading in the World Cup Final, 'If we win, this crowd will tear us apart.'

But as the second half began, it was Argentina who had the chances to extend their lead: Stábile missing a decent opportunity and then Varallo firing a looping shot which hit the angle of post and bar. Not only had his chance of personal glory been thwarted, but in taking this shot Varallo aggravated the knee injury that had kept him out of the semi-final and had nearly prevented him from taking part in the final. Now utterly injured, he spent the next part of the match ineffectively out of the way on the wing before having to go off altogether, unable to walk.

A goal then would have changed everything, putting Argentina well within reach of victory, but instead it was the moment that fate pointed its fickle finger towards Uruguay. Instead of going 3-1 down, Uruguay had soon levelled the scores at 2-2. That equaliser came 12 minutes into the second half when Héctor Scarone looped a ball over the full-backs Della Torre and Paternoster to find Uruguay's top scorer at the finals, Pedro Cea, who tapped in.

Uruguay's third had come when the soon-to-depart Varallo had lost possession, leading to Santos Iriarte scoring. Héctor Castro added the *coup de grâce* in the closing moments, beating Della Torre to Dorado's cross and heading over Botasso for Uruguay's fourth.

When the referee signalled the end of the game, it also indicated, yet again, that, for all of Argentina's wins over Uruguay at other times, when it came to handing out the global medals and trophies destiny was not on their side. A celebratory pitch invasion was all the excuse needed for the referee Langenus to make his planned swift exit, while the victorious players were carried from the pitch by their adoring fans. The joyous mood of the hosts extended into the following day which was declared a public holiday in Uruguay in celebration of their team's achievements, with the players each rewarded with a house gifted by the state.

In Buenos Aires, though, the mood was darker. A throng of angered fans threw stones at the Uruguayan embassy late that night, while there were several other flashpoints as disappointment turned to despair. Some Uruguayan expats in Buenos Aires were enjoying their victory in the city streets, but reports of gunfire and police dispersals showed that those celebrations were perhaps ill-advised in the midst of a disappointed nation. Where pre-match there had been joyful, hopeful marches and flag waving, now the Argentinian marches took on a more funereal air, with flags bowed as if in mourning.

The fallout was not restricted to the fans, however. The Argentinian football association broke off official relations with their Uruguayan counterparts in a fit of pique, in large part due to the intimidatory tactics of Uruguay's players, officials and media. As noted by Argentina's *El Grafico* afterwards, 'The Belgian referee Langenus let the Uruguayans go unpunished with violent challenges, while the Argentinians were doing what had been previously agreed, not to make violent fouls and use fair play.' The report went on to highlight several other factors, 'I also complain about the off-pitch behaviour of the Uruguayans, threatening players with anonymous calls and letters during and after the game against France, the press articles that brought Monti's morale down, and the mistake of the delegates that forced him to play, and that picked an injured Varallo over a fit Scopelli.' A post-match report in *El Grafico* lamented Monti's contributions in the final, saying the great midfielder 'was standing, literally soulless, without being the great playmaker that in normal circumstances he would have been, in the middle of the park'.

It is clear that the much-diminished effectiveness of one of their most influential players had a deep impact on proceedings. Had the death threats directed his way never occurred, would Argentina have been so physically dominated in the match? Would his influence on the play have crafted more opportunities for Argentina to build their lead? We will never know, but it seems inconceivable that Argentina would not have produced a more effective performance, and would have dished out as much physicality as they took, had Monti been at full tilt.

Other critics scathingly turned their anger on to those they perceived as having let Argentina down. *La Prensa*'s comment noted, 'Argentina teams sent abroad to represent the prestige of the nation in any form of sport should not be composed of men who have anything the matter with them. We don't need men who fall at the first blow, who are in danger of fainting at the first onslaught even if they are clever in their footwork.'

This astonishing reaction reveals the degree to which the defeat prompted a national analysis about why they lost. The question became not 'Why did we lose a football match?' but more 'What is it about our nation that is failing us?' With Monti, the symbol of Argentinian power, the player who was supposed to be there to impose that sense of power over Uruguay, resolutely failing to do so in the final, the soul-searching led to questions of virility. 'It's about manliness, bravery, strength, fitness, all those masculine characteristics,' Dr Peter Watson explained. 'Are we really man enough? Are we fit enough or strong enough? We haven't gained that sense of national discipline that's needed for success.'

Incidents such as the disorder around the Uruguayan embassy in Buenos Aires simply added to this, leading to questioning whether it revealed a deeper malaise in how Argentinian people are. Forgetting how well they had played to reach the final, instead the unexpected, shocking defeat to a perceived inferior nation left Argentinians focusing on the fact that they had failed when it mattered most. 'They looked at it as though questioning if this was a war, a battle when it really mattered, is that where we also fail?' added Watson. With national representation at stake, the idea of sport as war by other means was one that resonated.

The bitter sense of loss was heightened by the swift break-up of the team. Eight of the players who took the field in Argentinian stripes in that 1930 final never played for the national team again. The loss of players to Europe, with the exodus to Italy in particular continuing apace, left Argentina increasingly unable to cope with the repeated talent drain. Most significantly, Luis Monti left to join Juventus following the World Cup.

He played again for Argentina once more in 1931 but once established in Italy, and with the impracticalities of playing for a nation thousands of miles away, Monti was soon playing for Italy instead. His unique place in history is to be the only player to take the field in two successive World Cup finals for different nations. That he would win with Italy in 1934 – along with two other Argentinians – where he had failed with Argentina in 1930, merely added to the disappointment.

Gone, too, was Guillermo Stábile, who had never played for Argentina prior to this World Cup and never played for them again after it. Having scored eight goals in his four appearances, he left Argentina for Italy, to Genoa and Napoli, leaving his legacy as a remarkable World Cup statistic, but a symbol of the opportunity missed in 1930. Beyond the sporting impact, these departures raised questions around immigrants, about whether the sons of migrants so prevalent in society, and in the national football team, were truly Argentine and, by extension, whether they gave their all for Argentina. Seeing them succeed elsewhere merely enhanced this view.

While Argentina, unlike Uruguay, did go to the 1934 World Cup, they were severely weakened by that stage, losing to Sweden in the first round; a shadow of the team who went so close to glory in 1930. They soon entered a period of international isolation during which a developing professionalism and their own *la nuestra* style emerged. Argentina would become increasingly bolstered with a sense of self-confidence, devoid of the comparison of meaningful international competition beyond the Campeonato Sudamericano. Victory in the 1957 Sudamericano sent Argentina into their next World Cup appearance, in 1958, with a casual expectation of success.

They ran into their awakening in the form of a crushing defeat by Czechoslovakia that demonstrated just how far both the delusions of grandeur had risen and their international standing had slipped. *La nuestra*, a style of extravagant skill that Argentina had stubbornly clung to, may have lived on as the ideal all Argentina longed for, but pragmatism and *anti-fútbol* took over, before the rise of idealism under César Luis Menotti finally brought Argentina to the World Cup summit they yearned for in 1978.

That long-awaited glory could so easily have come nearly half a century earlier in the very first World Cup. The pain may have dwindled to nothing as the memories of 1930 fade as much as the grainy images of those pioneering days. But for those whose time that was, it was a pain that never left them. In an era when Uruguay gained international acclaim, the sense that Argentina were at least their equal was an itch that the country's teams of the day remained unable to scratch. For all of the regular victories over Uruguay, to lose out in both of the global titles the two contested was an enduring frustration.

The clear sense that Argentina had been the best side in the 1930 World Cup, and indeed for much of the final until injury took its toll, is a view that is frequently overlooked when the history of the competition is told. Some 80 years after that disappointment, the striker Francisco Varallo remained convinced his side would have won, even with the handicap of the understandable loss of focus and influence of Monti, were it not for the injuries leaving them undermanned at a critical time, 'I still remember it so well and it makes me so angry. I still wonder how we let it slip … In my whole life I've never felt such a bitter pain as losing that final.'

Just how different may Argentinian and world football history have been had that match, the biggest match there had ever been at that time, gone Argentina's way? 'The thing is that we were winning comfortably, really, really comfortably,' recalled Varallo only months before his death in 2010. 'At half-time the score was 2-1 to us, but it could have been more. We were making them dance.'

2

Austria 1934

In a way he had brains in his legs. Sindelar's
shot hit the back of the net like the perfect
punchline, the ending that made it possible
to understand and appreciate the perfect
composition of the story, the crowning of which
it represented.

Alfred Polgar

THEY WERE born of the coffee houses of Vienna, that haven for the free-thinking bourgeoisie of Austrian society in the early 20th century. It was here that the issues of the day were discussed: politics, finance, education. Also among the discussion points was football, as the game became an intellectual pursuit elevated beyond the realms of mere sport. The ideal of a football style, that would reach its ultimate expression with the *Wunderteam* of the early 1930s, was conceived in the grand, equitable surroundings of this breeding ground of thoughts, ideas and debate.

It is this environment which gave rise to one of the finest international sides of all time, whose peak burned brightly but briefly, and whose rapid style brushed many an opponent aside. They were an era-defining team developed through innovation and revolution, whose tragic destiny transcended sport but whose pinnacle has been overshadowed in the annals of history: a period of greatness almost forgotten.

The Danubian school of football, as it would become known, pushed the clubs and national teams of central Europe to the forefront of the game. In Hungary and Czechoslovakia too, these ideas and influences were developed into hugely successful teams. Both would, in fact, go further in a World Cup in the 1930s than Austria. But it was the Austrians who made a style of football their own, who developed a method that was truly pioneering, and whose footballing ideal was made flesh in their inventive, tragic hero.

The Austrian national team in the early 1930s were seen as being a more sophisticated side than any other during this period. Where English football in particular was all hustle, bustle and physicality, in Austria it was the opposite: a delicacy of touch, and a speed of movement making them ahead of their time. It took Austria on an extensive unbeaten run against some of the finest opposition around. At their peak they were arguably the best in the world. That the *Wunderteam*'s peak ultimately came along just too soon in terms of global tournament success, however, allows Austria to lay claim to be the world's first truly great team to fail to win the World Cup: the first of the great unfulfilled national sides.

It was all done with such style and swagger; a groundbreaking approach that not only brought them success but would also serve as a pathfinder for some of the great sides of the future. They played a sophisticated model of football that led some to dub them the 'godfathers of Total Football'. This is no idle exaggeration as the fluid, organic style saw players interchanging regularly in what became known as the Danubian Whirl, or the *Scheiberlspiel*: a system in which the technical excellence was all directed towards the collective rather than the individual. The Austrian players, generally slight in stature but fleet of foot, could move seamlessly and quickly from defence into attack and back again, without the need for the team to settle themselves into position. It was a vision of football's future, as the player in possession was supported by multiple team-mates, any gaps being filled by whoever was in position to do so. It also proved impossible for many to stop other than by brute force, and led to a string of notable victories, particularly in a lengthy unbeaten run in 1931 and 1932 as Austria manoeuvred into a position to mount a real challenge at the 1934 World Cup.

In an age of fixed W-M playing positions, this was truly revolutionary, and it was this fluidity which would in turn influence some of the great sides of the future. The likes of the 1950s Hungary showed clear stylistic roots in Austria's Danubian Whirl, which was taken yet further by the 1970s Dutch Total Football. Atop that footballing family tree, in international terms at least, sit the Austrian *Wunderteam*, the forefathers of the football revolution occurring in central Europe in the 1920s and 30s.

Hugo Meisl, the great pioneer of Austrian football and *Wunderteam* manager, had absorbed the influences which led to their high-tempo rapid passing style in the early 20th century. An English influence on Meisl from the gentlemen of the Vienna Cricket and Football Club in his formative years as a player was enhanced by the touring Scottish club sides who visited Vienna at the start of the century, as Meisl moved into a career as an international referee and then secretary of the Austrian FA.

A 1905 tour by Rangers saw the Glasgow giants hammer their hosts as other tourists had done before them, but they did it in such a style as to deeply influence Meisl, and, through him, much of Austrian football over the next three decades. When Meisl ascended to the position of national team coach in 1912 he wanted to mould his side in the image of that Rangers team, whose quick passing and movement had so absorbed him. Although he won his first match in charge against Italy, it was following a frustrating draw with Hungary that Meisl sought out greater coaching expertise in the build-up to the 1912 Olympic Games.

The English referee of that match, James Howcroft, recommended Jimmy Hogan to Meisl. Hogan would later go on to gain great credit for the development of Hungarian football, but his influence on Meisl and Austrian football was significant too. Like Meisl, he was an advocate of a short passing style complemented by dynamic, proactive movement off the ball and a focus on technical development. It was a match made in heaven, two minds coming together in the right place at the right time.

Together, they went to the 1912 Olympics where a 5-1 victory over Germany marked Austria's emergence on the international stage. That they went on to lose 4-3 to the Netherlands in the quarter-final didn't damage Hogan's image in the eyes of Meisl, who offered him the job of coaching the side into the next Olympic cycle. Hogan warmed to Austria too, putting on coaching sessions for Vienna's top club sides, and seeing their football as 'light and easy' like a waltz, which suited him. War soon intervened and Hogan's future lay across the border in Budapest, but the grounding he had laid, the vision he had helped define in Meisl's mind, would stand Austria in good stead in the interwar years.

Viennese football boomed in the 1920s. In 1924, the Austrian capital became home to the first fully professional league outside Britain. Football had become embedded in Viennese culture, and, later that year, the *Neues Wiener Journal* ran a feature where it hailed Vienna as 'the football capital of the European continent'. Amid regaling the pre-eminence of its footballing development, the writer posed the question, 'Where else can you see 40,000–50,000 spectators gathering Sunday after Sunday at all the sports stadiums, rain or shine? Where else is the majority of the population so interested in the results of the games that you can hear almost every other person talking about the results of the league matches and the clubs' prospects for the coming games?'

Nowhere else in continental Europe, certainly. Vienna, and latterly Budapest and Prague, was not only the stage for a rapid rise in football's popularity, but also its creative hub. Each club had its own café where players, fans and club directors would meet and dissect the latest goings-on, but it was the Ring Café which would become the centre of the football scene. As described in *Welt am Montag*, it was, 'A kind of revolutionary parliament of the friends and fanatics of football; one-sided club interest could not prevail because just about every Viennese club was present.'

This was the intellectual, free-thinking school which saw the development of some of the finest players of the pre-war era, whose intelligence and willingness to take on the ambitious direction of Meisl would build on the foundations he and Hogan had laid. This mix produced a style akin to that of the Scottish sides so loved by Meisl, with the added embellishment of wide-running half-backs, an attacking centre-half given the gift of creative freedom, and a slightly deep-lying centre-forward to confound the rigid opposition structures, drawing them out of position and creating space to be exploited. It required an intelligence and speed of thought that suited the players produced by the coffee-house culture of Vienna.

Meisl's Austria would produce a brand of football that led Brian Glanville to eulogise, 'Soccer became almost an exhibition, a sort of competitive ballet, in which scoring goals was no more than the excuse for the weaving of a hundred intricate patterns.' It had evolved so far beyond the style found in England that it became seen as an entirely separate model of football, where technical excellence within a sophisticated yet disciplined team structure was key, far more so than physicality.

The influence on Meisl was felt further afield than just Austria when he set up the first continental club tournament in 1927: the Mitropa Cup. Played between the best club sides from central Europe, this tournament aided the development of teams and players in this era, not only in Austria, but in Hungary, Czechoslovakia, Italy and other countries. Rapid Vienna enjoyed great success in this tournament in its early years, reaching three of the first four finals between 1927 and 1930, winning the last of those. A year later he had a hand in the creation of a national team equivalent, the Central European International Cup, with each edition lasting around two years. For the nations involved, from Italy in the south, to Poland in the north, it was a crucial step in their footballing development and exposure to different style and approaches.

For Austria, this was just the tonic to push their burgeoning talents to the next level. Meisl's central European competitive creations aided him significantly when it came to his squad selection. Not only was he able to choose the cream of the significant pool of professional players in the Viennese league, but many of them were used to international competition and an exposure to different styles and approaches.

Through the 1920s, the standard of the Austrian national team had been steadily improving, and though the passing style was embedded, it was still some way from what the *Wunderteam* would become. Meisl, at this time, was still fixated on the view that his side needed a strong, physical centre-forward to lead the line. In part, this was an adherence to the style he'd fallen in love with, where the passing approach play still necessitated a physical presence up front. But it was also a pragmatic approach, given the biggest Austrian football star of the 1920s was Josef Uridil, a force of nature in all aspects of his life but particularly on the football field.

His nickname, *der Tank*, was well deserved, such was his robust style, bludgeoning opponents aside should they deign to try to get in his way. He scored eight goals in his eight Austrian internationals in the 1920s and was the focal point of Meisl's plans, and those of the rising Rapid Vienna team. He was central to Austrian popular culture too, with a dance hall hit written and sung in his honour, and a film starring Uridil himself playing in the cinemas.

The chalk to Uridil's cheese was Matthias Sindelar. Both as players and people, Uridil and Sindelar were as different as night and day. But this contrast serves to highlight the final tweak to the Austrian team which would ultimately make them great. Sindelar, the leading footballer of his generation, was a slight, almost frail-looking forward, blessed with sublime skills but next to no physical presence. It was he, rather than the more charismatic Uridil, who would eventually become the figurehead of Austrian football.

Looking back on Sindelar's career in 1939, Alfred Polgar wrote in the *Pariser Tagezeitung*, 'He would play as a grandmaster played chess: with a broad mental conception, calculating moves and countermoves in advance, always choosing the most promising of all possibilities. He was an unequalled trapper of the ball and stager of surprise counterattacks, inexhaustibly devising tactical feints.' Initially, however, having first been selected for the national team by Meisl in 1926, he was to be restricted to the role of a bit-part player through much of the rest of the 1920s. Despite scoring on his international debut, and scoring four in his first three games for Austria, he represented a breaking of the mould that Meisl was hesitant to pursue at this stage, turning back to the more traditional centre-forward abilities of Uridil. Where Uridil was the tank, Sindelar was *der Papierene*: the paper man.

Only sporadically selected over the preceding couple of years, and having played in a 2-0 win over Switzerland in late 1928, it would be more than 18 months before Sindelar played for Austria again. During his enforced absence, the team struggled, only winning two of their seven matches. But when he did pull on the national team jersey again it was as the embodiment of a new approach: one that would take Austria to the top of the world game.

Sindelar was the personification of the intellectual ideal of football as espoused in the coffee-house debates, as well as sharing their socialist political leanings. His football abilities involved no end of tricks, ceaseless flamboyance, and a free-spirited devotion to new moves and methods. He was the leading playmaker of European football, and made a virtue of doing the unexpected, frequently slipping past the clutches of close markers and through tight defences, and taking visible delight on the occasions that his team-mates were on the same wavelength as his virtuoso displays.

Sindelar had learned his skills in the confined surroundings of streets of the immigrant community in Vienna's Favoriten district. His talents were initially spotted by Hertha Vienna who brought him into their youth set-up, before Austria Vienna, at the time known as Wiener Amateur, took him to a bigger stage when he was 21.

He would become synonymous with Austria Vienna for the rest of his career, playing more than 700 times for the club over the next 15 years and scoring an incredible 600 goals. 'He was truly symbolical of Austrian soccer at its peak period: no brawn but any amount of brain,' wrote Hugo Meisl's brother, the hugely respected football journalist Willy Meisl, of Sindelar. 'Technique bordering on virtuosity, precision work and an inexhaustible repertoire of tricks and ideas. He had a boyish delight in soccer exploits, above all in unexpected twists and moves which were quickly understood and shared by his partners brought up on the same wavelength, but were baffling to an opposition only a fraction of a second slower.'

Sindelar was one of those players for whom time seemed to move more slowly when on the football field. He had the time and confidence to put his foot on the ball, assess the position and space of every player on the pitch and choose the right option, be it a short pass, a long pass, a run, a shot. His reliance on grace and guile rather than grit imbued the team with the confidence to commit even more fully to this style. As noted by David Goldblatt in *The Ball is Round*, 'Viennese café society at last had a player and a game in their own image: cultured, intellectual, even cerebral, athletic but balletic at the same time.' His image, style and physique could not have been more different from that of Josef Uridil, and the same could be said of the club he played for. Where Uridil's Rapid Vienna represented a working-class community, Austria Vienna were the club of the bourgeoisie, the coffee-house intelligentsia, the free-thinking that Sindelar was the very embodiment of.

Naturally, therefore, he was the darling of the coffee houses, and when he was excluded from the national team by Meisl it became a hot topic of debate. The bohemian spirit of the coffee house, having taken football to their hearts, embraced Sindelar and his style: the triumph of mind over muscle, artistry over endeavour. Meisl hadn't cast Sindelar aside purely for footballing principles, however. The strict disciplinarian supposedly took umbrage at the perceived lack of such from the individualistic Sindelar: the authoritarian and the free spirit not seeing eye to eye. But the groundswell of support for Sindelar's return strengthened with each poor result the national team endured, the relative struggles provoking much debate, with the absence of their hero seen as the answer to all ills.

It was a call that Meisl would eventually heed. The story goes that Meisl was cornered by a group of leading football writers and authorities in the Ring Café in 1931, all arguing for Sindelar's return with an emphasis on how his abilities, his ingenuity, that spark of unpredictability could lead Austria forward. Meisl, finally convinced by the persuasive argument, changed his mind. His already disciplined, highly organised and hard-working team would gain its ingenious playmaker: the creative spark that would prove their inspiration and talisman.

The pieces were now all in place with Sindelar playing as the deep-lying centre-forward, dragging the opposition out of position and dictating both the play and the tempo.

The other crucial new idea was the use of Josef Smistik, a strong, versatile player renowned for his speed and range of passing, as a progressive centre-half, freed from the rigidity of the defensive thinking of that time. The combination of these two innovations made Austria unique, and released their latent potential. The *Wunderteam* was born.

On a spring day in May of 1931 in Vienna, Meisl's men took on one of the British giants when Scotland visited the Austrian capital for the first time. Given the significant affect of Scottish football on Meisl, and through him on Austrian football in general, the opposition on this day was fitting. It was admittedly a depleted Scotland side, shorn as they were of their Rangers and Celtic players for the tour, and featuring only three of the 11 who had beaten England 2-0 just seven weeks earlier. However, this was an age when British football could still be assumed as among the strongest in the world. Scotland, like England, were still significantly ahead of many European nations, though the gap was closing across the continent. In central Europe, the Danubian school of football was not merely catching up but was poised to surge ahead.

Sindelar, as the deep-lying central striker, a false nine long before there was such a thing, dominated and dictated the play. He scored his first international goal in five years as Austria brushed Scotland aside in a 5-0 drubbing, signalling the arrival of a new world power. It was a signal that went largely unheeded in Britain though. The Scottish sports press may have been effusive in their praise of the Austrians – 'Outclassed!' was how the *Daily Record* described it – but their ready-made excuse of a weakened squad meant the warning went ignored, as it had been in England when their touring side had been held to a goalless draw in Vienna the year before. Austria followed this victory up with a 6-0 victory over Germany in Berlin, and again 5-0 back in Vienna in September 1931. Hungary were similarly dismantled 8-2, Italy and Sweden beaten, as Austria surged to the top of the international game.

The groundbreaking style, with the team's distinctive movements and tactical innovations, enabled Austria to go on a 14-match unbeaten run in 1931 and 1932, all the while enhancing and perfecting their approach. As impressive as the results had been though, it was a narrower victory which made the rest of Europe, Britain excluded, begin to take notice. Beating Italy 2-1 in April 1932 to win the Central European International Cup, Austria's first title, confirmed their status as the real deal. With a World Cup now looming on the horizon, Austria had manoeuvred into a position from which they could mount a real challenge.

The increasingly influential forward line was complemented by wide half-backs, notably the left-half and team captain Walter Nausch. With the ability to play in virtually every position on the pitch, Nausch may not have had the more obvious impact of Sindelar but was rated as one of the best in the world in his position, and would later in life take charge of the Austrian national team after the Second World War. He was equally crucial to Austria's rise, though was sadly to miss out on the 1934 World Cup through injury, Smistik taking over the captaincy in his absence. Austria could boast talent in goal as well, with Rudi Hiden, one of the greatest interwar goalkeepers, as their last line of defence.

By 1932, Austria had earned what Meisl had yearned for: a chance to take on England once again, becoming only the third continental side to be invited to England. In December 1932, they visited Stamford Bridge where a crowd of 60,000 saw the Austrians give their hosts the fright of their lives. The Austrian public were captivated by their football heroes taking on England with huge crowds back in Vienna filling the Heldenplatz to listen to a radio broadcast of the match.

They were initially disappointed as England raced into a 2-0 lead but Austria's technical precision saw them dominate after the interval in an inspired fightback. Austria would ultimately lose 4-3, but had laid down another marker in their progression. With their habit of dropping back behind the ball when not in possession and their constant quick-fire passing, the Austrians left England confused and chasing shadows at times, though ultimately it was the lack of an incisive cutting edge that cost them a draw or better.

'English Team Lucky to Win' ran the headline in the *Manchester Guardian*, adding, 'There could not be the slightest doubt that as a team [Austria] were the superiors.' *The Times* succinctly noted, 'It was victory and no more,' while the *Daily Mail* declared the visitors 'a revelation'. Sindelar came in for particular praise, the *Daily Herald* match report stating, 'Sindelar is the best centre-forward continental Europe has ever known. I don't remember a play, a touch or a feint of him made not for the benefit of his own team.' While the nod to continental Europe suggests the underlying assumption of the English press that there may not have been better in Europe and belief in England's superiority remained, this was still high praise.

The lessons would go unheeded by England, who would wait another two decades before their wake-up call in the form of the Hungarians of the 1950s, with the game essentially seen as a triumph of England's more physical approach over the more subtle finesse of the Austrians. For Austria's part, they rued the missed opportunity to write their name into history. 'It was in that first half hour that Austria lost her chance of bringing off a sensation compared with which Hungary's victory at Wembley in 1953 would seem unimportant,' Willy Meisl wrote years later.

The additional cutting edge would later arrive in the form of Josef Bican, whose scoring exploits added a greater clinical nature in front of goal. Bican remains to this day one of the most prolific scorers of all time, amassing more than 800 goals in a stellar career. His composure, allied to his clinical two-footed striking ability, saw his feats rate among the greatest in the game. He was just 21 at the time of the 1934 World Cup but formed an effective combination with Sindelar, interchanging at will and confounding the defensive structures of the opposition.

Austria hadn't taken part in the first World Cup in 1930, deciding against travelling to Uruguay for similar reasons to many other European nations at that time. The cost was, of course, prohibitive, as was the time it would take given the distance involved. Additionally, while Austria, having had a professional league for several years, had no issues of players risking losing their jobs while on World Cup duty, many clubs were not willing to see their prize assets spending weeks away for a tournament that was an unknown quantity at this point.

There had been an increasing call from some within the game to send a squad to Uruguay though, with articles devoted to pushing Austria's participation being seen in Viennese newspapers in early 1930, citing the 'enormous economic, sporting and propaganda advantages of an Austrian expedition to Uruguay'. Many of the players felt the same way. The defender Roman Schramseis was quoted as saying, 'We would surely show the South Americans that we can also play football in Austria.'

But there was a lack of interest from those in a position of authority, and a fear that several players may choose to stay in South America to pursue their careers far from home. This lack of will meant that Austria ultimately opted against participation. The disappointment in Austria missing the inaugural World Cup is heightened by the fact that the up-and-coming power never got to meet the other great international sides of that era.

Austria had not taken part in the 1928 Olympic football tournament, where Uruguay and Argentina had dominated. Uruguay would not travel to the 1934 tournament in retribution for the perceived snub they had suffered from European non-attendance in 1930, while Argentina were much weakened by then. It is a great imponderable question to consider what may have happened had Austria been able to take part in 1930; however, given that Austria were still to find their ideal formation and line-up, they were still a year or two from their peak. Sindelar, for instance, would have been no part of a 1930 squad, still watching from the outside as Meisl had yet to bring him back in to the fold. Perhaps, therefore, the 1930 tournament came too soon for Austria. And with the *Wunderteam*'s peak coming in 1931 and 1932, the fear was that the next World Cup in 1934 would come too late.

In order to qualify for the tournament, Austria had to come through a group containing Hungary and Bulgaria. Despite being drawn against one of Europe's strongest, qualification was achieved with consummate ease. With Hungary beating Bulgaria twice and Austria doing likewise in front of 25,000 at the Praterstadion, Bulgaria, knowing they could no longer qualify, withdrew from the tournament saving the others the trouble of having to play out the remaining schedule. Austria had been very impressive in their one qualifying victory, winning 6-1 thanks to a hat-trick from Johann Horvath, a veteran inside-forward and another of the prominent players of the era, well suited to the technical, passing style of play.

It was only four weeks later that Austria played their opening match in the World Cup finals, by which time they had won or drawn 28 out of their previous 31 games, scoring more than 100 goals in the process. Not quite at their earlier peak perhaps, but without doubt very much a contender for the World Cup prize. Significantly, they had beaten Vittorio Pozzo's Italy a few months beforehand with a 4-2 victory in Turin in February 1934 in a Central European International Cup match. Tellingly, the Austrian performance that day would cause Pozzo to rethink his tactical approach and personnel ahead of a tournament his Italy side were under intense political pressure to win.

With this victory under their belt, Austria travelled to Italy again for the World Cup as one of the favourites to win. Meisl was more pessimistic, though. Austria would be without their great goalkeeper, Rudi Hiden, through injury, while Meisl also felt that many of his players were worn out from tiring foreign tours with their clubs. Another factor was that Austria was a nation in the midst of political turmoil in the lead-in to the tournament. With Vienna descending into three days of open warfare in February 1934, there is little doubt this will have impacted on the whole squad. Increased political conflicts between the Right and the Left amplified tensions already stirred by the lasting economic effects of the early 1930s Depression. The Austrian chancellor ordered the army into Vienna to stamp out the armed uprising, having earlier tried to ban several political parties. Amid this turmoil, Austria made their way to the

World Cup. Perhaps, given this backdrop, their sluggish start to the tournament was little surprise.

With the 1934 tournament taking a straight knockout format right from the start, Meisl's Austria would face France in their last-16 clash in Turin's Stadio Benito Mussolini. France were coached by the Englishman George Kimpton, a former Southampton player credited with bringing the W-M formation to French football. Ahead of this clash with Austria in which his France side were clear underdogs, he attempted to nullify the Austrian attack by implementing some rigorous man-marking on Austria's key man. 'You can follow Sindelar everywhere, even to the toilet,' he told his midfielder Georges Verriest, in an effort to stifle Sindelar's creativity, denying him the space to control the game.

France took the lead early in the first half, thanks to a Jean Nicolas shot which flew past goalkeeper Peter Platzer and into the top corner. How much Nicolas knew about it is open to debate, given he had suffered a bad head injury not long beforehand, and would spend much of the match as a passenger. Sindelar equalised moments before half-time to ease Austrian nerves but France, effectively a man down for most of the game, had defended resolutely leaving the much-fancied Austrians struggling to find a way through. With no more scoring in the second half, this would be the first match in World Cup history to go to extra time. Austria were quick out of the traps having had the chance to regroup, and Anton Schall soon gave them the lead for the first time in the 93rd minute.

Schall, a stalwart forward from Admira Vienna, was another of Austria's highly prolific forwards, and deserves his place alongside Sindelar, Bican and the rest as one of Austria's greats. He was pacy and skilful, and could occupy several different positions thanks to his intelligent reading of the game. A predominantly left-footed winger or inside-forward, it was from this position that he broke through the French defence to fire his side ahead.

Shortly into the second half of extra time, Bican made it 3-1 from close range, his only goal of the tournament, shooting past a leaping Alex Thépot in the French goal in what history records as a controversial winner with a hint of offside. The goal stood, though, and Austria were seemingly on their way. There was time for a late French penalty to reduce the deficit, but Austria clung on for a 3-2 victory and a place in the quarter-finals.

This was not how things were supposed to have begun, however. A year earlier, Austria had triumphed 4-0 over the same opposition in Paris, but the impact of tactical adjustments intended to disrupt the Austrian flow was significant, so much so that they had struggled to beat a team playing with an injured player for nigh on two hours of football.

Up next was a much sterner test in the form of the Austria's near neighbours from Hungary. It was a full-blown battle in Bologna's Stadio Littorale in a game Meisl would later describe as 'a brawl, not an exhibition of football'. Horvath gave Austria the lead in just the eighth minute with a stinging left-footed shot from Karl Zischek's cross. Zischek himself added another early in the second half from a fine Bican pass. With Hungary struggling to get a foothold in the match, things began to get rough as frustrations started to rise. György Sárosi pulled a goal back from the penalty spot, but while Hungary pressed for an equaliser the Austrians remained calm amid some severe provocation, seeing out a victory that could have been clearer had Sindelar's late effort not been brilliantly saved by Antal Szabo in Hungary's goal.

It was another win, another close encounter, but an altogether more satisfying victory than the France match had been. Austria had found their groove to some extent, brushing off the cobwebs of their opening match, but there was a sting in the tail. The rough nature of the game saw Hungary have a man sent off while Austria suffered an injury to Horvath, rendering him unable to take any part in the upcoming semi-final.

Austria's match in the final four would be one that most observers felt was the game to decide the World Cup, albeit coming along prematurely at the semi-final stage. This would have been the natural final, with the two foremost teams of the time, led by two of the most dominant figures of European football. As with many great encounters, it was to be a clash of styles with the slick, deft approach of the Austrians contrasting, almost jarring, with the brutish physicality of Pozzo's Italy. Crucially, the lessons handed down by Austria a few months earlier had caused Pozzo to ensure his team would not seek to go toe-to-toe with the slick Austrians, but would seek to prevail in a more robust manner.

Wary of how Austria had dominated them just months before, Pozzo had earmarked the Argentine-born Luis Monti, stalwart of the 1930 Argentina team but now an Italian, to closely mark Sindelar. The role of stifling the opposition's main threat would be one that the tough Monti, expert in the physical dark arts, would relish. He hassled and harried, kicked and pulled, smothering the slight Austrian's impact on the game. At one point he caught Sindelar in the face, leaving the paper man bleeding, bruised and bewildered. The referee didn't even see a foul. Sindelar, schooled in aesthetic footballing beauty not rugged physicality, became a frustrated figure, unable to take control in his usual manner, at times peripheral to the key action. The loss of Horvath was also keenly felt given the impact of his performances so far and the crucial support he had been able to give Sindelar.

Austria's play would be further hampered by a brief deluge which had occurred prior to kick-off, leaving the San Siro pitch heavy, wet and muddy – not conditions conducive to Austria's slick passing. Rain had poured on what should have been Austria's parade. To add to Austrian woes, the surface was uneven and dotted with areas of sand, but they persisted with their usual style regardless, sticking to their ideological guns.

Sindelar and Zischek, probably the least physically commanding of the Austrian stars, would struggle particularly with the heavy surface. Equally, with the highly effective smothering job being handed down by the savvy Italians, Austria couldn't control the tempo, couldn't impose themselves and struggled to make their usual impact. They barely registered a shot all match, although defensively Austria were almost as robust as the Italians, with Smistik putting in an exemplary performance at centre-half, linking the play to the talented forward line.

In keeping with the physical nature of the game, the only goal was brutal in its nature too. Platzer had dived to gather a relatively innocuous cross, but as he did so the Italian forward Giuseppe Meazza barged into him, sending ball and man sprawling. Amid the pile-up, Enrique Guaita poked the ball home and bundled Platzer into the net in the process. It was a goal that would never have stood in the modern age but it was one that the referee, Swede Ivan Eklind, saw nothing wrong with. The rumours swirling around Eklind, both during this tournament and in the years that followed, leave something of a question mark around his performances in 1934, however. He was rumoured to have dined with Mussolini the night before this semi-final, and was felt to have favoured Italy in both this game and the final which followed.

Austria, looking tired and heavy-legged in the tumult of a partisan occasion and the muddy surface, produced by far their best spell of the game early in the second half, pouring forward with a renewed energy. What they couldn't do, though, was carve out the clear chances that their improved showing warranted and they desperately needed amid the suffocating performance of the Italians. But in such a close game with it all on the line there is often that one opportunity that falls the way of the team chasing the game, one chance to save themselves. For Austria, this late chance fell to Zischek, latching on to a clearance from Platzer and surging through the tiring Italian defence with barely a minute remaining. When he shot wide, Austria's hopes were gone.

Beauty had been slain by the beast, artistry losing out to physicality. Austria, those idealists of inventive exquisiteness, had been bullied out of the match and out of the tournament; the *Wunderteam*'s chance of World Cup glory had gone. The combination of bad weather, a well-prepared opponent, and a lack of an alternative plan when faced with such physicality left Austria unable to earn the place in history that their talent warranted. This semi-final saw the two best teams of the tournament face off but it was Italy who went on to win the trophy that could have been Austria's. The final, had Austria reached it, would have been a Danubian delight as Czechoslovakia, of the same Danubian school, were the opposition who took on Italy and so nearly beat them.

Austria, distraught and frustrated by the manner of their exit, understandably failed to rouse themselves for the third-place play-off against Germany. A goal down in the opening minute, and two down soon after, they were always chasing the game and eventually lost 3-2 against a team they had beaten many times in recent years.

It would be the start of a slow but steady decline. The higher the peak the sadder the demise, and so it was for the *Wunderteam*. Sindelar was into his 30s now, and like this team in general, save for the likes of Bican, was past his peak. There would be one final glorious swansong in 1936, a last glimmer of greatness. In a victory over England in May that year, Meisl showed he had learned from the past defeats to both England and Italy, and adapted his approach sufficiently to overcome a more physically strong team. Overwhelming England early on, he ensured Austria took the initiative in a way they had been unable to do in the World Cup semi-final. Sindelar repeatedly dragged the English centre-back out of position as Austria stormed into a 2-0 lead and held on for a narrow victory. An Olympic silver medal a few months later in Berlin gave a tangible reward on a global stage, but the nation that beat them that day was the same as had beaten them in 1934: the new powers of European football, Italy.

While much of the *Wunderteam* was further past their peak, there was still the opportunity to right the wrongs of 1934 in the next World Cup, held in France in 1938. Austria had again qualified, this time winning a one-match play-off with Latvia with a narrow 2-1 victory in October 1937. This had been achieved with Sindelar still in the team, but they were no longer led by their great authoritarian leader Meisl. He had died in February 1937 of a heart attack, leaving behind a legacy as strong as any international manager before or since. It also left a team facing competitive action without Meisl at the helm for the first time in almost two decades and 127 official internationals. Qualification had been achieved under Heinrich Retschury, who had also briefly led the team as a caretaker during the First World War while Meisl was otherwise engaged in the fighting. Before the World Cup the following summer though, Austria was a wholly different place. In March of 1938, the German army had marched into Vienna and the subsequent Anschluss amalgamated Austria into the Nazi Reich.

Stemming from the intellectual, predominantly left-wing, coffee-house culture, many of those involved in Austrian football were less than sympathetic with the Nazi ideology. Sindelar, for instance, had never hidden his opposition to the Nazi viewpoint. With Austria ceasing to exist just months ahead of the 1938 World Cup, so too the Austrian national team ceased to exist, their place in the finals at one point being offered to England, although in the end the tournament went ahead with no Austrian replacement.

There would be one last hurrah for the Austrian team, and the players of the *Wunderteam,* however. What was now named the German region of Ostmark was instructed to play one final game against the German national team in what was dubbed the Reconciliation Match, as the Nazis wanted to showcase their expansion, celebrating Austria's absorption into the Reich. Sindelar, initially reluctant, agreed to play, reputedly on the condition that the Austrian team could wear their traditional red colours.

The symbolism of the event meant that a score draw was deemed the most diplomatic result; however, there was a clear disparity in quality. The Austrians, showcasing their talents to the full, ran rings around the German team. Myth may have embellished the reality but many contemporary reports make mention of the host of easy chances that the Austrians missed in the first half. The story goes that Sindelar deliberately spurned several, placing the ball narrowly wide as if to show how easy it was for him to put the ball wherever he wanted. He was widely, and likely accurately, assumed to be mocking the Germans in the best way he knew how.

In the second half, his patience finally wore thin. He scored, following another exquisite period of play from the Austrians before celebrating gleefully, and perhaps unwisely, in front of the watching Nazi dignitaries. Fellow forward Karl Sesta later added a second with a vicious strike from distance. The large crowd in Vienna's Praterstadion were roused from their fearful silence into cheers of 'Österreich! Österreich!' celebrating the expression of patriotism for the nation they had just lost.

Going into the World Cup, the German authorities were clear about the way in which they expected the national team to be composed. 'In our sphere as well as in others a visible expression of our solidarity with the Austrians who have come back to the Reich has to be presented. The Führer demands a 6:5 or 5:6 ratio. History expects this of us.' Several Austrians did indeed join the German team led by future World Cup-winning coach Sepp Herberger, although all that resulted in was two teams within a team. The dressing room was full of resentment and tension, and when the team played the two factions were clear, as Austrians passed to Austrians and Germans passed to Germans. Germany's miserable tournament was played out against the backdrop of vocal anti-Nazi protests from the French crowds, and following an initial draw in their first-round match with Switzerland, Germany were thumped 4-2 in the replay, and sent home with the boos of thousands of protesters ringing loudly in their ears.

One Austrian who was not at the 1938 World Cup was Matthias Sindelar. He may have been convinced to play in the reconciliation match, but his principles would not allow him to heed the call for the German national team. Despite Herberger's repeated requests, Sindelar refused to play, instead focusing his attentions away from football and on the café he had purchased from a Jewish acquaintance when Austria's Jews were forced to give up their business interests. Within a few months, however, Sindelar was dead.

Speculation has been rife for decades of Nazi involvement in his death following the twin shame of his celebrations when scoring in front of the Nazi command, and in refusing to go to the World Cup. He died of carbon monoxide poisoning in his home, but the truth of the mystery seems far less sinister than any foul play. He lived in a block of flats where several other residents had complained about the chimneys in recent weeks and one night he and his new partner died while they slept. The greatest footballer in Austrian history, the inspiration and star of the *Wunderteam*, the key piece in the jigsaw around whom the whole revolutionary style developed and relied on, was dead at the age of 36.

His funeral procession in Vienna was witnessed by more than 20,000 people lining the streets to bid their hero farewell in an occasion that has since been described as 'Vienna's first, and last, rally against the Nazis' by the writer Robin Stummer. Sindelar's death wasn't just the passing of a hero, but it also symbolised the end of the golden period in Austrian football, the end of Vienna's Danubian dream. Alfred Polgar, who felt Sindelar's death had been suicide for the lost love of his homeland and the team in which he represented his nation, poetically lamented, 'The good Sindelar followed the city, whose child and pride he was, to its death. He was so inextricably entwined with it that he had to die when it did ... For to live and play football in the downtrodden, broken, tormented city meant deceiving Vienna with a repulsive spectre of itself. But how can one play football like that? And live, when a life without football is nothing?' Austria's great generation and their football dreams had died, and, with it, so had Sindelar.

Romanticism aside, Austria's *Wunderteam* deserve to be remembered as one of the greatest sides never to lift the World Cup: the first of the era-defining greats to fall short. Their legacy is seen most in the style they developed, later enhanced by Hungary in the 1950s and perfected by the Dutch in the 1970s. Austria's tale is less well known, however, faded in the mists of time, belonging to a different age. This is the case in Austria, too. Modern Austrian football fans already have to look back in time for any hint of success, the stars of the 1970s and 1980s remaining prominent in people's thoughts. 'With that already being well in the past, the need to look back further diminished even more,' Tom Middler, a Vienna-based football writer and commentator explained to me.

There is also an understandable reluctance to look back with any fondness on the 1930s, with the war, and Austria's role in the spread of fascism, obscuring that era of history. 'The subsequent reformation of football was little more than a side note in a much larger historical matter. Only the most ardent of fans look back on that period, and for the average fan those decades are mostly forgotten,' added Middler.

With neither Meisl nor Sindelar surviving beyond the 1930s, the *Wunderteam* also lacked the natural legacy of other generations, its two key protagonists unable to write football history beyond the 1930s. And yet their achievements made them the first truly great side to fail to win the World Cup. There may have been a flimsiness to them, as exemplified by their paper man, but the team represented everything that was progressive about Viennese society, its imagination and its critical thinking.

While it would be Czechoslovakia who took the Danubian school further in the World Cup in 1934, as did Hungary in 1938, it was Austria who had pushed the style the furthest in this era and reached the higher pinnacles of style and influence. Meisl and Sindelar stand as icons of the Austrian game: two people who saw the game differently to the majority, two people who defined a nation's footballing identity and the *Wunderteam* which symbolised it.

3

Brazil 1950

*Everywhere has its irremediable national
catastrophe, something like a Hiroshima. Our
catastrophe, our Hiroshima, was the defeat by
Uruguay in 1950.*

Nelson Rodrigues – playwright, journalist and novelist

FOR ALL of Brazil's footballing grandeur, all of those
glittering prizes, those moments when their canary-yellow
shirts dazzled as the sun shone on their crowning glories,
it is a moment of sporting tragedy that remains the most
morbidly fascinating to Brazilians.

They may have since won the World Cup five times,
but they will never be able to go back and win the one they
were supposed to win more than any other. They can never
return to Rio de Janeiro's Estadio do Maracanã on 16 July
1950 to fulfil their destiny. A destiny, what is more, that a
whole nation felt would crown its emergence as a modern,
confident nation with a positive future. Instead, the defeat
seemed to confirm the feeling of inferiority that lurked not
far below the surface. No football result has ever had such

a deep and enduring impact on the emotions and outlook of a nation as the fateful final of 1950.

The renowned Brazilian anthropologist Roberto DaMatta saw fit to describe the 1950 defeat as, 'Perhaps the greatest tragedy in contemporary Brazilian history. Because it happened collectively and brought a united vision of the loss of historic opportunity. Because it happened at the beginning of a decade in which Brazil was looking to assert itself as a nation with a great future. The result was a tireless search for explications of, and blame for, the shameful defeat.'

To understand the impact of this defeat, we need to understand just why the 1950 World Cup was such a national priority to Brazil and its people, and how certain victory had seemed to those caught up in the contagious enthusiasm of that home tournament.

Brazil, at that time, was a troubled country with a weak economy, limited infrastructure and volatile political establishment. A military coup in 1945 had rid the country of the dictatorship of Getulio Vargas, but the ensuing free elections failed to yield a stable government as one dictatorship was merely replaced with another. Against this backdrop, the idea of hosting the 1950 World Cup was conceived, having previously mooted a bid for the 1942 tournament. With the descent into the Second World War, the 1942 event never took place, and by the time FIFA met again in 1946 no European country was in a position to host a World Cup, leaving the path clear for Brazil.

The Brazilian government, far from secure in their position, saw an opportunity to enhance their popularity domestically and to showcase Brazil and its push for modernity to the rest of the world. To create a sense of Brazilianness, Vargas had looked to popular culture, to football and samba, using their popularity as a means to foster a sense of nationhood in a vast, regionalised country. 'The two are fused together,' Dr Peter Watson, Latin American Studies Fellow at Leeds University, noted to me. 'As the game was growing, both became politicised and symbolic of what Brazil is, what unites us and what we care about.' Race was an important factor too, only 62 years after the abolition of slavery in Brazil as the 1950 World Cup took place. There had been a real attempt to integrate black Brazilians, to see what they could contribute to Brazilian nationhood: style, exoticism, the cunning of *malandrismo*.

With football's increasing popularity making it an integral part of Brazilian life and local identity, a successful team would seal what Brazilians saw as their rightful place at the pinnacle of world football. 'This was the chance for Brazil to emerge,' Watson continued. 'All of those things were bound up together to make football culturally, politically and nationally really significant. That expectation, that sense of destiny, comes to make it seem that they just have to turn up and win.' And they would do it in a new stadium in central Rio de Janeiro to serve as the crown jewel in the country's efforts to demonstrate the grandeur of Brazil's national aspiration.

More a national monument than simply a football stadium, construction began on the Maracanã in 1948, to be completed on a tight schedule in time for the 1950 tournament. Many critics argued that the money spent on the stadium would have been better served being focused on hospitals or education, but the need to have a visible embodiment of Brazil's progress meant the stadium was a priority for the government. 'It was sort of an opportunity to tell the world about 20 years of Brazilian development and also Brazil's football prowess,' wrote David Goldblatt in *Futebol Nation*. 'The debate of the Maracanã was most emblematic: Are we going to build the kind of stage that sends a message to the world?'

Crucially, there was a need to project themselves as on a par with the old world of European colonial powers. It mattered to Brazil, for their prestige and self-respect, how they were portrayed back in Europe. But equally, for the government, it was about projecting this image internally too, to convince Brazilians, many living in poverty, that the nation was progressing.

While it wasn't fully complete by the time the tournament began, scaffolding and wet cement just about holding in place, the Maracanã was intended as a monument worthy of sitting alongside Rio's other iconic landmarks: Christ the Redeemer, Sugar Loaf Mountain and Copacabana beach. Its location was therefore crucial, right at the heart of the city, emphasising football's importance to Brazil with its sheer scale.

'Today, Brazil has the biggest and most perfect stadium in the world, dignifying the competence of its people and its evolution in all branches of human activity,' went an editorial in the Rio-based *A Noite* newspaper. 'Now we have a stage of fantastic proportions in which the whole world can admire our prestige and sporting greatness.' The links to nationhood and a reawakening of Brazil's very soul were the theme of many such articles. With the entire 1950 World Cup so directly linked to Brazil's need to portray themselves on to the world stage, success on the field was needed to justify the vast expense and to seal Brazil's status. Brazil had created the stage. Now they needed the team to grace it.

Brazil had been to all three previous World Cups, although it wasn't until the 1938 tournament that they achieved anything of note. They had fallen at the first hurdle in the inaugural 1930 competition, losing to Yugoslavia before beating Bolivia 4-0 in their final group match when already eliminated. In 1934 they fared even worse with a 3-1 loss to Spain seeing them eliminated after just one match. Brazil's scorer that day was Leônidas da Silva, an agile and prolific forward, one of the most important players of the first half of the 20th century. He would inspire Brazil to the semi-final four years later in 1938, before missing out on the clash with Italy in which Brazil were beaten.

The 1938 tournament captured the imagination of the Brazilian people, with large crowds gathering to listen to the games together on the outdoor speakers set up by the local authorities. The team's performances struck a chord with the public, boosting national confidence in Brazil's football prowess. This was aided by the fact that the team's play had developed an exuberance and style that was seen as the personification of the Brazilian attitude to life. 'The Brazilians play as if it were a dance,' wrote the sociologist Gilberto Freyre of Brazil in the 1950s and of the influential exoticism brought by Brazilians of African descent, 'for such Brazilians tend to reduce everything to dance, work and play alike.'

Brazil's growing strength was built on the style introduced to the country by the itinerant Hungarian coach Dori Kurschner at Flamengo in the 1930s and with the national team in 1938. This system was tweaked by Flavio Costa, who would go on to lead Brazil in the 1950 World Cup with his diagonal formation – positioning a wing-half a little deeper on one side, and pushing the opposite inside-forward higher. It was this system that Brazil would take into the 1950 tournament.

Costa had been appointed to the national team job in 1944 having won four Rio league titles at Flamengo, and would ultimately combine the Seleção role with the coaching job at Rio club Vasco da Gama. In an age when Vasco were known as the 'Victory Express', he led them to both domestic and international glory. Costa drew many of the players who would form the core of his World Cup team from his Vasco squad.

A staunch disciplinarian, Costa was also somewhat ahead of his time in his preparations, ensuring he watched other national teams play when he could, aiming to keep up to date on tactical developments and the threat of potential World Cup opponents. He was convinced that, in order to win the World Cup, Brazil would need to find a way past England, and he became focused on the dangers the English would pose. It was a needless concern as it turned out. England's disorganisation and complacency saw them eliminated in humiliating style, but this level of foresight shows what was, for the time, an uncommon degree of preparation.

Costa knew the South American opposition well, though. A year before the World Cup, Brazil had won the Campeonato Sudamericano in style, ending a 27-year wait for continental success, scoring a phenomenal 46 goals in their eight tournament games, more than double any other nation's tally. Hindsight gives us the ability to see one troubling portent for the Brazilians, however. In the round-robin format of the competition, Brazil only needed a draw in their final match against Paraguay to win the tournament, but lost, forcing a title play-off against the same opposition. They recovered to thrash Paraguay 7-0 on that occasion, in a display of attacking excellence, but the parallels in the final group match of that tournament, and the position Brazil would find themselves in at the World Cup a year later, are clear. Any warnings about complacency and over-confidence when within touching distance of glory went unheeded, though, amid the euphoria of the play-off win.

Uruguay, the team who would become Brazil's 1950 nemesis, were summarily brushed aside 5-1 in that Campeonato Sudamericano victory. Indeed, Uruguay, a year ahead of being crowned world champions, were only able to finish sixth best out of eight. Brazil knew the Uruguayan team well though, with the two sides meeting three times shortly before the 1950 World Cup in a series of friendly matches in preparation for the tournament. The first of those saw the *celeste* of Uruguay come back from a 3-0 half-time deficit to win 4-3, with Brazil narrowly winning the other two matches. Far from the crushing victory of the year before, the indications immediately prior to the 1950 tournament were that there was very little between the two sides. There were two close encounters with Paraguay shortly before the World Cup too, Brazil earning a win and a draw.

Confidence remained sky-high, however. Since the performance at the 1938 World Cup, and the successes of Brazil's clubs in continental competition, Brazilians had increasingly viewed themselves as the 'land of football', a narrative positively encouraged by the populist regime: a place where the game had been developed in a style that was both exuberant and effective. A World Cup victory was not only a clear expectation but a requirement. The team simply couldn't let them down.

Due to a handful of late withdrawals, the tournament went ahead with only 13 teams. Nevertheless, Brazil was ablaze with anticipation and excitement with World Cup posters popping up in streets and shops, while the Rio Carnival that February had featured World Cup-themed floats in the parade. Lamartine Babo, one of Brazil's most important popular composers, wrote an early instance of a World Cup song with his 'March of the Brazilian Team' urging the Brazilians, 'Let's cheer with faith in our hearts, Let's cheer for Brazil to be champions.'

The Seleção opened the tournament against Mexico on a warm Saturday afternoon in a barely complete Maracanã amid a party atmosphere. A 4-0 win was the perfect start for the hosts who were missing the best player of this Brazilian generation, Zizinho, who had suffered a knee injury shortly before the tournament. Without him, Ademir scored the first two of the goals that would make him the top scorer in the competition. If this had been a straightforward beginning, things would be more awkward in the second match as the team travelled to São Paulo to take on Switzerland.

The rivalry and bitterness felt between the Rio and São Paulo-based players in the Brazilian squad had been intense during the 1930s and 1940s, and although it had lessened by 1950 it was still significant enough to cause a change in Costa's selection policy. In a sop to the São Paulo crowd, he made several changes with the whole midfield being made up of players from São Paulo state. The team had never trained together in this adjusted formation, let alone played a match together. Despite this, Brazil twice led, only to be pegged back on each occasion. When Switzerland's second equaliser came just minutes from time, it was the prompt for the São Paulo crowd to serenade the team with a shower or boos and whistles. The 2-2 draw, an embarrassing lapse, left Brazil in a precarious position. With only the group winners progressing to the next round, Brazil now trailed Yugoslavia in the standings. Therefore, when Brazil took on Yugoslavia back at the relative comfort of the Maracanã, they had to win to qualify. A draw would see Yugoslavia through instead: Brazil's nightmare scenario.

Yugoslavia had been silver medallists at the 1948 Olympics and, as their results in Brazil so far indicated, they were a formidable opponent. The situation was already tough enough when the two sides met in front of a desperate and vociferous 142,000 crowd in Rio without an ill-advised intervention from the Rio mayor, Mendes de Morais. He addressed the stadium prior to kick-off, pointedly laying out in no uncertain terms what was expected of the players, 'The battle for the world championship has two parts. By constructing the stadium, Rio de Janeiro did theirs. Now you have to do yours.'

Fortune lent Brazil a favour when the Yugoslav striker Rajko Mitić badly cut his head on a low-lying metal beam on his way on to the pitch, a result of the unfinished stadium construction. Mitić missed the opening 20 minutes of the match while his profuse bleeding was stitched and bandaged. With Yugoslavia playing with just ten men for that opening period, Brazil, with Zizinho now in the team, threw everything forward. After only three minutes, Ademir fired them ahead, settling the nerves jangling throughout the stadium. Zizinho, still clearly in pain with restricted mobility, fired a vicious shot past the Yugoslav goalkeeper to seal a 2-0 win. Relief surged from the watching thousands in the stands and on to the pitch in the form of the Brazilian press corps who spilled on to the playing surface in cathartic celebration. Brazil had survived; the dream was still alive.

The 1950 World Cup would uniquely feature a final group stage with no one-off final at all. Fate would lead us to a decisive match regardless, but it was a format born out of the need for Brazil to recoup as much revenue as possible from a tournament that had seen their massive investment in the showpiece venue. To do this, they needed more games, and ideally more involving the home nation.

The hosts were joined in the final group by Spain, who had eased through with three wins including despatching a lacklustre England. Sweden had also qualified having overcome the reigning champions Italy in their group. Italy, though, were a depleted side in 1950, far from their 1930s pomp, with the loss of the players in the great Torino side, killed in the Superga plane disaster the year before. And then there was Uruguay. The *celeste* had been the beneficiaries of the raft of withdrawals, leaving them with only Bolivia to face in their group. Having spent the first week of the tournament with little to do but prepare, they then despatched the Bolivians in some style in an 8-0 victory, with Óscar Miguez, Uruguay's great striker of the era, firing a hat-trick.

Lots were drawn between the final four to decide the playing order, with Brazil's schedule decided as Sweden, Spain and then Uruguay. Thanks to some steadfast lobbying from the Brazilian federation with the tournament organisers, it was decided that all of Brazil's final stage games would be held at the Maracanã, leaving the others to have to travel between Rio and São Paulo.

If Brazil had stuttered their way into the final stage, shredding the nerves of their devout followers in the process, any jitters were put behind them with their finest display of the tournament so far against Sweden. It took little over quarter of an hour for Brazil to break the deadlock, Ademir easing any lingering tension as the near 140,000 in the Maracanã screamed their delight. By half-time it was 3-0 and when, by the hour, Ademir had not only completed his hat-trick but had gone one better to become the only

Brazilian to score four goals in a World Cup game, the rapture was unparalleled.

The final score of 7-1, which still stands as Brazil's biggest World Cup win, was a victory so absolute that Brazilian optimism had been replaced by near certainty. When they followed this by tearing Spain apart in an astonishing 6-1 victory full of flair and invention, there seemed nothing that could stop the Seleção from fulfilling their destiny and their nation's needs.

Against Spain, the intricate skills of Zizinho and Ademir were evident in glorious synchronicity, showcasing everything that was great about Brazilian football: deceptive feints, flicks, dribbles, delightful build-up and clinical, spectacular finishing. This was a team in their prime, enjoying the adulation of the huge crowd who had been celebrating in carnival atmosphere since the first half when victory was already assured. Many of the 153,000 present were waving white handkerchiefs in the air and chanting 'olé' with every Brazilian touch, creating a spectacular backdrop as the players, inspired by the adulation, continued to delight and captivate. There was even an impromptu rendition of a popular carnival song, 'Bullfighting in Madrid', to serve as a contemptuous 'adios' to their outclassed Spanish opponents. The world's media were equally impressed, with the acclaim universal. Italy's *La Gazzetta dello Sport* delighted in Zizinho's role as chief instigator, 'Creating works of art with his feet on the immense canvas of the Maracanã pitch.'

Brazil's first two games in the final group reaffirmed the aura of invincibility, such was their dominance and swagger. The wave of euphoria seemed to confirm everything that the Brazilian nation already knew in themselves to be true: that they were destined for victory, that their superiority was supreme, and that the final match with Uruguay was therefore little more than a formality. The final whistle in the Spain match prompted people across Brazil to party as if the tournament was already won. In so many people's minds, it was.

On the morning of the final, Rio's *O Mundo* declared, 'These are the world champions,' alongside a picture of the Brazilian team. In the lead-up to the final match, the players had been presented with gold watches inscribed to commemorate their anticipated victory. It's not hard to imagine the weight of expectation now bearing down on the players, building to an intolerable crescendo, largely not of their own doing. The international validation Brazil craved through sporting success meant that their achievements carried a burden that now threatened to become increasingly difficult to bear. There is little evidence, though, that the players themselves were attempting to approach the final with any complacency. 'Nobody was thinking we would just walk all over them,' was Ademir's recollection. 'We knew the Uruguayans too well to have any such thought.' Familiarity with their Uruguayan counterparts meant the players knew there was a job still to be done, even if the majority of Brazilians felt differently.

But there was a real sense of fear, born of the fact that there was little glory to be gained. A fear, now that it was taking hold, that would threaten to hamstring the Brazilians when their crowning glory beckoned, their composure and cohesion negatively affected. In the eyes of most Brazilians, the best the team could hope to achieve was to meet their expectant nation's minimum demand. The players must deliver what was expected of them; the only alternative would see them castigated as a catastrophic failure.

In the tournament so far, Brazil had been enjoying the relative seclusion of their base far from the madding crowds of central Rio, in the swanky up-market Joa hills a few kilometres along the coast. It had been a place of refuge, for reflection and focus, an escape from the brewing storm their victories were whipping up. Now, only a few days before the final match, the decision was made by the Brazilian federation to move the squad to a new base at the San Januario, Vasco da Gama's stadium, in the heart of the city.

This wasn't done with the welfare and preparation of the players in mind of course. With victory apparently already achieved, what might be best for the team was of minimal importance. Rather, the move was to enable the endless stream of politicians, dignitaries, celebrities and media greater access to the would-be world champions. The players, with barely a moment's respite, were called upon to gratify frequent requests for photo opportunities, interviews and to attend whatever function the power brokers deemed necessary.

Ademir had to go to a hospital the day before the final to bless a boy. Others were repeatedly pestered for exclusive interviews. Politicians, not wishing to miss the bandwagon and the public popularity it engendered, invaded the base at will to grab their opportunity. The camp was more a scene of bustling revelry than a place for the players to rest and prepare for their one final challenge in the biggest match of their lives.

The noise continued through the evening with Costa only able to finally send his players away from their hijackers around 10pm. Too wired to sleep, many stayed up until the small hours playing cards, trying to unwind. One player, the midfielder Juvenal, instead decided to spend the night drinking in the city. Even the following morning, the day of the final match of the World Cup no less, with a bedraggled Juvenal in tow, the players couldn't escape the distractions of the obligations placed upon them. They were taken to a mass at Rio's Capuchinhos church, not for prayers to see them to victory, but instead to support the launch of a radio station. They were mobbed by fans of course, and again had to spend longer than they should glad-handing and posing for photographs. Back at the San Januario later in the morning, what should have been a time for lunch and a rest before making their way to the stadium was instead turned into another circus as the presidential candidate, Cristian Machado, interrupted proceedings to make a speech hailing Brazil's success.

Instead of a relaxing lunch at their base, they escaped to the Maracanã early – out of the frying pan and into the fire. The stadium was already overcrowded as the team arrived, their bus having a collision among the crowds which caused the team's captain, the Vasco defender Augusto, to receive a cut to the head. To the backing of the crowd already in full-on party mode, noisily hailing their heroes, the players ate lunch in the changing room before bedding down on mattresses on the floor to attempt their post-lunch nap.

On entering the arena, past the pitchside samba band who were ready to play their recently composed song, 'Brasil Os Vencedores' – 'Brazil the Victors' – once victory was confirmed, the Brazilian players were welcomed by a hail of fireworks and rockets, as confetti wafted over the stands filled with flag-waving fans. They were met, too, with a speech from the Rio mayor, the same Mendes de Morais who had ratcheted up the pressure with a similar speech ahead of the Yugoslavia group match. This time, he took things to new extremes.

'You players, who in less than a few hours will be hailed as champions by millions of compatriots,' he proclaimed. 'You, who have no rivals in the entire hemisphere. You, who will overcome any other competitor. You, who I already salute as victors!' All of this prior to the start of a match in which a strong opponent was yet to be overcome, a match in which defeat would spell disaster.

But what of their opponents, those indefatigable Uruguayans? The opportunity was there for them too. While a draw would be good enough to see Brazil crowned champions, for Uruguay the task was more straightforward. Win, and reclaim the world title they had won 20 years earlier. Amid the tangible tension of the occasion, the Uruguayan sense of battling the odds, of taking on an opponent who looked down on them, had been enhanced by the seemingly endless Brazilian proclamations and rhetoric. It was fuel to the flames for a team with their own sense of destiny, and to their captain and leader, Obdulio Varela.

Varela, 'El Negro Jefe' as he was known, the "Black Chief", was a tenacious, tough, no-nonsense midfielder with an iron will and imposing personality, who was more than a mere leader to *la celeste*; he was their inspiration. When presented with a copy of *O Mundo* on the morning of the match by the Uruguayan consul, on seeing the headline proclaiming the Brazilians as champions, he took several copies of the newspaper into the toilets and laid them out on the urinals before encouraging his team-mates to go in and show exactly what they thought of the Brazilian overconfidence. This incident has gained mythical status given what followed, but it served as a clear statement that this underdog would not go quietly into the night.

Having come through their opening group tie against Bolivia with ease, Uruguay initially seemed to struggle to adjust to the higher standard of the final group. After the speedy winger Alcides Ghiggia had given them an early lead against Spain, Uruguay soon fell behind and only a late equaliser from Varela salvaged a draw. Against Sweden, Uruguay trailed 2-1 with less than quarter of an hour to go, before Miguez fired in an equaliser in the 77th minute. He scored again in the final moments for a dramatic victory, in the process maintaining Uruguay's record of never having been beaten at the World Cup. And what is more, they now knew that if they could beat Brazil, it would be they that would be crowned world champions instead of the hosts.

And yet the manner of Brazil's victories over Sweden and Spain contrasted sharply to the close encounters the Uruguayans had come through. Brazilian confidence was well founded, even while it was massively over the top. In front of the biggest football crowd in history, the Uruguayans were in a situation that no team has ever had to face before or since. Nobody else ever has (or likely ever will) entered a bear pit of an arena packed with around 200,000 fans in a delirious, expectant frenzy, all utterly against them, with a World Cup on the line. They were no shrinking violets, however. On walking out into the stadium, the noise deafening, the stands shaking, Varela turned to his team-mates, urging them, 'Go out calmly, walk slowly, do not look up. Never look at the stands. The match is played below.'

They needed their focus. Brazil, with an unchanged line-up, flew out of the traps as they had in their previous final-round matches, seeking to gain an early advantage to ease their nerves. Unlike those matches, when seemingly everything they tried turned to goals, asserting their dominance was less straightforward on this critical occasion. Zizinho burst straight into the Uruguayan box from the outset, winning a corner from which Friaça went close with a zipping shot. Ademir had two early efforts saved and Jair sent a free kick narrowly off target, all within a frantic first few minutes.

Ademir continued to spearhead the siege, creating several more first-half chances, going closest with a bullet header forcing the Uruguayan goalkeeper, Roque Máspoli, into a spectacular save. In all, the Brazilians crafted 17 shots on goal in the opening period. But in the statistic that counted the most, the honours remained resolutely even. Uruguay's back line, protected by Varela in front of them, had fought like dogs to keep their team in the contest. With the attacking impetus mostly one way, it was seemingly only a matter of time before the hosts took the lead.

That said, the best chances of the half actually fell Uruguay's way in their sporadic surges upfield. Juan Schiaffino and Rubén Morán both missed good opportunities presented to them by a nervous Brazilian defence. Then, eight minutes before the interval, Miguez caused numerous heart palpitations in the stadium when his shot smacked off the post with Moacir Barbosa in Brazil's goal well beaten. Despite these chances, Uruguay had been second best overall, fortunate that Brazil's profligate finishing meant they were still in a match they needed to win.

Uruguay had landed another punch, in a more literal sense, during the half as well. Bigode, Brazil's left-half, was struggling to contain the pace and skills of Ghiggia, resorting to fouls to stop the flying winger. On one occasion, having barged Ghiggia over, Bigode was on the receiving end of a clip around the ear from the nearby Varela, only too happy to extend his captaincy duties into the realms of intimidation; a characteristic he frequently exuded by his mere presence and general demeanour. Varela's actions weren't violent as such – Bigode, no shrinking violet himself, was more surprised than hurt – but they served to send a message of rebuke. It was a small victory in itself, but Bigode's continued troubles in this match, his apparent inability to be as influential and dominant as usual, make it seem appear significant nonetheless.

As frustrated as Brazil were by their lack of first-half goals, they were still performing well. They began the second half in much the same way, but this time they got their reward. Only two minutes of the second period had elapsed when Friaça fulfilled the dreams of many a Brazilian: to score in a World Cup Final in the Maracanã. Released down the right by Ademir's neat reverse pass, Friaça's shot bobbled its way into the left corner of the net, sending the massed crowd into rapture.

A goal ahead and playing well when only in need of a draw, Brazil could now almost touch the trophy. The momentum, already heavily in their favour, could have easily overwhelmed the Uruguayans now. Varela, wily, savvy and street-smart, stepped in once again, pursuing the linesman while holding the match ball under his arm, to berate him for a perceived offside in the build-up to Brazil's goal. Really, though, he was playing for time. Time for the crowd to settle from their initial euphoria, time for the tidal wave of Brazilian momentum to be stemmed and interrupted, time, too, for his Uruguayan colleagues to settle themselves for the task ahead.

His intervention certainly took some sting out of the moment, the noise now more focused on criticising Varela rather than pure celebration. 'Let them shout,' Varela told his half-back colleague Rodriguez Andrade before the match restarted. 'In five minutes, the stadium will seem like a graveyard, and then only one voice will be heard. Mine.'

Uruguay responded positively, with Schiaffino shooting narrowly wide soon after. Brazil kept going forwards too, though with notably less abandon than before, seeking to play on the counter-attack given Uruguay's expected desperation. Ademir sprinted into the box before being felled and appealing unsuccessfully for a penalty, and then Jair fired a free kick narrowly over the bar. With Varela's defensive duties easing though, as a result of Brazil sitting back a little more, he was able to move further forwards himself. In the 66th minute, he fed a pass wide to Ghiggia, who raced past Bigode once again. As he neared the byline, he pulled the ball back into the goalmouth where Schiaffino had edged ahead of his marker, Juvenal, and shot firmly past Barbosa.

At 1-1, Brazil were still set for glory, but the atmosphere had utterly changed. Where there had been a carnival atmosphere before, now the nerves had begun to jitter, and the noise had become muted and subdued, almost eerie in fact. It was having an impact on the home team. Costa would later claim that the silence of the crowd had unsettled the players as much as the equaliser itself had. Passes were going astray, the earlier vigour and seamless attack now disjointed and ragged. Uruguay, on the other hand, were playing with renewed energy. Ghiggia continued to torment Bigode, firstly crossing for Schiaffino who headed wide, and setting up another chance, missed by Morán. The warning signs were there for anyone who wanted to see them, but with Bigode apparently unable to prevent it, there was no Brazilian adjustment to assist him. When Ghiggia broke past him again, Brazil's world would collapse around them.

Miguel Perez played a one-two with Ghiggia before then releasing the winger in another chase with the exasperated Bigode. Ghiggia raced into the area with Schiaffino once more surging towards goal for the anticipated pull-back. That was certainly what Barbosa expected to happen. He had stepped slightly to his right, away from his near post, setting himself to either block the cross, or to stifle Schiaffino's shot. Juvenal, too, was lunging in towards Ghiggia in an effort to block the cross. But the cross never came.

Instead, Ghiggia fired a low shot towards the near post. Barbosa, straining his body to recover the gap he had left, got a hand to the ball but not enough to stop it. Footage of the defining moment is hazy, with the cameraman as confused as most others by what was happening. The image pans across goal as if searching for the ball before finding it nestled in the corner of the net, Ghiggia racing through the background, arms aloft. The camera then focused on Barbosa, clambering up from his knees, head bowed, the personal torture that would remain for a lifetime having begun.

'Gol do Uruguay,' said the Brazilian commentator Luiz Mendes on the Radio Globo broadcast, before repeating himself, with a tone of disbelief, 'Gol do Uruguay?' He answered himself, repeating the same phrase a further six times as the shock gave way to resignation, his voice that of a broken nation, of a hope extinguished.

The Maracanã fell silent: this footballing shrine as quiet as a tomb, disbelief etched on the face of the thousands of stunned witnesses in the stands. Brazil had just ten minutes in which to rescue themselves in a match in which victory had been a given. You would expect ten frantic minutes with Brazil throwing everything at Uruguay in their desperation. Instead, while Brazil did indeed attack, their rhythm and belief had been eroded to such an extent that they seemed incapable of playing with conviction. The shell-shocked observers looked on in a near-funereal atmosphere. As Jules

Rimet himself put it, 'The silence was morbid, sometimes too difficult to bear.' When the final whistle came, the tears flowed on the pitch, in the stands and around the entire country. While Uruguay celebrated, the Brazilian players entered a personal hell. Having been tasked with securing a nation's international pride, to have failed in such a manner left a nation bereft.

Varela received the trophy from a flustered Rimet among a pitchside huddle of tearful policemen and devastated onlookers. Having celebrated noisily in their changing room afterwards, the drive back to their hotel made it clear to the Uruguayans what pain they had inflicted on their hosts. The streets were unnervingly empty, many bars and restaurants staying closed as a nation hid itself away in mourning, turning in on itself, its worst fears realised.

While many of the Uruguayan squad remained celebrating at their hotel, Varela and a few others chose to venture into the city. 'I sat at a bar and I started to drink sugarcane hoping that no one would recognise me, because I thought that if they did, they would kill me,' he recalled in an interview in 1993. 'But they recognised me straight away and, to my surprise, they congratulated me, they hugged me and many of them stayed to drink with me into the night.'

But make no mistake, the pain inflicted on the defeated nation cut deep. As Alex Bellos describes in *Futebol: The Brazilian Way of Life*, 'The adjective fatidico, fateful, has, to all intents and purposes, been copyrighted by 1950.' Every aspect of the match is described using this adjective, referring to far more than merely the game of football it decided. It was a national humiliation which transcended football and sport, and to many Brazilians confirmed a long-held inferiority complex. Not only had they lost to their much smaller near neighbours, but they had done so in the newly built edifice to Brazilian progress and achievement and when the political need to promote Brazil internationally had required this crowning glory. When even football, their great expression of Brazilianness, had failed them, the sense that Brazilians were a naturally defeated people took hold again. The 'stray dog complex', as discussed by the popular Brazilian writer Nelson Rodrigues, may have existed prior to 1950, but it was amplified by the events in the Maracanã.

Second place in the World Cup was, at the time, Brazil's best-ever finish, and yet it felt like a colossal defeat as the prospect of failure had simply not been countenanced. An excess of confidence and the unbearable weight of expectation had certainly contributed to the defeat, but for a nation unable to accept that Uruguay had simply been the better, more composed team on the day, the impression was forged that the defeat was the natural conclusion for a nation unsure of its place in the world. Victory would have vindicated the national optimism, but defeat exposed how fragile that was.

The self-esteem of a nation was damaged, a huge mark left on the Brazilian psyche. David Goldblatt explores this theme in *Futebol Nation*, 'When you nail your colours to *futebol* the way Brazil had done in the 1930s and 1940s, that's the catch, isn't it? It's a capricious thing. Brazil really did buy into it. They bought into it in a very serious way, and suddenly, the cupboard was bare. As far as the projection to the outside world, they were left asking themselves, what is Brazil?'

Many Brazilians didn't like what they saw when contemplating that question. For a young nation, ill at ease with itself and with no particular experience of national tragedies of any description, or significant nationally remembered moments, its people weren't psychologically prepared for defeat. It was a historical void which the pain of 1950 filled. Viewed in hindsight, it's easy to dismiss these reactions as excessive, unwarranted and lacking any sense of perspective. When viewed through the context of the time and place, however, the inextricable link between its football fortunes and the nation's politics, economic development and sense of self-worth at home and abroad make it understandable to some extent, even if it still seems irrational.

In the *Jornal dos Sports*, the novelist Jose Rins do Rego wrote, 'I saw a nation defeated – more than that – one without hope. That hurt my heart. All the vibrancy of the first minutes reduced to the ashes of an extinguished fire. And suddenly a greater disappointment, it stuck in my head that we really were a luckless people, a nation deprived of the great joys of victory, always pursued by bad luck, by the meanness of destiny.' It's remarkable to modern eyes to think that football caused Brazilians to feel this way, given all the success that has come their way since, but the scars truly ran deep.

The concept of the Maracanãço was born, meaning the agony of Maracanã, the millstone around the neck of Brazilian football that would remain the omnipresent haunting reminder of national failure for years to come. Pelé, just nine years old at the time of the 1950 tournament, would recall both his own and his father's tears. Legend has it that the young boy destined to become a legend sought to reassure his distraught father, telling him that he would one day win the World Cup for Brazil. That moment of cathartic fulfilment was still eight long years away, however, when a still-teenage Pelé would inspire his country to a first World Cup victory in Sweden in 1958. That Brazil's ultimate football hero would be a black man contrasts somewhat with the treatment of the scapegoats of the 1950 side.

Defeat had caused a lot of self-reflection, reopening issues of self-worth and race, laying bare the old emotions and feelings that had yet to fade into the background. The question became, what is it about our nation that is failing us? In the search for scapegoats, the whole concept of what it meant to be Brazilian was questioned, reigniting theories about Brazil's national lack of character stemming from the racial mixture in a nation that was only 62 years beyond the abolition of slavery. Thus, in many a Brazilian newspaper the blame was pointed squarely at the three black players in the team: Bigode, Juvenal and the goalkeeper Barbosa.

Black Brazilians were associated with slavery, and therefore with a lack of character or education, and with laziness. 'All those characteristics are easily built upon and criticised,' explained Dr Peter Watson. 'It's easy to do that, and Barbosa is the one that suffers it. But it's part of a national conversation that's been ongoing about trying to assimilate so many things and questioning whether they are worth it.'

Bigode had been tormented by Ghiggia throughout the match, but the moment when Varela had seemingly got into his head, putting him off his naturally aggressive game with the clip around the ear, was cited as the moment Bigode disappeared against Uruguay. This fails to consider the instruction he'd received from Costa to rein in his naturally antagonistic style, which some of his team-mates later claimed had impacted his whole performance. Juvenal, too, was earmarked for his perceived weakness in dealing with the twin threat of Ghiggia and Schiaffino. But neither Bigode nor Juvenal suffered the levels of vitriol aimed at Barbosa.

Considering he was voted by journalists as the best goalkeeper of the 1950 World Cup, for Barbosa's contribution to be ultimately remembered for one fateful moment is painfully unfair. More poignantly, his whole career, and indeed his whole life, would be defined by the goal that lost the World Cup.

As part of the great Vasco da Gama team of the 1940s, Barbosa had helped his side win numerous domestic and continental titles. For the Seleção, he had established himself as not only the first-choice goalkeeper but Brazil's first black goalkeeper. And yet he became the personification of the defeat and would only play once more for Brazil following the Maracanaço, and that was some three years later in a Campeonato Sudamericano victory over Ecuador in 1953. He then suffered a bad injury which scuppered any hope of going to the 1954 World Cup, but the reality is that he was largely excluded from the international set-up following the trauma of 1950, victimised and castigated for one moment among a collective failure.

He remained one of Brazil's best goalkeepers, though, continuing his fine form for Vasco, playing for them until 1960. Upon his retirement three years later, aged 41, he took a job for the organisation responsible for managing Rio's sports venues. As a result, Barbosa had to work in the shadow of the scene of the defining moment of his life. In 1963, he hosted a barbecue for some friends at his home on which he burned the Maracanã posts, a symbol of his pain sent up in smoke in what he described as a 'liturgy of purification'. It may have helped his internal demons, but to the wider Brazilian public he was still reviled: the personification of a nation's failure.

He recalled an incident in 1970, the year that Brazil's *jogo bonito* reached its perfect zenith in their third World

Cup victory. When shopping at a market a woman pointed at him and told her young child, 'Look at him, son. He is the man that made all of Brazil cry.' Barbosa would never escape the shadow cast by the seismic defeat. He was refused entry when trying to visit a national squad training camp in 1993 lest he bring them bad luck. Not long before his death in 2000, he was quoted as saying, 'In Brazil, the most you get for a crime is 30 years. For 50 years I've been paying for a crime I did not commit. Even a criminal when he has paid his debt is forgiven. But I have never been forgiven.' He added, 'I'm not guilty. There were 11 of us.' He would take this pain to his grave; a man broken by the twists of fate on a day in 1950 which could have been the crowning moment of his career.

Others, too, were not immune from the backlash. Costa was replaced as coach of the Seleção by Zezé Moreira, who revamped Costa's man-to-man marking approach, so exposed in the Uruguay defeat, and steered Brazil on the beginnings of the path to the 4-2-4 which would see Brazil dominate in the years down the line. So, too, the lessons of the flawed logistics and the chaotic levels to which the players were exposed in the final days of the tournament were learned. By 1958, there was a greater level of professionalism to prevent such obvious mistakes from happening again.

The shirts worn on the fateful day in 1950 were also tarnished through association with defeat. Brazil had always worn all white up until this point, but they had now become a symbol of national humiliation. They weren't replaced immediately, indeed Brazil wore white when winning the 1952 Pan-American Championship – including a victory over Uruguay – but a competition had been launched across the nation seeking artistic submissions for a new kit incorporating the colours of the Brazilian flag. It was won by a teenager named Aldyr Schlee, who designed the iconic yellow with green trim and blue shorts that was worn at the 1954 World Cup. This design is now so utterly synonymous with Brazil, its football and its success, the glamour and flamboyance, as to make the fact that they previously wore white seem almost implausible. That Schlee hailed from close to the Uruguayan border and supported Uruguay rather than Brazil was a bitter irony.

Perhaps the failure of 1950 was a necessary step for a nation carving out a place for itself in the world. While Brazil's football history did not begin with the 1950 defeat, it does mark the starting point of its modern history; an essential rite of passage, a turning point in the rise of the country who would become one of the finest exponents the game has ever known. The Brazilian nation's modern history is marked out in World Cups, the biggest collective celebration of Brazilianness on a global stage, which helps to explain why the Maracanaço holds such a place in Brazil's history and has remained forefront in the minds of Brazilians for so long.

The team buckled under the weight of pressure and the expectation of a desperate nation; its national wellbeing tied so closely to its football success. The trauma was eased once World Cup victories came along in 1958 and 1962, but it's arguable that Brazil only regained its assuredness following the 1970 win when they enjoyed a victory so perfect as to finally ease the pain. It couldn't erase it completely though. In facing Uruguay in the semi-final that year, memories of 1950 haunted Brazilian thoughts, with references to events two decades earlier inevitable and painful. In 1970, Brazil may have become the best football team, playing the best football with the best footballer in the world, but that feeling remained, as described to me by Dr Peter Watson, 'That we couldn't win it in our own country when we were supposed to, when we'd built it up into the biggest deal that we were ever going to have.'

The year 1950 has become the comparison by which all other Brazilian World Cup defeats are measured. The parallels to the humiliating disaster the next time Brazil hosted a World Cup, only to be thrashed 7-1 by Germany in the 2014 semi-final, are stark. That defeat prevented the opportunity to erase the memory of the Maracanaço by returning there for another World Cup Final. Instead, it lingers still, but no longer stands alone as the measure of Brazilian football failure; '2014 has put 1950 in perspective,' Fernando Duarte, author of *Shocking Brazil*, told me. 'But make no mistake: the defeat to Uruguay will linger.' Its impact was keenly felt in 2014. 'It rekindled the feeling that Brazil needed to win at home, and that put huge pressure on the players.' Just as it had in 1950.

Hosting the World Cup again in 2014 provided no cathartic, cleansing home victory, instead foisting a new nightmare on the Brazilian sporting consciousness, but the lasting impact on a nation's psyche, though not insignificant, wouldn't match that of the 1950 defeat. Where 1950, therefore, stands above Brazil's 2014 disaster is in the links to nationhood and national self-esteem. As Paulo Perdigão wrote in *Anatomia de uma Derrota* (Anatomy of a Defeat), 'It continues being the most famous goal in the history of Brazilian football ... because none other transcended its status as a sporting fact ... converting itself into a historic moment in the life of a nation.'

Such moments are seared into the collective consciousness of the nation, immortalised in countless analyses of Brazil and Brazilianness. Defeat was felt so deeply in large part because it was one of the first events to embed itself in the national memory. Brazil had fought no major wars or faced hugely significant national events. But the 1950 defeat was one such event; a nation-building moment forged through pain. To have the expected victory snatched away, Watson added, 'It does become a national tragedy as it dominates the national discussion. And it's still seen this way today.'

They had been within reach of a first World Cup trophy. Victory had been hailed, the fanfares ready, a nation's emergence as a vibrant, confident powerhouse set to be confirmed. When Ghiggia scored and the Maracanã fell silent, a nation wept and mourned; a stray dog kicked into submission by their more successful neighbours from Uruguay.

The national team has gone on to be the most successful in the world in terms of World Cup victories, but the Maracanãço will remain in Brazilian consciousness as a reminder that their modern history began not with victory but with defeat. Just as the Maracanã, the monument to Brazilian progress and modernity, will never escape the fact that it began life as the scene of a national humiliation.

4

Hungary 1954

If someone was to wake me up tomorrow
morning and remind me of that match, I'd
burst into tears.

Gyula Grosics

ONE DEFEAT. One single defeat in four years. It had been
a run of success that had taken in 32 matches and brought
Hungary fame and glory. The Magnificent Magyars had
not only achieved unparalleled success on the field, they had
also inspired and raised the profile of a nation. Most of all,
though, they had revolutionised the way football was played,
creating a style that was as delightful as it was effective: a
mesmeric, sophisticated style that pointed the way forwards
in tactical development and lifted Hungary all the way to
the 1954 World Cup Final.

Yet, on the day that World Cup glory beckoned, the
Hungarian players stood in the sodden, muddy surroundings
of the Wankdorf Stadium in Bern looking on as Fritz Walter,
the West German captain, raised the World Cup in victory.
Their destiny had deserted them. It was meant to have been

their time, the moment the preceding years of astonishing glory had all been building towards, the moment that the greatest team the world had seen would be crowned as such. And yet fate decreed otherwise. The 1954 World Cup Final would be the one full international match the great side of Puskás, Kocsis, Czibor and Hidegkuti would fail to win in almost six years of action in the 1950s – four years prior to the 1954 World Cup, and two years following it.

It was a glorious era for the team who would be dubbed *Aranycsapat*: the Golden Team. On the field, it would end in crushing disappointment, while off the field, it would all ultimately crumble amid uprising, revolution and defection. But what a team it was. They left a legacy that elevates them above most others, and indeed above the West German team that would inflict defeat on them. They were the symbol of Hungary abroad, seen by the political hierarchy as emblematic of Hungarian national success amid a period of oppression imposed by their Soviet overlords, while also an obvious source of national pride for the Hungarian people.

Hungary had been one of the key football powers in central Europe in the pre-war years, a power whose first real peak would come in the 1930s, culminating in reaching the 1938 World Cup Final before losing to the great Italian side of the era. Having not entered the first post-war World Cup in 1950 due to the costs involved for a war-weary nation, this 1954 tournament represented Hungary's next assault on football glory, 16 years on from finishing as runners-up. The end result may have been the same as in 1938, but the manner of it would capture the imagination of the world.

Hungarian football thinking had developed with a strong influence from their Austrian neighbours, and the passing, technical style aided by involvement with the English itinerant coach Jimmy Hogan. He ultimately continued his career in Budapest, influencing the development of football across Hungary, but particularly with Budapest club MTK. The seeds sewn by Hogan would ultimately lead to the revolutionary approach that Hungary refined at international level.

Having come through a tumultuous time in the Second World War, Hungary had been freed of Nazi partnership and occupation and become a part of the Soviet Union's sphere of influence under the hard-line leadership of Mátyás Rákosi. Amid the huge political turmoil and transformation, the deputy minister for sport and staunch communist, Gusztáv Sebes, was appointed as national team manager, and left free to run the national team in his own way. A former player under Hogan at MTK, he was no football coach, however. His skills lay in management rather than tactics, gathering around him the coaching team and support for the players he felt would get the best from the talented squad at his disposal.

Sebes would always maintain a level of separation, acting as what the great goalkeeper of the era, Gyula Grosics, would describe as 'a dictator with the power over life and death'. Sebes sought to combine the pass and move style with the highly flexible positional interchanging of another great team of the late 1940s, Dynamo Moscow: a team in which the system not the individuals, as it was in communism, was everything. Equally advanced were his changes in making the Hungarian kit more aerodynamic, using low-cut, lightweight boots to aid the quick style of play, and a greater focus on health, both physical and mental.

Hungarian football was also going through structural change, taking on a more Soviet-style mode. Professionalism was ended, and the best clubs in the country were placed under the ownership of government departments, trade unions and industries. Hungary's defence minister, the Moscow-trained Mihály Farkas, with an eye on pleasing his Soviet masters, made sure that the army had its choice of clubs and so instructed Sebes to find a suitable, Budapest-based team to take over.

Sebes, ever the canny operator, saw potential advantage he could gain for his national team with a consolidated core of players playing together regularly. As a result, Kispest, a relatively small team located on the outskirts of Budapest, became the army club and was soon renamed Honvéd, meaning 'protect the homeland'. The entire staff of players and coaches were given military ranks, and were supplied with new kit, new boots and improved training facilities. Crucially though, for Sebes, two of the national team's most important players were already there: József Bozsik and Ferenc Puskás.

Nobody is more synonymous with this team and this era than Puskás. Fast, skilful and powerful, Puskás was a force of nature who had been part of the national team since 1945 and was already racking up the goal tally with his hammer of a left foot. His free rein would, at times, mean he was afforded a degree of latitude not available to other players for both Honvéd and Hungary, but his talents, extraordinary vision and improvisation made him the indispensable star of Hungarian football. He and Bozsik, a deep-lying midfield playmaker with elegance and poise, had been childhood friends, growing up in the same apartment block. In terms of character they were poles apart, but their friendship endured through their mutual progression from local playing fields to Kispest, its transformation into Honvéd, and into the national team.

Sebes wanted more of the national team players to join Bozsik and Puskás at Honvéd. The first to receive their call-up papers, drafted into the army in little more than name only, were the Ferencváros pair Sándor Kocsis and László Budai. Kocsis was the most prized and would go on to become the principal goalscorer for the national team. These close friends had first met in the Ferencváros youth team, quickly developing a strong bond on and off the pitch. Budai was a direct winger who used his burst of pace to beat his man and fire in a cross from the byline, invariably in the direction of Kocsis who habitually scored. The move to Honvéd merely made their combination more prolific as Kocsis, a clinical goalscorer, benefitted from the additional potent attacking talents around him for both club and country. From his international debut in 1948 to his departure from Hungary in 1956, he would score a remarkable 68 goals in his 75 international appearances.

The central defender Gyula Lóránt was another Honvéd conscript shortly after, as was the goalkeeper Gyula Grosics – perhaps the finest custodian of the early 1950s, and a player who had previously been banned for a year following an arrest for trying to escape Hungary. Part of his punishment had been conscription into the army during his playing ban, and so once Honvéd became the army club, he could simply be told to play for them.

Sebes was initially hesitant to bring Grosics back into the international fold, however, disliking him both personally and politically. But following a 5-3 defeat to Austria in Vienna in 1950, he laid a portion of the blame on the goalkeeper he had chosen, Géza Henni. Lacking alternatives and accepting that Grosics was far and away the best Hungarian goalkeeper, Sebes eventually came to see that the national team would be best served with him guarding their goal. Despite their mutual loathing, Grosics made his international return later in 1950. Hungary's defence was immediately improved, helping the team to remain unbeaten through the rest of the year.

A year later, one more of the key internationals also joined Honvéd: Zoltán Czibor. Czibor was something of a free spirit, making him far from the ideal military conscript and not the kind of player Sebes would normally tolerate in his team. Like Grosics, Czibor had been banned for trying to escape Hungary, but he would only serve one month of his ban once he was called into the national team. There was simply no other left-winger in Hungary remotely in his class, with such dedication and will to win.

The Hungarian style had also been evolving during this time, prompted by a defeat to Czechoslovakia in 1949. 'After that game the issue could no longer be avoided,' wrote Puskás in his autobiography. 'Hungary had to evolve an entirely new method of play if we were to make any headway in international football.' What followed was the enhancement of the sophisticated, fluid structure with players constantly changing position, leaving many an opponent confused and confounded. This evolution set Hungary on the first steps of their astonishing unbeaten run in the early 1950s, and on the path to their first great challenge: the 1952 Helsinki Olympics.

Sebes took his team to Moscow shortly before the Olympics began for two matches against Soviet selections in what were unofficial internationals; Hungary winning one and losing one. While politically nobody in the power halls of Budapest would quibble over a loss to the Soviet Union, there was certainly a concern about how the side may perform in the Olympics, when the chance to promote Hungary on the world stage would be best served by victory.

Sebes's solution came from one of his managerial rivals, the MTK coach Márton Bukovi. MTK, the club of the

Secret Police, home to the principal Hungarian players who were not conscripted to Honvéd, had been playing through the late 1940s with a centre-forward withdrawn into a position where there would be more space to exploit, the two wingers pushing further forwards to compensate. In also pushing a half-back practically into the defence, this formation had served MTK well and was particularly suited to a squad that lacked a strong, battering-ram-style centre-forward. Instead of forcing another player to play out of position, it made more sense to adapt the system to suit the skills of the players available.

When this approach proved successful for MTK and then latterly at Honvéd too, it was a small step to see this implemented by the national team. While Nándor Hidegkuti would go on to become synonymous with the withdrawn centre-forward role for Hungary through 1953 and 1954, he was initially a winger at MTK, and so it was Péter Palotás who Sebes first picked in this role, with Hidegkuti on the right wing. Palotás, no natural goalscorer, thrived in this position, acting as a pivot between the defence and attack supplying the wingers and inside-forwards.

With the Hungarian league officially amateur, with players employed by government agencies, unions or the army, it was a full-strength Hungarian team which took part in the 1952 Olympics: Hungary's first date with destiny. In a straight knockout tournament, Hungary's start was gradual rather than spectacular. They faced a preliminary-round clash with Romania, scraping a 2-1 win. Hungary had struggled to find their rhythm, not aided by the fact that Kocsis was sent off for the only time in his career. This near disaster led to a further tweak in personnel. József Zakariás would come into the team at left-half to partner Bozsik in the midfield, covering for his more forward-thinking colleague when Hungary attacked. And attacking was something Hungary did almost at will.

Hungary beat Italy in a dominant display to win 3-0, before a quarter-final 7-1 thrashing of Turkey was followed by a 6-0 win over Sweden to send Hungary into the gold medal match. Hungary's play, and incredible scoring rate, was now drawing the attention of others, for its scintillating style and sophistication, as well as its success. As Puskás noted, 'We were already a great side, but it was during the Olympics that our football began to flow with real exhilaration ... We had positional freedom and when we attacked, everyone attacked, from the defenders to the strikers.'

It was captivating to those observing, such as the head of the English FA, Stanley Rous, who invited Hungary to face England the following year having witnessed their semi-final victory. But it needed a gold medal to really signal the arrival of a new power. On 2 August 1952, they took the field at Helsinki's Olympic Stadium in front of nearly 60,000 spectators to take on a very strong Yugoslavia side. Politically this was an awkward opponent, given the way the Yugoslav leader Tito was steadfastly refusing to run his country the way the Soviets had attempted to dictate. Yugoslavia had knocked the Soviet Union out in the first round too, meaning that for Hungary's politicians, this represented an opportunity. A Hungarian win could restore the honour of communism and earn the Hungarians some plaudits from their Moscow masters. Therefore, it was little surprise that Rákosi phoned Sebes the night before the final to inform him, 'The political situation for us is very difficult at the present moment, Comrade Sebes. You have to win.'

A nervy first half was short on chances for either team, and when the Hungarians did create they were ably rebuffed. Even a Puskás penalty was weak, mishit almost, and easily saved. Shortly after the half-time interval though, things clicked into gear. After two Kocsis strikes had been disallowed, Puskás finally scored with an irresistible shot to make it 1-0. Czibor added a lobbed long-range effort in the closing moments to seal the gold medal and a 2-0 win, and, with it, the *Aranycsapat*, the Golden Team, were truly born.

'I felt an overwhelming sense of relief,' Sebes told FIFA when looking back on this triumph. 'We had done what we had to do, and we had done it in style. All of a sudden, the international press was showering us in praise. Those Olympics put us on the map.' Puskás stood atop the podium to receive the gold medal from the current Miss Universe, beaming from ear to ear as he received the adulation of the crowd. That would be nothing compared to the adulation that greeted them on their return to Hungary, however.

'On the train home, once we left Prague, the train kept stopping at every station to allow crowds to greet us,' Puskás recalled. Tens of thousands crammed into the streets around Budapest's Keleti station to welcome them home. 'We were ecstatic,' continued Puskás. 'That was our first great victory and our hearts were still so young.' Suddenly, everything was different. The players became the centre of attention in Budapest, feted as celebrities. None more so than Puskás, who was now rated the best player in the world. It led to a rise in expectation not only from the public but also from the political regime.

The first match following that victory came a little over a month later, and the pressure seemed to have got to the Olympic champions. Trailing 2-0 to Switzerland in a Central European International Cup clash, Sebes substituted Palotás for Hidegkuti, in part to test out the 30-year-old Hidegkuti's stamina, but also his suitability in the withdrawn role. This move signalled what was arguably the most significant personnel change for Hungary. They came back from their deficit to win 4-2 with Hidegkuti hugely influential.

Hidegkuti had been in and out of the national team since the end of the Second World War and had rotated with Palotás in the Olympic squad, but now the role was truly his own. He played in such an intelligent way, a forerunner to some of the midfield pivots around which more modern teams are built, linking up with the other forwards, principally Puskás and Kocsis. His quick, short passes often led to him receiving the ball back straight away, playing in what modern eyes would see as between the lines. In this way he could keep the ball moving, keep the attacking momentum and, crucially, leave the opposition chasing shadows, not knowing whether to close him down or remain in their formation.

With the first-choice 11 now firmly established, 1953 would be a momentous year for the Hungarians. Firstly they travelled to Italy, crushing their hosts 3-0 in Rome's newly built Stadio Olimpico, securing Hungary's first Central European International Cup title – Puskás scoring twice in his 50th international. As impressive and significant as this victory was, it was nothing compared to what followed later in 1953 when Hungary travelled to Wembley to face England for the Golden Team's finest hour.

Prior to heading to London, Hungary were held to a 2-2 draw by Sweden, whose English coach George Raynor had demonstrated the way in which Hungary's main threat could be nullified. By man-marking Hidegkuti, taking away the space he often found when dropping deep, Sweden stifled Hungary's attack, while the rest of the team sat deep, creating a defensive barrier.

The English weren't paying attention, however. Fielding a handful of the world's best players, such as Stanley Matthews and Tom Finney, England were confident in their superiority in spite of their ignorance of the task ahead. Famously, as the teams lined up in the tunnel to come out on to the Wembley pitch, England's captain Billy Wright noticed the low-cut boots of the Hungarians and whispered to striker Stan Mortensen, 'We should be all right here, Stan – they haven't even got the proper kit.' England's ignorant confidence meant there would be no man-marking of Hidegkuti, or anyone else. It was against England's ingrained approach to attempt to adjust their formation to cope with the opposition's threat, and this game would be no different.

Freed from any special attention, Hidegkuti dominated the opening moments. In the very first minute he received the ball completely unmarked, had the time to set himself, dummy the onrushing centre-half and fire a shot that silenced the Wembley crowd to give Hungary the lead within 45 seconds of kick-off. Although England recovered to equalise ten minutes later, there was to be no respite. Hidegkuti soon made it 2-1 before Puskás scored the most famous goal of the match, nonchalantly dragging the ball back to leave the desperate Wright looking clumsily foolish – famously described by Geoffrey Green in *The Times* as 'like a fire engine going to the wrong fire' – before calmly beating Gil Merrick in the England goal. Puskás made it 4-1 soon after, and though England clawed one back before the break, and came close to another only for Grosics to make a good fingertip save, it was clear to all who the superior team was.

In the England dressing room at the interval, confusion reigned. Harry Johnston, the centre-half, sought clarity on what he should do with Hidegkuti, and in doing so neatly summed up the tactical conundrum the Hungarians were inflicting on opponents unused to such flexibility, 'If I follow him, into midfield, then I leave myself exposed at the back, but if I stay where I am, he is unmarked to do as he damn well pleases! I am bloody helpless!' He was not alone in his confusion, however. Matthews was muddled by his direct opponent, Czibor, who kept changing wings, and also by the fact that there were three men closing him down when in possession. Wright, too, was struggling to cope with the movement of those he was tasked with marking, ending up attempting to contain Bozsik, Zakariás and Puskás. England sought solace in their standard fallback option: try to beat them with physicality.

Within ten minutes of the restart though, Hungary had scored twice more. Bozsik rifled in the fifth following a rebound after Kocsis's shot had hit the post, and then Puskás set up Hidegkuti to complete his hat-trick with a neat volley. It ended 6-3, and in the shell-shocked aftermath of defeat, the English press corps hailed their conquerors not only for their victory, but for the way in which they had achieved it. In the *Daily Telegraph*, Frank Field described the performance as 'the most brilliant display of football ever seen in this country'. The players felt much the same. 'The result did not truly reflect the Hungarians' overall superiority,' commented Matthews, while Johnston, the perplexed centre-half, later wrote, 'To me, the tragedy was the utter helplessness. Being unable to do anything to alter the grim outlook.'

English football may have ignored the warning signs for years but the Hungarians had caused the penny to finally drop. As Puskás told the press conference the next day, 'We demonstrated the golden rule of modern football, and that is: the good players keep playing even without the ball.' The Magical Magyars were the new masters and were serenaded as such by huge crowds on their return to Budapest in the now-familiar fashion.

The message still hadn't been heeded by all, however. Viewing the defeat as an off day, Stanley Rous asked for the opportunity to play again, in Budapest; a request the Hungarians were only too willing to accommodate. The two sides would meet again in May 1954, shortly before the World Cup was due to begin. The Wembley victory, however, had raised expectations in Hungary to new heights, and it was political gold dust too. Through its football success, Hungary was global news, its name associated with forward-thinking, elegance, style and panache.

Once England arrived in Budapest in May 1954, the clamour for tickets to the match was unprecedented in Hungary with 90,000 ultimately cramming in to the Népstadion in the biggest attendance for a match in the country. In the splendid sunshine of a May afternoon, Hungary produced what is arguably their finest display of football. Sebes had been so convinced that England would alter their tactics that he urged caution from the start until England's game plan became clear. Soon enough it was apparent, though, that while England may have changed some of their players, they were rigidly sticking to the same formation and tactics that had seen them humbled at Wembley. In Budapest, they were simply torn apart.

Hungary won 7-1 in a display of exquisite magnificence. 'We were just glad the ordeal was over and to get off the pitch before the score reached double figures,' was the England captain Billy Wright's reaction. Puskás, Kocsis and Czibor in particular were in scintillating form, but the team as a whole had been magnificent. It was, as England's Tom Finney succinctly reflected 'like carthorses playing racehorses'.

The point had been made once again: Hungary were on another level, at their real peak in fact. As Czibor put it, 'Everything came together. Everything just clicked.' This was the Magical Magyars at their very best, the pinnacle of several years of magnificence. They didn't know it at the time, but it was to be their greatest triumph: the 6-3 and 7-1 wins over England remaining revered by Hungarians to this day in a way they surely wouldn't have been to quite the same degree had they been eclipsed by World Cup victory soon after. Three weeks later, with the cheers of the astounded home crowd still ringing in their ears, the World Cup began in Switzerland, with Hungary as the clear favourites. It's hard to think of another team going into any World Cup on such a run of success.

Hungary had qualified without having to kick a ball, thanks to the withdrawal of their only qualifying opponent, Poland. The Polish, as with some other eastern European nations, didn't want to risk humiliation on the world stage at such a developmental time for European communism. Hungary, on the other hand, harboured no such fears.

The 1954 finals adopted a uniquely odd format for the group stage. Drawn into a group featuring South Korea, West Germany and Turkey, the Hungarians would only have to face the two non-seeded teams in their group. For Hungary, this meant going from one extreme to the other, facing the weak Koreans before taking on the rather more significant challenge of West Germany. The group winner would go straight through to the quarter-finals, with the next two best facing each other in a play-off for the final place in the knockout rounds.

Hungary's tournament began in Zürich against a South Korea side that had only arrived in Switzerland two days earlier following an arduous week-long journey from the Far East. The 9-0 scoreline, including a Kocsis hat-trick, could easily have been so much more had Hungary really turned the screw and the match not been constantly interrupted late on due to frequent cases of cramp in their exhausted opponents.

Having been tested less than they had in their pre-tournament warm-ups against local Swiss league clubs, Hungary were back in action just three days later facing West Germany in Basel in what ought to have been a truer test of their credentials. Under Sepp Herberger, who had been manager of Germany in the 1938 World Cup and up to 1945 when the team was barred from international football, West Germany came into the tournament as something of an unknown quantity. They came to Switzerland with a strong squad, but one that was short of international experience. On being readmitted to FIFA in 1950, West Germany struggled to find opposition willing to play them. When they did play matches they were barracked almost continually. Herberger himself had been banned for his Nazi involvement but had made his return to guide West Germany through qualifying. He took a fairly pragmatic approach to this group match with Hungary, aided by the fact that they had already comfortably beaten Turkey.

Reasoning that Hungary would likely beat a full-strength West Germany anyway, leaving the Germans only a few days to recover before facing Turkey again in a play-off, Herberger selected a weakened side, making seven changes. Hungary settled for just two changes, including Hidegkuti replacing Palotás as the number nine. Hungary battered the Germans, winning 8-3, Kocsis again demonstrating his goalscoring prowess with four, including the opener in just the third minute.

Puskás scored early too, but he was subjected to some close attention from the tough West German defender Werner Liebrich. He repeatedly landed his studs on to Puskás's legs, eventually flooring him with a vicious kick to the ankle resulting in a serious hairline fracture of his left ankle. It may not have affected the outcome of this match but the implications for Hungary's tournament were severe. The loss of their most significant and most important player was a major blow. The esteemed football writer Brian Glanville went so far as to later describe this incident as 'the foul that won the World Cup'. Puskás hoped for a swift recovery, not for the upcoming quarter-final or indeed semi-final, but only for the final should they get there. He later admitted to crying bitterly every night during his battle for fitness in the coming days, drying his bedding each morning so that his team-mates wouldn't see the tear stains.

Hungary may have been without their talisman, but they had won their group and would now face Brazil in the quarter-final in an eagerly anticipated clash, with both sides capable of playing attractive, attacking football. Brazil, still haunted by their 1950 trauma, entered the knockout phase with an anxiety that may have helped to cause what was one of the most cynical, brutal and unpleasant matches in World Cup history. In what would become known as the Battle of Bern, three players were sent off amid a stream of fouls that caused the referee, Englishman Arthur Ellis, to note, 'They behaved like animals. It was a disgrace. It was a horrible match.' Amid the anarchy, some football broke out too, with Hungary racing into an early 2-0 lead, something that their focus on physical preparation and proper warm-ups meant was a fairly frequent occurrence. Hidegkuti and Kocsis scored the goals.

Both teams then scored a penalty apiece, police having to disperse the aggressive Brazilian complaints at the disputed spot kick they conceded. Mihály Lantos scored it anyway to restore the two-goal advantage. Brazil pulled one back soon afterwards, before both sides were reduced to ten men when Bozsik and Nilton Santos were sent off for fighting. Djalma Santos escaped similar censure despite chasing Czibor across the pitch behind the referee's back, spitting and gesticulating at him, while Hidegkuti stamped on Indio's legs, having pushed him to the ground.

Brazil came close to an equaliser too, hitting the woodwork more than once. With four minutes to go, another Brazilian, Humberto Tozzi, was sent off for a near assault on Kocsis, who exacted revenge in the way he did best, adding a fourth goal shortly before full time, heading in Czibor's cross from the right. Hungary were far from innocent in the chaos that had unfolded but were certainly more frequently victim than perpetrator of the excessive violence.

The day was far from done, however, as the final whistle failed to herald a cessation in hostilities. Rather, it was the signal for any pretence at discipline to be abandoned altogether with numerous clashes including the non-playing Puskás supposedly hitting Pinheiro on the head with a bottle. The Brazilians also took the fight into the Hungarian dressing room, Sebes needing stitches as a result of a boot to the face.

Nevertheless, Hungary were through to the semi-finals where they faced Uruguay. The reigning champions were arguably a stronger side than the one that had shocked Brazil to win the 1950 tournament, and had to this point never lost a World Cup match. It would go down as one of *the* great World Cup matches, pitting world champions against Olympic champions, the undefeated best of the recent past versus the unequivocal best of the present. Two elegant teams littered with talent, charisma and solidity produced a game in stark contrast to the quarter-final that Hungary had just come through. Unusually for a game of such significance, symbolic and sporting, it was a game of immense quality that was, at least until Brazil's seminal clash with Italy in the 1982 World Cup, often cited as the greatest World Cup match: the game of the century.

Uruguay had beaten England in the quarter-finals, having also demolished Scotland 7-0 in the group. Like Hungary, it had been a bruising quarter-final for the Uruguayans, losing three players to injury during the match including influential captain Obdulio Varela, who would miss the semi-final as a result.

Hungary were again without Puskás, but otherwise had recovered from their ordeal with Brazil. Palotás came into the side to play as the withdrawn centre-forward, with Hidegkuti moving left to play in Puskás's position, although the two swapped positions repeatedly throughout. Bozsik retained his place, despite his sending off in the previous match. The sense was that the winners of this semi-final would go on to win the tournament, as the other semi-final featured the two teams who had finished behind Hungary and Uruguay in the group stages: West Germany and Austria.

Despite starting a little more slowly than usual, Hungary had gone close through Palotás and Hidegkuti before they took the lead in just the 13th minute: Hidegkuti's chipped pass to the edge of the box was nodded down by Kocsis for Czibor to fire unnervingly, low into the net. Uruguay then forced two good saves from Grosics, who also raced out of his box twice to intercept what could have been dangerous breaks, with Juan Schiaffino proving an awkward opponent to stifle. Hungary were a touch quicker and more incisive, however, and deserved their half-time lead.

Despite the frenetic nature of the second half, Hungary still exerted a level of control and were soon 2-0 up, Hidegkuti scoring with a diving header. This only spurred Uruguay on, however, and they began to dominate while an increasingly nervous Hungary began to appear uncharacteristically flustered. Grosics would later admit that he kept looking at the clock behind his goal every couple of minutes, yearning for it to move more quickly. Uruguay duly pulled a goal back through Juan Hohberg, setting up a tense finish to the match.

The final quarter of an hour was a frantic frenzy of chances at either end as a place in the final was within reach. Both teams had more than one effort cleared off the line, and then with four minutes left Schiaffino again set Hohberg through. This time Grosics got a hand to the ball as Hohberg tried to go past him, but that just pushed it behind the Uruguayan who turned sharply to fire a snapshot into the goal. Hungary had been just four minutes from the final, but now it was Uruguay who had the momentum as the match entered extra time.

Hohberg again was the key threat, shooting wide early in the additional period and later hitting the post. Hungary weathered the initial storm and began to impose themselves again, scoring six minutes into the second half of extra time through the much-tested combination of Budai crossing for Kocsis, who leapt high to head Hungary back into the lead. Five minutes later, the provider was different but the outcome the same, as Hidegkuti crossed for Kocsis to head Hungary's fourth. There was no coming back for Uruguay now, and on the back of an astonishing 11 goals for Kocsis in the four tournament games so far, Hungary were back in the final, 16 years on from their previous showpiece appearance.

'Never have I seen such an outstanding performance between two teams playing at their highest level,' said Sebes after the match. Many of the Hungarian players were effusive in their praise of the opposition, calling Uruguay the best opponent they had ever faced. This semi-final performance would stand alongside the wins over England as a tribute to the greatness of this Hungarian side. It had it all: controlled possession, wonderful team goals, assured defending, and a strong fightback withstood. *World Soccer* magazine would look back on this match in 1960 and declare it 'the greatest ever football match'. Surely now World Cup glory awaited the Magical Magyars; a triumph to eclipse all else they had achieved, and just reward for their years of dominance? Their sternest challenge overcome, Hungary were now overwhelming favourites for the final against the team they'd so soundly beaten just a fortnight earlier, West Germany.

Before that though, the Hungarian players enjoyed what Grosics described as 'a little party', with the squad not arriving back at their hotel until around 4am on the Saturday and the final taking place on Sunday. But there was another concern which dominated the days leading up to the final. Would Puskás be fit to play?

Puskás, of course, was certain that he was ready. In the days of no substitutes though, the fear was naturally that, should his ankle fail him, Hungary could be left playing the World Cup Final with ten men. Even if it held up, another concern was whether his ability to change direction at pace would be compromised. In one sense, the big fuss about the need for Puskás's return was odd, given how well the team had played without him. But on the other hand, he was their star player. His 68 goals in 57 internationals to this point stood as testament to his abilities, although his overall influence went well beyond mere statistics. He was the captain of the team, the symbol of its success, and, if anyone was to lift the trophy for Hungary in their moment of glory, surely it would be him. The thought was that he was around 80 per cent fit on the day of the final.

Instead of simply restoring Puskás to the now-standard line-up, though, Sebes attempted to mitigate against his lack of full fitness by adjusting the team in other areas. Budai, who had played well on the wing in the semi-final, was dropped, with Czibor moving to the right in his place. The player brought in to play on the left, where Czibor would normally play, was Mihály Tóth, a popular man among the squad but one that even his colleagues were stunned to find in the line-up for the final. Would these adjustments blunt the Magyar magic?

West Germany, too, were a completely different side than the one Hungary had beaten so convincingly in the group. Now at full strength and with the momentum of three consecutive knockout victories, including a 6-1 crushing of Austria in the semi-final, they would present a far sterner challenge than they had done two weeks earlier.

Hungary's arrival at the stadium was also hampered by the sheer number of fans outside, causing their bus to get stuck, the team arriving late and a bit flustered. The weather was seemingly against the Hungarians too. It had been a bright morning in Bern, but by the time the teams walked out on to the pitch to play, the rain had been teeming down for several hours. The mist covering the city and the nearby mountains gave the occasion an air of gloom, conflicting with the exuberance in the stands. The sodden conditions meant the pitch would be a heavy, waterlogged quagmire. Far from ideal for the quick, light-touch speed of the Hungarian team. By contrast, West Germany were pleased. Not only was the more robust German style of play more suited to these conditions, but they also benefitted from newly developed screw-in studs, courtesy of close ties between Adidas and the German team, which meant they could use longer studs in the sodden, muddy conditions.

If it suited the cherry-red-shirted Hungarians less, however, it didn't appear so as the match began. Puskás seemingly justified his selection by scoring after only six minutes, driving a powerful shot in with his gilded left foot after Kocsis's shot had cannoned off a German defender. He celebrated in his usual style, stood like a statue, his back arched, chest puffed out and arms aloft, as if frozen in the celebratory moment. Two minutes later it was 2-0. Under pressure from Kocsis, defender Werner Kohlmeyer and goalkeeper Toni Turek got themselves in an almighty muddle, gifting the ball to Czibor who nudged it into the empty net.

Two goals up after only eight minutes, this was a start beyond the wildest dreams of the Hungarians. Following the pattern of so many of the matches in Hungary's astonishing unbeaten run, they had surged into an early lead that most watching on now assumed was unassailable. It may well have been so had West Germany not scored themselves a mere two minutes later. A cross from the left was only partially blocked by Zakariás, which merely served to tee it up for Max Morlock, who slid the ball home.

Having been seemingly down and out after eight minutes, such a swift riposte gained the West Germans some vital momentum. Astonishingly, before the final had even reached the 20-minute mark, they had taken this and used it to fashion another goal. Grosics failed to claim a Walter corner and Rahn, thundering in at the back post, scored the equaliser.

It's tempting to assume that Hungary had got complacent, having taken such an early, apparently dominant lead, but West Germany had given them little time to rest on their laurels. Having lost their lead, Hungary didn't crumble, however. Rather, they reasserted control, doing everything but score as they laid siege to the German goal. Soon after the equaliser, Hidegkuti had an effort well saved, and early in the second half, Tóth twice had efforts cleared off the line. Hidegkuti hit the post, Kocsis hit the crossbar, while numerous other attacks were repelled by save after save from Turek in the German goal.

This remained the pattern other than the occasional foray forwards from West Germany. But the goal wouldn't come for Hungary. Instead, with just six minutes remaining, disaster struck. A cross into the Hungarian box was headed clear by Lantos, but only as far as Rahn on the edge. He wrong-footed the defenders before firing a skidding shot narrowly beyond the reach of the diving Grosics and into the net. 'Tor! Tor! Tor! Tor für Deutschland!' yelled the famous German commentator Herbert Zimmerman, in words that are now a part of German folklore.

There was still time left for Hungary, though. In desperation they poured forwards once more, and just two minutes after going behind came the most agonising of moments. A through ball by Tóth was flicked on by Kocsis to Puskás. The great Galloping Major of Hungarian football fired in what seemed an equaliser. 'Öcsi has done it! How wrong were they to doubt Puskás!' went the commentary of György Szepesi, broadcasting to the enthralled Hungarian nation.

For a fleeting, blissful moment, Hungary looked to have saved themselves, thanks to the predatory instincts of their unfit idol. It was a brief moment of joy, before utter despair would set in. 'Oh, no, wait a second – the linesman is waving his flag,' continued Szepesi. From the referee's perspective, the goal looked legitimate and he appeared happy to award it, but he deferred to the linesman, who was, in theory, better positioned to judge.

At such a stage of a World Cup Final, this was a momentous decision no matter which way his verdict had gone. Looking at it now from the only camera angle available, it is hard to ascertain for certain whether the decision was correct or not. What is true is that the German players mostly appeared devastated to have let the lead slip, only one player belatedly claiming for offside. Puskás himself remained adamant to his dying day that he was denied a legitimate equaliser. 'That was a perfectly good goal. I can never forgive him,' he wrote in his autobiography. 'Unfortunately, it was no dream or nightmare from which one could awake. This was a sad reality.'

We can only speculate what might have happened had the goal been given, but given the almost overwhelming nature of the Hungarian attacks and the increasingly frantic nature of the German defending, it's reasonable to suggest that the more likely winner would have been Hungary, whether in the remaining minutes or in extra time. There was still time for a last-minute chance, when Czibor's close-range shot was stopped by Turek.

When the final whistle went moments later, it not only ended dreams of Hungary's crowning glory and their incredible unbeaten run, but it also heralded one of the greatest upsets in football history. Hungary had dominated the Germans with 26 shots to seven, and across the tournament they had been comfortably the highest scorers with an incredible 27 goals from five games. Kocsis alone had scored 11 to claim the Golden Boot, far ahead of the next best in the tournament. It mattered little in the final reckoning, though.

'The end, my dear listeners. The end,' was Szepesi's response to the final whistle on Hungarian radio, signing off his commentary in tears and despair. After trudging despondently back to their dressing room, several players sat openly crying, while others, a dumbfounded Sebes included, sat silently contemplating what had just unfolded.

Back in Hungary, the defeat was greeted with total disbelief. The crowds listening in at the Népstadion and in their homes were at a loss, having expected an afternoon of celebration. One of the few bright spots of Hungarian life at the time had been their football team. When the glimmer of pride endowed on the nation by their footballing heroes proved fallible, despair took hold. A rumour spread that the players had thrown the match in return for brand new Mercedes cars, while workers were already removing a giant Hungarian flag from the main station that had been decked out for their triumphant return.

Despair in turn led to disorder as windows were smashed and frustrations bubbled over. The protests were quickly quelled, but the authorities had been scared by how little control they had over a large angry mob. The public could see that too, and wouldn't forget how easily they could frighten the regime.

The Hungarian players had expected a warm greeting on their return to Budapest. After all, they had performed excellently overall, and reached levels few other nations could attain. Instead, though, their train was intercepted at the border, and redirected to the Olympic training base in Tata to sit out the unrest in Budapest. The situation at home came as a massive shock to all of the players, stunned that their defeat could have unleashed such chaos. This unexpected isolation also gave them too much time to mull over the defeat, as the fresh wounds festered.

Some blamed Sebes's inclusion of Tóth for the final, and the exclusion from the squad altogether of Karoly Sándor, who could have deputised well for Puskás. Some blamed Puskás for coming back too soon, and wanting to have the moment of glory for himself. Others blamed the officials, with many convinced, some still to this day, that the dubious offside decision was part of an anti-communist conspiracy to ensure the Germans won. There was also the question of the West Germans having been seen injecting themselves with something at half-time. The Germans claimed this was vitamins, but we now know that it was amphetamines, a product now banned but not breaking any rules in 1954, if not entirely in the spirit of fair competition.

The fine margins of a World Cup Final; the bounce of the ball, the marginal decisions, the countless moments that fall for one side or the other, these are the factors that really decided the 1954 denouement in West Germany's favour rather than Hungary's. Perhaps it was simply one of those games where the best team doesn't get their just reward. It was the end of a sporting dream, but was soon to be the end of so much more.

The footballing fortunes of Hungary and West Germany had come together momentarily but would now diverge significantly in the coming years and decades. Where West Germany used this unlikely success as the springboard to become a dominant power in world football, also contributing greatly to a sense of regained international recognition, for Hungary this was the beginning of the end.

The national team would never again reach such heights, while the defeat and the national despair it induced was cited as a contributing factor in the general discontent in Hungary. The public reaction to defeat became, in essence, demonstrations against the regime. 'In those demonstrations,' recalled Grosics later in life, 'I believe, lay the seeds of the 1956 uprising.'

The national team remained a successful one between 1954 and 1956, maintaining a new unbeaten run of 18 matches until defeat eventually came in Turkey in early 1956. Sebes's reputation suffered following the World Cup defeat, his standing in the corridors of power never the same again. Following two further uninspiring performances, he was relieved of his duties.

Later that year, political tensions spilled over into the Hungarian uprising. As the revolt raged, Honvéd were due to play a European Cup tie against Athletic Bilbao. Given the ongoing turmoil at home, they switched the first leg to Spain, meaning that when the Soviet tanks rolled through Budapest the squad were out of the country. Many chose not to return. Among 200,000 or so Hungarians who fled the country, Czibor, Kocsis and Puskás defected to start new lives in the west, all ultimately settling in Spain and playing there with distinction: Puskás with Real Madrid, and Czibor and Kocsis joining another Hungarian, László Kubala who had defected some years before, at Barcelona. Others did return home, but the great Honvéd side, and the national team as a consequence, would never be the same again.

The national under-21 side was also abroad at the time of the uprising, and defected en masse. With the senior squad decimated and the young prospects all gone, and with them the culture and knowledge that had produced these players, Hungarian football's finest age was over. The regrets would linger a lifetime, though. 'When I go to bed at night or wake up in the morning, I am still thinking of the *Aranycsapat*,' said Grosics, citing both his gratitude at having the fortune to be a part of such a great team, and his frustration at dreams unfulfilled; an enormous sense of personal loss.

It is *the* missed opportunity of Hungarian football, but also the glories of the Golden Team have unwittingly hindered every Hungarian national team since, constantly compared unfavourably to the greats of the 1950s. They had set an unattainable precedent for all generations to follow. Beyond mere sport though, they had given Hungary a place in the world's consciousness. As David Bailey, author of *Magical Magyars*, told me, 'The Golden Team was responsible for putting Hungary on the map. People all around the world still know the name Puskás and the great team he captained, but only at a push can they name any other famous Hungarians. That is the Golden Team's legacy; that they made the world notice Hungary.' They did more than just notice too, captivated and confounded in equal measure by the groundbreaking style and manner of their play.

The pride of Hungarians at the time has echoed through the years. The protagonists of the 1950s are national heroes, with all Hungarians deeply aware that their nation once produced the greatest football team in the world. While World Cup defeat in 1954 had denied Hungary their apparent destiny, they left a legacy that has endured. Their tactical concepts, the players interchanging roles to confuse the opposition were enhanced and perfected by the Dutch in the 1970s.

Hungary may not have won in 1954, but their pride and their curse is to forever know they were the best team in the tournament. No other team discussed in this book can lay claim to such a period of dominance as this Hungary team can. Years of greatness interrupted by just one defeat is a reality that brings both glory and despair at a dream unfulfilled. Football, though, is more than titles, more than mere victory. The greatest team in the world had lost the one match that mattered more than any other in four years without defeat, but history would judge them as one of football's most revered teams of all time. One of the very greatest to have failed to capture the ultimate prize, they remain football's tragic heroes, but heroes nonetheless.

Defeat was bitter, and the aftermath traumatic, but the legacy remains. 'What is true, is true,' ran Szepesi's closing remarks to the listening nation as his commentary reached its tearful conclusion. 'We lost that match. A West German team won 3-2. They won the World Cup. For four years we were unbeaten. And now we've lost.'

5

Portugal 1966

No finer sporting team ... This was football
at its best, magnificent in every department.

Albert Barham, *The Guardian*

TO AN Anglo audience, the 1966 World Cup was all about England. Played out in the Swinging Sixties when British cool was being exported around the world from music to fashion, from The Beatles and the Rolling Stones to Twiggy and Jean Shrimpton, the cultural values of a nation were changing at the same time that England welcomed the football world. It was a summer that would be fondly remembered in England as the lone occasion in which football not only came home, but stayed for a glorious conclusion.

But scratch beneath that surface and there was a player and team who dazzled and enchanted to a greater extent than the ultimate English victors did. The play of this genius and his colleagues was the most expressive of a strait-laced World Cup, winning affection at every turn. Almost as iconic as the image of Bobby Moore lifting the trophy is that of Eusébio leaving a trail of helpless defenders in his wake, or thumping in another ferociously unstoppable goal. So, too, the impression of sportsmanship and respect that he encapsulated. The 1966 World Cup was the setting for Eusébio's transition from being among the best to being *the* best for that moment in time: a greatness confirmed on the grandest stage of all.

The Portugal side of 1966 had been built on the foundations of a superb Benfica team. In Eusébio, they featured a player whose intoxicating mix of astonishing skill and boundless dynamism made him unplayable at times, a cut above all bar Pelé of his contemporaries. Like many of the true greats, he was a player whose impact extended beyond simply football. Eusébio was representative not only of his nation, but also of Africa in a tournament denied the presence of any African nation. He was far from the only talent in the team, though. And while 1966 was Portugal's first World Cup appearance, it was a performance that took them to within a whisker of the final, all achieved while delighting audiences with the flair and style that so nearly took them all the way.

Portugal may have been raw debutants on the international stage, but in the club game it was another story. Benfica had lifted the European Cup in 1961 and 1962, taking over the significant mantle of Real Madrid, and were then twice runners-up in the years following that. The core of that side was the fulcrum of the national team, replete with players of international renown. Portugal may not have graced a World Cup before but they arrived in England with considerable pedigree. The 1966 Portuguese vintage was one of the finest in Europe at that time, and despite that lack of World Cup experience they grew through the tournament into becoming one of the strongest contenders for glory, and one who would test England to the limit.

This may not fit the usual English narrative when it comes to 1966 – that of Charlton, Moore and Hurst, of Alf Ramsey and the fulfilment of a nation's footballing destiny – but that perception is skewed by the years hailing that victory. Each blinkered rewatching of those images from long ago reaffirms the English stance of the worthiness of that triumph, but they were just one of many strong teams, with the astonishing Portuguese perhaps the most elegant, exciting and impactful. They would cross paths in the semi-final, and it's no great stretch of the imagination to envisage that clash going the other way, thanks to the glorious brilliance of the Portuguese team and the player whose claim to greatness became increasingly validated as the World Cup progressed.

Eusébio da Silva Ferreira arrived in England as the reigning European Player of the Year, having made his reputation at Benfica as one of the most gifted of performers. Beyond being a Portuguese hero, Eusébio was the first star of African football, arriving at Benfica almost by accident. Growing up in the Portuguese colony of Mozambique, his footballing development came with Sporting Clube de Lourenço Marques, a feeder club for the Lisbon giants Sporting Club de Portugal, Benfica's fiercest rivals. Even as a teenager, Eusébio had a reputation that was extending beyond the confines of Lourenço Marques, Mozambique's capital city, known today as Maputo. The former Brazilian international José Carlos Bauer, who had played for Brazil in the Maracanaço of 1950, was one of those to have witnessed the explosive talents of the teenage prodigy first-hand. When he bumped into the legendary Benfica manager Béla Guttmann in a Lisbon barbershop of all places, Bauer gave such a glowing report on the young player that Guttmann was soon on his way to Mozambique to see what all the fuss was about.

Guttmann was so impressed with what he saw that he persuaded Eusébio to sign for Benfica then and there, stealing him away from Sporting, who were understandably rather put out at losing the player they had been patiently nurturing. Such was the outcry, that on arriving in Portugal in December 1960, Eusébio hid out in a remote village in the Algarve for a time while the fuss died down.

Eusébio first took the field in the famous red of the Lisbon club in May 1961 in a pre-season tournament, announcing his arrival by scoring a hat-trick in a 4-2 victory in typically explosive style. A competitive Benfica debut soon followed in bizarre circumstances, with the club forced to play a cup game the day after the European Cup Final which Benfica had won against Barcelona. Playing in an effective reserve line-up, Eusébio scored again, though the young team were beaten. He repeated this scoring feat in his league debut soon after too.

For all this impressive beginning, it would be in a friendly tournament over the summer of 1961 when Eusébio's talent truly burst on to the scene, bringing him to wider prominence. Benfica faced Santos, Pelé and all, with the young Eusébio starting on the bench. With Benfica trailing 4-0 in the second half and the game beyond them, Eusébio was sent on: a player destined to be one of the world's best up against the undisputed current king.

In the space of 17 minutes Eusébio scored a hat-trick. He may have been unable to stop his side from slipping to defeat, an outclassed Benfica losing 6-3 in the end, but this was the moment that a star was born. Such was the impact of his arrival on the scene, in a match that was considered a serious contest between the European champions and the celebrated, globetrotting Santos and their global icon, that Eusébio's talent had already marked him out as a potential heir apparent. It wasn't Pelé who was featured on the cover of *L'Équipe* afterwards. It was Eusébio, the new genius.

Eusébio was a hugely talented, highly skilful phenomenon. He had everything. To add to his wondrous skills, he was also blessed with supremely explosive speed and strength, magically quick feet and a mesmeric dribbling ability that, if anything, was underutilised by the great man. He also displayed an incredible knack for goalscoring. In his career with Benfica, spanning some 15 years, he played 440 times and scored an astonishing 473 goals. He was a one-man wrecking ball, storming through opponents seemingly at will. An unstoppable force of nature, decades ahead of his time in terms of how a striker played and the sheer dominance his abilities made possible.

For Benfica, already European Cup winners ahead of Eusébio's ascent to the first team, the emergence of their new hero ensured a place at the top table of European football for much of the rest of the 1960s. With Eusébio as their inspiration, Benfica won through to the 1962 European Cup Final against a Real Madrid side seeking to reclaim what they saw as their rightful possession, something only temporarily on loan to Benfica.

In the final in Amsterdam's Olympic Stadium though, the outcome could be viewed as a symbolic handing over of the baton of excellence from one generation to the next. In Real Madrid white that day were Ferenc Puskás and Alfredo Di Stéfano: two of the finest exponents of the game but whose heyday was on the wane. Puskás still scored a hat-trick, including sending his team into an early 2-0 lead, but Benfica fought back and in the second half pulled clear, with the final two goals in a 5-3 victory coming from Eusébio, grasping the mantle held by Puskás and Di Stéfano and making it his own. Hindsight affords us the chance to see this moment as a symbolic progression from the old guard to the new superstar, but this was a 20-year-old Eusébio we are talking about at this point. To have grabbed hold of such an occasion against such illustrious opposition at such a young age was, certainly in the early 1960s, truly a remarkable thing.

Eusébio would lead Benfica to three more finals in the 1960s, enhancing his reputation with every step. Similarly enhanced was the symbolism of his mere presence as one of the very few prominent black players at the time in Europe, certainly at such a high level. This all served to focus the attention of a continent on him, as each new achievement broke new ground in the sport.

Eusébio's emergence had a further impact on Benfica, and ultimately on the national team too. To accommodate his new star, the Benfica coach Béla Guttmann adjusted his team, 'I was able to play Mário Coluna deeper, more as a wing-half than an inside-forward. He did not like it at first because he did not score so many goals, but he became my best player.' The parallels to Hungary's Nándor Hidegkuti in the 1950s are clear. Coluna's creative potential was released and heightened by a deeper starting position, not only unleashing his own abilities, but serving to provide a greater structure for the team to flourish. With many of the same players involved, what had proved successful at Benfica was mirrored in the national team.

Coluna, another supremely talented player to hail from Mozambique, had followed a similar career path to Eusébio, making the journey to Lisbon some years earlier. He scored in both the 1961 and 1962 European Cup successes, but it was in his partnership with Eusébio that he flourished even further, eventually settling on a central or attacking midfield role from which he could dictate a lot of the play. On the left wing, for both club and country, was António Simões. He had broken into the team around the same time as Eusébio, and, in fact, became at the time the youngest player ever to win the European Cup, in 1961, marginally younger than Eusébio.

Partnering Eusébio up front was the 'Kind Giant' José Torres, a powerful, tall striker who proved the perfect foil for Eusébio, and would go on to manage Portugal in the 1986 World Cup. The right wing was the domain of José Augusto, a player of such skill he was once dubbed the 'Portuguese Garrincha'.

What linked all of these great names of Portuguese football was not only that they were a part of Benfica's 1960s rise to prominence, but that they were all fundamental to the Lisbon club for the majority of their careers. They had developed together as senior players, working together so closely for so long that they instinctively knew what each other were doing. When this experience and quality was transposed into the national team, international success finally seemed possible. Hindsight makes the transition of success from club to country appear inevitable, yet in the early 1960s the Portuguese national team was not one of any particular renown.

Indeed, not only had Portugal never qualified for a World Cup before, they hadn't even come close. Having entered for the first time in 1934, Portugal were soundly beaten by Spain in a two-legged clash, including a 9-0 loss in Madrid. They came closer four years later but lost out to Switzerland in a one-off tie for a place at the 1938 tournament. The subsequent war years stifled what football development there had been with a lack of any meaningful competition. When they fell to a 10-0 friendly loss to England in 1947, it seemed Portuguese football was a long way behind.

This was born out in qualification for the 1950 World Cup, where Portugal were again beaten by Spain, though they did succeed in drawing the home leg 2-2. The 1954 tournament followed a similar pattern, losing 9-1 in Austria before saving some face with a fairly meaningless goalless draw back in Lisbon. Considering this was just some 12 years prior to the great achievements of Portugal in 1966, an astonishing rise took place through the late 1950s and early 1960s.

Portugal won a World Cup qualifier for the first time in the 1958 qualification phase, beating Italy 3-0, but still finished last in the group. There is a significance in that the first of the great Benfica forwards, Mário Coluna, featured in two of these qualifying matches, and with a squad drawn largely from the three powers of Portuguese football, Benfica, Sporting and Porto, standards were belatedly on the rise. The national team was ultimately benefitting from the huge quality the big professional clubs had developed rather than any grand planning on behalf of the definitively more amateurish national federation.

By the time of the 1962 qualifiers, Portugal had already reached the quarter-finals of the inaugural European Nations' Cup – the European Championship today – in 1960, overcoming East Germany before losing to a strong Yugoslavia side. In World Cup qualifying, Portugal beat Luxembourg and then drew 1-1 with England in Lisbon. If ever a result signified their emergence as a rising force, this was it. And if ever a result demonstrated what still needed to be improved, losing 4-2 to Luxembourg a few months later made that apparent. This inauspicious result in October 1961 was significant in other ways though, as it marked Eusébio's international debut, scorer of Portugal's first goal in an otherwise disastrous game. Defeat at Wembley soon after ended any faint hopes of reaching the 1962 tournament but the steady improvement was clear, and would now continue apace.

The side were led by another Benfica man, as the coach taking Portugal through their qualifiers and into their debut World Cup, Otto Gloria, had been a part of Benfica's transformation and development in the late 1950s. Gloria had helped create the environment which enabled the flourishing of their huge potential into the early 1960s. He was also the driving force behind the broadening of Benfica's horizons when it came to recruitment, searching for players from beyond the more traditional but narrow confines of Lisbon, to the provinces, and beyond to the African overseas territories. Coluna arrived on Gloria's watch, and seeds had been sown for the talent still to come.

By the time of the 1966 World Cup, Gloria had gained experience at all of Portugal's top clubs, going from Benfica to Belenenses and then Sporting. After a brief interlude in Marseille and back in his native Brazil at Vasco da Gama, he returned to Portugal in 1964 to coach Porto for a season before taking on Sporting once again in the 1965/66 season. It was while in these latter two positions that he also took on the task of leading the national team, his unique experiences making him ideal to blend the talents available across Portugal.

When the time came for qualifying for the 1966 tournament, the team was built around the attacking talents of the great Benfica side, with a significant addition of defensive solidity from their city rivals Sporting, and the Belenenses goalkeeper José Pereira. The qualification campaign may not have ended unbeaten, but it was a group in which Portugal dominated from the start. Drawn to face Turkey, Romania and, most significantly, the 1962 World Cup runners-up Czechoslovakia, Portugal won their opening four matches, Eusébio scoring in all four victories with seven goals in total. This included the only goal in the hugely critical 1-0 win away in Bratislava against Czechoslovakia which went a long way to securing Portugal's place at the World Cup. While their opponents took points off each other, a goalless draw in Porto in the return against Czechoslovakia was enough to guarantee Portugal's qualification with a game to spare. That they then lost in Romania mattered not one jot, other than to dented pride.

Despite such a successful campaign, Portugal didn't enter the 1966 World Cup with particularly high hopes, given the paucity of any accomplishments of note in international football. When placed into a group featuring reigning two-time world champions Brazil, Olympic champions Hungary, with their new star Flórián Albert, plus a tough Bulgaria side, Portugal were not the obvious pick to dominate. Expectations in Portugal were low, and the feeling that Portugal had a genuine place at football's top table was far from people's minds as Ricardo Serrado, a Portuguese football historian and author of *História do Futebol Português*, explained to me, 'No one expected that Portugal could pass the group stage. Furthermore, the social and cultural outlook of Portuguese people was very pessimistic, as if Portugal was not strong enough to claim an honorific place in international sport.'

With Brazil opening the group with a straightforward 2-0 victory over Bulgaria, Portugal's World Cup began the next day in Manchester taking on Hungary at Old Trafford. As World Cup debuts go, for Portugal to take the lead in the first minute was an entrance very much to the point. When Augusto rose above a hesitant Hungarian defence, and a catastrophically indecisive goalkeeper, to head a simple goal into an unguarded net, Portugal could barely have wished for a better start. But Hungary soon found their rhythm as the game became quite open. It was little surprise when Hungary equalised in the second half but that was the signal for more Portuguese pressure at the other end. Eusébio, now sporting a bandage on his head thanks to an earlier collision, was proving an elusive, all-action thorn in Hungary's side. His slick interplay with those around him caused repeated panic in the Hungarian back line, and the attention he drew created more space for others to exploit.

When a loose cross was sent in by Torres from the right only a few minutes after Portugal had conceded, the Hungarian goalkeeper made his earlier mistake seem trivial by comparison. He came to catch Torres's apparently harmless cross only to nudge the ball straight at Augusto, who nodded it into the goal. Two mistakes, two Augusto headers, two easy goals. But the simplicity of the way Portugal had taken the lead again was just reward for the pressure they were exerting on Hungary.

For all of Portugal's fine play, and the clearly apparent quality of their attacks, when they secured victory with a third goal it was simplicity itself once again; Torres heading in from a corner to complete an impressive 3-1 win. Hungary had their chances too, however, as noted in the match report in *The Guardian* which was fairly damning of Hungary's wastefulness, claiming, 'Hungary will never forgive themselves for the opportunities they wasted this night.' But Portugal's victory was just reward for their slick play. Some deficiencies in the defence to tighten up, sure, but when going forward Portugal were already displaying a fearsome attacking ability.

More was to come with a comfortable 3-0 win over Bulgaria, which, combined with Hungary beating Brazil in a bruising encounter, left Portugal in prime position at the top of the group. Eusébio scored his first of the tournament against Bulgaria, with a typically incisive burst into the penalty area to latch on to a wonderful through ball from his Benfica colleague, Simões. In an instant, Eusébio fired into the far corner, too quick for the goalkeeper to do more than get a soft hand to it as it flew past. The 'Black Panther', as he was dubbed, showed the first of the familiar exuberant celebrations he would repeatedly bring to the World Cup party, enthusiastically celebrating the goal with his team-mates. As against Hungary, Portugal had benefitted from some lax defending for their other two goals, but again it was, in part, a result of the pressure they were exerting, and the panic induced by both the formidable pace and guile they were playing with. The opposition defences simply couldn't cope.

Going into the decisive final group match with Brazil, the build-up was heavy with symbolism. Aside from the obvious sporting drama, there was also the weight of history of a past colonial power versus its former colony, plus the much-anticipated meeting of two of the world's finest and highest-profile players, meaning the layers of symbolism on a single football match were many. It was a game in which Portugal only required a draw to ensure finishing top of the group, and they went into it with growing confidence, inspired by their talisman.

And yet there remained that ever-present doubt. Brazil had been so dominant for so long, and Portugal had been so poor in previous years, that for many Portuguese, facing Brazil was an almost impossible task. The feeling that Brazilian football was some distance ahead had been seemingly entrenched following a clash between Benfica and Pelé's Santos in the 1962 Intercontinental Cup in which Pelé outclassed the Portuguese players in a blistering 5-2 triumph. 'The difference was so big, and the Brazilians had such superiority to the Portuguese footballers, that the Brazilians said that in Portugal the ball was square,' explained Ricardo Serrado, illustrating the supposed inability to perform the basics of football in comparison to the Brazilian masters. For Portugal, if victory was to come, it would represent a massive breakthrough for a nation unused to competing at such levels.

Brazil had their troubles ahead of this match too. Pelé, their inspirational focal point, had been subjected to some vicious tackling in Brazil's opening victory over Bulgaria, leaving him unable to play in the defeat to Hungary. He did start the final group match with Portugal at Everton's Goodison Park but was clearly far from fully fit, included perhaps for the psychological impact his presence might have, more than anything else. The huge crowd had been looking forward to the clash between the legendary Pelé and his heir apparent. But with the Brazilian clearly uncomfortable and impeded, Eusébio shone far brighter, thrilling the crowd with his dominant performance.

Brazil, facing the unenviable task of having to win to avoid early elimination, had not only brought Pelé back into the side in an act of apparent desperation but had made eight other changes to the line-up from their previous defeat, seven of whom had not appeared in either of their opening two games. Brazilian panic would be even greater after just 15 minutes when a Eusébio cross wasn't dealt with, presenting Simões with an easy headed chance to give Portugal the lead.

By this stage it had already become apparent that Portugal were not averse to demonstrating their steel as well as their style. The principal defensive game plan was clear: stop Pelé by any means necessary. Within the first few minutes, more than one crunching tackle had stopped Pelé in his tracks, chopped down before he could inflict any damage. This tight marking had another, less cynical benefit as it allowed Portugal to establish dominance in the midfield, forming the base from which they could unleash Eusébio's talents. Turning in a tournament-defining performance, Eusébio seized both the match and the headlines in a startling display.

The veteran Brazilian defensive midfielder Orlando, a stalwart of the victorious 1958 World Cup squad, had been recalled for this match in a move ostensibly designed to nullify Eusébio's threat. But against such speed, strength and explosive ability, Orlando and his defensive colleagues were helpless at times. Eusébio doubled Portugal's lead midway through the first half with a near-post header, but his finest moment of the match was to come later.

Before that, however, the other defining image of the match was seeing Pelé scythed down by João Morais on the edge of the Portuguese box. Pelé got straight up, retaining possession, only for Morais to cut him off at the knees again, twice within as many seconds. 'A brutal, inexplicable double foul,' as described by Brian Glanville in his book *The Story of the World Cup*. Morais escaped punishment from the referee but Pelé was not so fortunate. He was carried off before returning after lengthy treatment – no substitutes were allowed in the 1966 World Cup – with his leg heavily bandaged, able to contribute little other than hobbling around out of the way on the wing, offering only sporadic interventions with the occasional fine pass.

Against the tide though, Brazil did drag themselves back into the match a quarter of an hour from the end, thanks to a fierce shot fired in from the edge of the box by the left-back Rildo. This was a fleeting moment of inspiration from the defending champions, however. They were eclipsed at every turn by a team superior to them in almost every way. And, in Eusébio, they had the tournament's emerging star.

In response to conceding, Eusébio grasped the mantle once again, firing a rasping shot from all of 40 yards out that was tipped over the bar. Then, five minutes from the end, came the greatest moment of his magical performance, the last and most decisive of the 17 shots he took aim with in this match. The ball fell to Eusébio to the right of Brazil's goal, at an impossibly narrow angle. He connected with a volley of such brutal force that the thud of boot on ball was almost immediately followed by the crackle of the ball hitting the net. The emphatic nature of the shot as it ripped into the goal exemplified the manner of Eusébio's performance. As European Player of the Year, he was hardly an unknown quantity, but his dominance of the now former world champion Brazil announced his arrival at a level above and beyond that which he had already achieved with Benfica. He was now a true world star.

As Brazil's players slumped to the ground in defeat, a new power was rising, claiming a place among the favourites for the World Cup as the tournament entered the knockout rounds. Portugal had shown, too, that their explosively artistic style could be combined with a physical approach to great effect. Beyond that, for Portugal, this victory was the moment that belief began to grow among the squad and back at home, where crowds gathered around televisions in cafés and bars to witness the action. 'In football terms it was astonishing,' explained Ricardo Serrado. 'Brazil had the most powerful national team, the best players in the world. The difference to Portuguese football was huge. The victory had a tremendous impact at all levels in Portuguese society. Winning against the world champion, against the best players in the world, was something thought almost impossible. Looking back, we can see the value of that Portuguese team, and victory was not so improbable. But, in 1966 it was seen as a David v Goliath duel.' Anything now seemed possible.

With the massive psychological boost of the win over Brazil, Portugal stayed at Goodison Park for their quarter-final to face another revelation of the tournament: North Korea. The tournament's only Asian representatives were unlikely opponents, but had shocked the world in beating the much-fancied Italians 1-0 to grab a quarter-final place ahead of the Azzurri. Their progression made possible one of the most remarkable and unforgettable matches in World Cup history, and one of the most epic games in the history of Portuguese football. It brought together the two visiting teams who had resonated most with their hosts, both having garnered extensive support from the locals through their class and endeavour. It would also be an occasion in which Eusébio would reinforce his rapidly escalating reputation, almost single-handedly rescuing his team in spectacular style, following a startling opening by the North Koreans. It would be perhaps the defining match in a career of astonishing highs, such was his impact on this Saturday afternoon on Merseyside.

Before Eusébio took over proceedings, however, it was North Korea who started in confident fashion, buoyed by their remarkable victory over Italy a few days before.

In conjunction with what appeared to be a touch of complacency from the Portuguese, North Korea stormed into an incredible early lead. Scoring not just once, or even twice, the Koreans surged into a 3-0 lead by the 25th minute of the match against one of the favourites to lift the World Cup, no less.

The first had gone in only a handful of seconds after kick-off, a fine shot from the edge of the box by Pak Seung-zin which flew past José Pereira in the Portuguese goal. It's tempting to speculate that this was such a shock to the system that Portugal struggled to settle at all following this, unable to assert themselves in the opening exchanges. Eusébio at this stage of the game was as ineffectual as the rest of the men in Portuguese red, as the North Koreans hassled and harried: a perpetual blur of busy motion, not allowing the superior Portuguese skill, or indeed physicality, to establish itself. Nothing exemplifies this as well as Eusébio mishitting a shot midway through the half, from which North Korea broke to make it 2-0, after Pereira had misjudged a cross.

Within three minutes it was 3-0, and the Portuguese players looked stunned and almost paralysed with disbelief, unable to comprehend what was happening. If ever a moment called for an intervention of greatness this was it. Portugal were committed to all-out attack even before they trailed 3-0, but now it was a necessity, with Eusébio belatedly grabbing hold of the match and imposing himself in career-defining style. Within two minutes of going 3-0 down, Eusébio had scored his first when Simões picked out his surging run into the box. Having finished emphatically, Eusébio rushed to retrieve the ball and raced to place it back on the centre spot to restart the game as quickly as possible.

It was already a different match. Korean energy was now pinned back amid the increasingly incessant Portuguese attack, but Eusébio would have to wait until close to half-time before scoring again, decisively despatching a penalty to make it 3-2 at the break. The newly established pattern continued in the second half, and by the hour Portugal would no longer be behind but in the lead, with Eusébio having scored all four. His third came following an angled shot after he'd been put through by another Simões through ball, before he earned another penalty. His boundless energy and relentlessly incisive running were proving more than the Koreans could cope with. As he surged into the box following an exhilarating run down the left, the only way he could be stopped was to be chopped down. Not that it changed the outcome. What was likely a fine fourth goal was instead another penalty. Either way, it was 4-3 and the Korean resistance was utterly broken, torn asunder by a player at the peak of his powers, earning his place among the very greatest.

When Augusto made it 5-3 in the closing minutes, it was against a Korean team that was now all out of both ideas and energy. The post-match comments of Portugal's captain, Coluna, seemed to have an element of rewriting history when he declared, 'We were not disturbed at any time. We knew we would beat Korea.' The evidence suggests otherwise, given the indecision apparent in Portugal's struggles. North Korea's blistering opening had left Portugal in a state of shock and many of those watching thinking they were about to witness an extraordinary upset. North Korea's remarkable story may have come to a close, but in having tested Portugal, had they revealed a defensive frailty at the heart of this great attacking team? With hosts England now awaiting Portugal in the semi-final, defensive solidity would be a necessity. As Otto Gloria claimed afterwards, 'Attack is our best defence. We do not like to play on defence. We do not know how to play on defence.'

In attack, though, Portugal were supreme, and this is why they exhilarated so many and why their performances remain so well regarded so many years later. With Eusébio clearly now the greatest forward in the world, and having just put in a performance for the ages, Portugal's attacking prowess had taken them to the semi-finals and could yet take them all the way. 'Portugal had shown themselves as sound in temperament as in technique and Eusébio stood in what, until a few days before, had been Pelé's place,' ran *The Observer*'s assessment. The new king of world football would take some stopping. The power, speed and technique that Eusébio showed against North Korea was simply extraordinary: a performance for the ages in a match for the ages.

A controversial spanner in the works would threaten to derail Portugal ahead of the semi-final with England, however. The World Cup schedule had this second semi-final set for Goodison Park, a venue where Portugal had by now become not only comfortable, but hugely popular with the local crowd thanks to their games against Brazil and North Korea. England, on the other hand, had played all of their games in the familiar surroundings of Wembley. Opinion seems divided on whose decision it was, but either the tournament organisers, FIFA or both changed the schedule to keep England at Wembley for their semi-final. Portugal had to travel south at short notice, interrupting their preparation for the match of their lives, and away from the place they had become familiar.

The official line was that the most attractive match should be played at the biggest stadium, generating the most revenue and enabling more England followers to attend. Instead, the West Germany v Soviet Union semi-final took place at Goodison. Eusébio and company would be taking on their English hosts, and a huge home crowd, at Wembley after a day of summer rain that made the pitch heavier than the Portuguese would have liked.

Last-minute train journeys to London aside, Portugal still came into this semi-final with confidence high. While the threat of Bobby Charlton and his England colleagues was a huge one, the potency of Portugal's attack was giving England concern too. It would need to be at its finest to penetrate the English defences, however. Gordon Banks's goal had yet to be breached in England's four matches so far: the sternest defence in the competition, marshalled by the superlative Bobby Moore. But they hadn't faced a threat quite like Eusébio yet.

Nobby Stiles, England's combative midfield spoiler, was assigned the unenviable task of marking the prolific Portuguese forward. He stuck to the dynamic genius like glue throughout, and while Portugal enjoyed a good amount of possession, Eusébio's influence on proceedings would be stifled. It may seem an easy tactical move to man-mark the main opposition threat, but against a player of the quality of Eusébio, to keep him shackled the way Stiles did through much of the semi-final required never-ending concentration and ceaseless energy. No easy feat at all.

In front of a noisy, celebratory and expectant crowd at Wembley, England initially kept a measure of control against Portugal that few had managed so far. This was, in part, thanks to the ever-present shackle attaching itself to Eusébio, but also to the fact that Coluna was having a busy day of his own, tracking Bobby Charlton. This rendered him less able to provide the creative outlet for Portugal, or the foil to Eusébio, that Portugal craved. Charlton was to be the standout performer in the match, scoring twice for England. His first came after half an hour following a quick break, the culmination of a few good opportunities that England had created up to that point. Roger Hunt, finding space between the Portuguese defenders, mis-controlled a long pass, nudging the ball a little too far ahead: too strong for him to reach, too weak to be an effective shot. Pereira raced out, sliding feet first to clear when he might have smothered, presenting the ball to Charlton who sent it right back at goal, firing into the unguarded net.

Portugal had been less effective in attack than usual during the first half, failing to create as many opportunities as usual. What they were showing, though, was a perpetual, dangerous movement. They had set themselves up to attack England, going toe-to-toe with their hosts rather than to contain, as many of England's previous opponents had attempted. This produced a magnificent spectacle, but up to this point it hadn't produced too many Portuguese opportunities. Given the proclivity for attacking within the Portuguese ranks, this was to England's credit, stifling the strongest attack in the tournament.

By far the best chance they did create fell to Eusébio, who hit a magnificent swerving volley from the edge of the box, which was destined for the corner of the net before Banks dived to push it away. But with Eusébio largely restricted, the tactic of aiming high balls for Torres was being comfortably dealt with by England's centre-back pairing of Bobby Moore and Jack Charlton. After the interval, though, Portugal would gain more forward momentum: the slick attacking verve restored to its most relentless flow, heading increasingly and unremittingly in the direction of Banks's goal. Shortly after the restart, a Simões cross from the right appeared to hit Stiles on the arm, prompting Portuguese claims for a penalty which were waved away dismissively by the French referee.

Portugal were playing with a greater level of energy and purpose now, but the inability to break the resolute English defence meant that, as the clock ticked on, Portugal's hopes began to fade. When Bobby Charlton scored his second with a little over ten minutes remaining, Portugal looked down and out. And yet, just two minutes later, their increasing second half pressure finally bore fruit. While the crowd were rejoicing what seemed a certain place in the final, a surging run forwards from Augusto saw the ball worked out to Simões on the right. His deep cross was headed goalwards by Torres, beyond the outstretched arm of Banks. Jack Charlton did what Luis Suárez would become vilified for more than four decades later in similar circumstances and thrust up an arm to push the ball clear. There was no red card for such an offence in 1966, but the resultant penalty was despatched with a nonchalant, calm authority by Eusébio, his eighth goal of the tournament, to make it 2-1. This was the first goal that England had conceded in the World Cup of 1966, and with seven minutes still remaining, it left the outcome hanging in the balance once again.

Portugal were now unleashing all attacking options in a desperate attempt to take the match into extra time. Only two more minutes had elapsed when they came very close to doing just that. Augusto, finding renewed resources of energy on the right, drilled a diagonal ball across the edge of the box for Torres, whose header looked set to fall to Simões, poised to bury the equaliser from short range. Before he could reach it, however, Stiles, vigilantly tracking any threat, stretched to nudge the ball out for a corner, preventing what seemed a certain equaliser.

England's nerves appeared shot, and within another minute their increasing levels of panic nearly presented Portugal with another great opportunity. Coluna headed back across the box, with the ball bouncing up and looking to strike Moore on the arm. As with the first-half penalty claim, the referee waved away any protests. Later still, Coluna forced a fine stretching save from Banks but, when the resultant corner was cleared the final whistle signalled the hosts' delight, and the end of Portugal's dream. This panicked ending is almost airbrushed from English football history, but Portugal so very nearly took England to extra time in this semi-final, where who knows what may have happened.

Eusébio, the man around whom everything was built in this Portugal side, was a gracious, yet forlorn figure at the end. He left the field in tears, being comforted by both team-mates and opposition alike. The frustration of not being able to get as strong a hold on this match as he had done in Portugal's previous matches made the defeat harder to bear, and his tears became the symbol of this match, and indeed of this campaign, to Portuguese observers. This match would become known as the *Jogo das Lágrimas*: the Game of Tears.

Eusébio himself recalled afterwards, 'I was really sad and asked, "Lord, what have I done to deserve this?"' But what he and his side had achieved was to have put Portuguese football firmly in the global consciousness, lauded for its exuberant play, and for the delight they had given so many. That they played such exhilarating football was one thing, but to do it with such grace, elegance and dignity, in a tournament where cynicism had become increasingly apparent, merely enhanced their allure. That England had to be at their very best to contain and overcome Portugal was clear.

England had certainly gained a respect for Eusébio and his colleagues, enhanced by the test their side had just been given: a far sterner and subtler one than they had needed to overcome prior to the semi-final. The English press were equally in thrall to the magnificent Portuguese. 'No finer semi-final match than that in which Portugal were defeated 2-1 could have been anticipated,' ran *The Guardian*'s match report the next morning. 'No finer sporting team have had to bow to England, at their best, in this competition. How the audience of 90,000 were held in the spell of this fine Portuguese attacking side, and of the great performance England put up against them to win. This was football at its best, magnificent in every department.' The report went on to extol the virtues of Eusébio, Simões, Augusto and Torres in particular, expressing significant relief that such a test had been overcome.

Many contemporary reports expressed doubts that West Germany would provide as awkward an opposition for England in the final. And while West Germany did indeed give England a difficult, albeit different, test, it remains true that Portugal had forced the very best of this England side, and had come ever so close to denying them, playing in more exhilarating style than anyone else in that World Cup. No team had played with such a technical fluency or effervescent dynamism as Portugal in the 1966 World Cup. No team provided such dazzling entertainment, and relentlessly free attacking. Portugal were a diamond amid a lot of rough in the tournament in England, as such joyful attacking was more the exception rather than the norm. They weren't recklessly carefree in their attacking, though, marrying it with a stringent defence that held many at bay, save for the stunningly surprising early blitz by the North Koreans, and the very best of the world champions to be, England.

Eusébio went on to score his ninth of the World Cup in a 2-1 third-place play-off victory over the Soviet Union: an achievement that only one player has since surpassed when Gerd Müller scored ten in 1970. His scoring feat was a phenomenal personal achievement, but so too was the manner in which he led his side to what was a hugely successful debut tournament. His status as a great of the game was assured, made more certain with each performance. The thousands who lined the streets of Lisbon on the team's return home were testament to the impact this success had on a nation unused to such international footballing achievement. Third place in the World Cup was viewed as an astonishing achievement, tempered by the fact that the manner of their performances made many believe Portugal really could have done even better. And yet the great achievements of 1966 would sit as a lone pinnacle amid an international wilderness for Portugal.

While Benfica still remained at the top of the European club game, again reaching the European Cup Final in 1968, for the national team there would be no return to a tournament for 18 years, and no second appearance at a World Cup for 20 years. There was no golden era of Portuguese football built on this grand platform. While Eusébio and co were reaching the heights with Benfica again, Portugal had failed to reach the 1968 European Nations' Cup. Only a few months after their World Cup zenith, many of the same players were in the team beaten by Sweden in Lisbon which set their campaign on a rocky path, ultimately finishing well behind Bulgaria in their qualifying group: a Bulgaria side that Portugal had brushed aside with ease in 1966.

By the time of the 1970 World Cup qualification, the great side of 1966 was beginning to break up, with the retirement of Coluna and others from the national team. But Eusébio, Augusto and Torres were still there for what was a disastrous attempt at reaching the next World Cup. Where before there had been such attacking potency, now there seemed a stuttering loss of confidence as Portugal slumped to last place in their qualifying group, winning only one of their six matches.

Just how had a national team gone from a history of no international achievement whatsoever, to third in the world, and then swiftly returned to the international wilderness despite all of the successes of Portuguese clubs? 'The Portugal team had one big problem,' explained Ricardo Serrado. 'The clubs were professional and had top conditions, but the Portuguese federation were amateur and had many problems. They didn't have the stability, the conditions or the people to support a professional national team.' This mismatch from the club game to the international one was never fully resolved until the 1990s, with any brief achievement prior to then the result of good fortune rather than good planning.

Eusébio's Portugal may not have remained among the world's best for long, but they captivated so many during their brief peak, before quickly fading into the darkness of international obscurity once again. For their peak to have come in Portugal's sole World Cup appearance prior to 1986 made it all the more startling. They secured not only a legacy as a popular team that had thrilled so many, but also as a multicultural team ahead of its time. In a World Cup without any African representation, the African confederation deemed unworthy of even one guaranteed place in the tournament, this Portugal side was that continent's effective representatives. In all, four of the 1966 squad hailed from Mozambique, with defenders Hilário and Vicente in addition to Eusébio and Coluna. That Coluna and, most significantly of course, Eusébio, were such stars of the World Cup was hugely symbolic, focusing attention not only on Portugal but on African football, even if it wasn't being achieved in Africa's name.

This Portugal side remain so beloved, both at home and beyond their borders, in part because of the style they portrayed but most of all because of Eusébio. A star already, he propelled himself to the very top of the top of the game as a result of his World Cup exploits, taking over Pelé's mantle, even if it was only temporarily on loan.

The symbolic passing of the baton from one great to another had come in the group match victory over Brazil. Eusébio had become the best player in the world at the time. He had emphasised that, with a magnificent World Cup performance, leading and inspiring his side to within touching distance of glory, while blazing a trail for black players at the elite level in Europe. It was a magnificent moment, but in international terms it was just that: momentary. Come the next World Cup and Portugal's failure to even qualify, the mantle of the world's best was decisively grasped back by Pelé, as he and Brazil elevated themselves to legendary status.

There was more personal and club glory for Eusébio but nothing in international terms. The brief international greatness for Portugal replaced by decades in the wilderness, with nothing but the memories of a golden summer. Those memories would serve as both a millstone and an inspiration for those who followed; Eusébio's individual greatness at once inspiring both Portuguese and African footballers. For all the great players to have followed for Portugal, from Figo to Rui Costa to Cristiano Ronaldo, Eusébio retains a place in the hearts of Portuguese fans as one of the nation's greatest.

This Portugal side are still seen as heroes of the Portuguese game, their legacy and impact as pioneers on the international stage enhanced by how close they came to glory, inspiring many of the generations to follow. 'They made an entire country believe that they can win against all the odds, against any players and against any national team, even the world champions, Brazil,' explained Ricardo Serrado. 'They made an entire country believe that Portugal – a team that no one knew at the beginning of the tournament – was capable of accomplishing great deeds.'

It so nearly took Eusébio and his team to the ultimate prize in 1966. Had they overcome the obdurate England, who would have bet against them lifting the trophy in the final? Portugal had played the finest football of the competition, pushing England to raise themselves to new heights in an epic semi-final that saw the two best teams of that World Cup going head-to-head.

As Otto Gloria said, following the semi-final defeat, 'Surely that was the final,' such was the quality of both teams on that day. Had Portugal prevailed, the ultimate glory could have been theirs: a glittering reward for an exhilarating team that had dazzled so gloriously, and one player touched with greatness. Had they done so, would this great generation have faded away so quickly? Instead, having so narrowly fallen short, Portugal returned to the international hibernation from whence they came. The pinnacle of Eusébio's Portugal may have been brief, but it could so easily have been glistened with gold.

6

Netherlands 1974 and 1978

*Sometimes, even when you don't lift the
trophy, in the end you're still seen as a winner.
Wherever I go in the world, people always
want to talk about our team in those days.
I think we earned more praise and respect
during the tournament than most world
champions before or since. I'm proud of that.*

Johan Cruyff

THE NETHERLANDS teams of the 1970s lifted
a nation from World Cup obscurity into the realms of
football mythology. Such was the revolutionary approach
and manner of the Dutch that they captivated the world,
set on a path to a destiny that would remain agonisingly
beyond reach. The anguish of unrewarded beauty in 1974
was followed by the ill fortune of the width of a post in
1978. Two World Cups, two finals, two defeats, but two
very different places in football history.

The flamboyant Dutch team of 1974 in particular evoke
emotions akin to appreciating fine art, grabbing the hearts

of so many who saw them play or have studied them since. It was a team that causes us to rethink our default perceptions of what the game is all about, what the purpose of football and the World Cup is. Is it simply a means to identify and crown a winner, all others falling by the wayside as all eyes become fixed on the victors? Or is it an entertainment, a way of delighting and inspiring, in which ultimate victory is not the be-all and end-all? Is art, beauty and a lasting memory just as important, or perhaps more important, than victory? Can success be measured in terms of legacy rather than victory?

When Johan Cruyff claimed that perhaps the Netherlands of 1974, a team of footballing rock stars that encapsulated a counterculture, were the real winners because they were remembered more than the victors, it wasn't the outlandish claim of someone struggling to accept that his crowning glory had been lost. It was a genuine sentiment, expressed to offer an alternative view. Naturally, it's a thought which occupies many of the views in this book, but when it comes to the Dutch team of 1974, it is perhaps truer than with any other.

This was a team which not only provided a revolutionary approach to the game, but also provided so many images and moments that are seared into the mind, played out in a style – of football, of attitude, of appearance – which spoke to and resonated with so many people. 'Dutch football culture is steeped in this mythology of Johan Cruyff and the 1970s,' Dutch football journalist Elko Born explained to me. 'From a very young age you're told these stories. Everywhere, the 1970s are always mentioned. There's this feeling deep down inside, even if I didn't see it myself, that this is the origin story, the most important thing that ever happened and something you can never surpass. It's just the founding mythology of everything.'

It went beyond the aesthetic beauty of the way they played the game into the realms of symbolising a cultural movement. This was a team that represented a nation and its people in more than name, colour and flag. It represented a way of being and a way of thinking: a gang of football rebels bringing a nonconformist approach to the world's game. They were representative of their time, fitting the changing world of the late 1960s and early 1970s, depicting a footballing cool, leaving the more strait-laced era of their forebears behind. It was the fulfilment of years of development in thought and deed. Is it any wonder they are so fondly remembered, more heralded than the ultimate winners – what was actually a very influential, successful and, in their own way, a relatively fluid West Germany team?

For all the impact that Dutch football would have on the world in the 1970s, it's easy to forget that before 1974 the Netherlands had barely registered in the international arena at all. There had been fleeting appearances at the 1934 and 1938 World Cups, both of which were over almost as soon as they had begun. Olympic participation was mostly restricted to the early pioneering days, while the first few European Championship tournaments had also passed by without the Dutch troubling the latter stages. Now this spectacular new generation were forging their own path in a football world that was unprepared for the impact they would have.

In club competition, Feyenoord were the first to make a mark on the European stage, reaching the semi-final of the European Cup in 1963, and it was they who became the first Dutch team to lift the trophy after winning in 1970 against Panathinaikos. Ajax then took up the mantle, winning the next three European Cups and raising the bar to extraordinary heights, their groundbreaking brand of football proving as effective as it was intoxicating.

Rinus Michels took over as coach of Ajax in 1965 with the club in the midst of a relegation battle. He steered Ajax to safety before leading them to the title the next year. Indeed, they would win four championships in six seasons under Michels. But beyond the trophies, it was the Ajax approach which was impressing in such exhilarating style.

On some fortuitous occasions, paths converge in the perfect place at the perfect time, and the young Cruyff was the on-field personification of the freedom Michels was poised to unleash. Cruyff was a free spirit of extraordinary talent, with a sophisticated and groundbreaking tactical understanding. He was a footballing rebel, but also a romantic and idealist. Perhaps the most influential idealist the game has ever seen.

He was a product of his time and place, and the Netherlands in the 1960s was a rapidly changing place. While the world was changing in terms of counterculture and free-thinking, the hippie movement burgeoning in America caused ripples in Europe too. It was in the Netherlands, and Amsterdam in particular, that this culture thrived: a place where free-thinking was encouraged, where freedom of expression and acceptance of new ideas was not only tolerated but normalised, inspired and validated by events such as John Lennon and Yoko Ono's 1969 bed-in at the Amsterdam Hilton.

It was also a country permanently at odds with, and creatively adapting to, its environment. In a country susceptible to flooding and lacking space, the Dutch have become well versed in adapting and making the most of the space they do have, or devising creative ways to generate new space. David Winner talks on this theme in his seminal book on Dutch football, *Brilliant Orange*, giving a compelling explanation of why it was in the Netherlands that the ultimate footballing adaption to, and use of, space developed.

The roots of the Dutch Total Football can be traced back through the influence of the early pioneering British coaches who ventured into Europe, and also the central European style of Hungary in the 1950s. But it was the Ajax that Michels set on their path to glory, and later the Dutch national team, who would not only push the boundaries of this style further but would come to define it.

Having given Cruyff the freedom to roam to wherever he felt he could do the most damage, Michels extended this to the rest of the team. When any player moved out of position the gap left was filled by a team-mate, establishing a high degree of fluidity as the players were freed from the restraints of convention. Anyone could be an attacker or a defender as players across the pitch pressured opponents in numbers when without the ball and sought space where they pleased when with the ball. Such fluidity was carved into a coherent strategy by Michels and Cruyff, the on-field manager. Ajax became a complex machine of perpetual movement, requiring a high degree of football intelligence and versatility; an approach which created the finest generation of revolutionary footballers propelling first club, and then nation, to extraordinary heights.

A core of what would be the Dutch national team of the 1970s were schooled in this way, from Arie Haan, Ruud Krol, Wim Suurbier, Barry Hulshoff and Sjaak Swart through to Johnny Rep and Johan Neeskens. *Totaalvoetbal*, Total Football, as it was dubbed, was not simply a tactical approach, however, but also a state of mind. All players are involved in the movement no matter how far they are from the ball, interchanging effortlessly, gliding seamlessly from one position to another, confusing opponents and stretching the pitch to its fullest extent.

'People talk of Total Football as if it is a system, something to replace 4-2-4 or 4-3-3,' Haan explained to *The Observer* in 1974. 'It is not a system. As it is at any moment, so you play. Not one or two players make a situation, but five or six. The best is that with every situation all 11 players are involved, but this is difficult. In many teams maybe only two or three play, and the rest are looking. In the Holland team, when you are 60 metres from the ball, you are playing.'

The need to constantly create space was central to the approach, requiring continual vigilance and concentration. 'We discussed it the whole time,' said the Ajax defender Hulshoff. 'Cruyff always talked about where to run and where to stand, and when not to move.' It was an incessantly proactive approach, intensely pressuring the opposition to win the ball back quickly and capitalise on a floundering foe. It stood in stark contrast to the defensive catenaccio style, or the overly physical approach so prevalent in the 1960s, providing such a refreshing, invigorating view of how beautiful and dynamic football could be. The shackles of conformity were cast away, the free-thinking counter-culture embraced, with Cruyff, the personification of freedom, style and idealism, its focal point.

It took Ajax to three European Cups in a row from 1971 to 1973, with Michels transposing the approach to Barcelona when he moved on following the first of those triumphs, only for his successor, the Romanian Ştefan Kovács, to push Total Football even further. When Cruyff also joined Barcelona at the start of the 1973/74 season, the great era of Ajax was at the beginning of the end.

But for the national team, the combination of the players schooled in the Ajax way, plus those from Feyenoord and the rising force of PSV Eindhoven, would ultimately create footballing majesty. The path to their peak would be far from smooth, however. In fact, had one offside decision in the final qualifying match in November 1973 been called correctly, this story simply wouldn't have been written, as the great Dutch team would have failed to qualify for the 1974 World Cup.

The Dutch were under the management of the Czech coach František Fadrhonc, who had spent two decades coaching in the Eredivisie before becoming the national team manager in 1970. Paired with neighbours Belgium, as well as the weaker teams of Norway and Iceland, the Dutch had fought their way through to a position where a draw in the final qualifier with Belgium would see them through.

Cracks had begun to show in the penultimate match in Oslo, however. Taking place in September 1973, it came a matter of weeks after Cruyff had left Ajax, citing eroded trust, having been voted out of the club captaincy by his team-mates. Against this backdrop, he had barely reached Barcelona before he was meeting up with many of the same players in the national team colours.

Perhaps it is little surprise, then, that the Dutch produced their most awkward performance of the qualifiers, only rescuing a victory over a Norway side they had beaten 9-0 ten months earlier in the final few minutes. When Hulshoff latched on to Cruyff's delightful back-heeled pass and rolled the ball home to grab a 2-1 win, it marked a fortunate escape in a game in which the Dutch had been more niggly than fluent, more argumentative than attractive. They had escaped, though, setting up that final decisive showdown against Belgium in November 1973.

Belgium were yet to concede in the group, including a goalless draw against the Dutch in Antwerp a year before in which they had come the width of a post away from winning. They would come oh-so close in the return match too. With only moments remaining, and the match still goalless, Belgium earned a free kick on the left for a final, desperate push for the goal they needed. As the free kick came in, the Dutch defence mistimed their attempted offside trap, while the cross evaded a flapping Piet Schrijvers in goal. The ball reached Jan Verheyen who volleyed home, only for it to be ruled out for offside.

While the angles available on YouTube are not quite up to the levels of the fine lines of a modern VAR decision, it seems abundantly clear that neither Verheyen nor any of his team-mates were offside. With that incorrect decision, Belgium, having not conceded in the whole campaign, were out. The Netherlands could celebrate a first World Cup appearance in 36 years, but only just.

But while the team that qualified was replete with all the familiar talents, they weren't yet adept in the carousel style of Total Football. As they entered World Cup year, the Dutch federation opted to replace Fadrhonc for the tournament with the man who had built the great Ajax side. Michels, still Barcelona coach, would combine that role with the Dutch position to lead his country into the World Cup; the ideal man to get the best from this phenomenal generation. In the short space of time he had prior to the World Cup, he moulded the national team in the image of Ajax, developing the style of play over a series of mainly underwhelming friendlies, save for a statement 4-1 win over Argentina.

Michels faced various issues in creating his vision, however. He needed to find a way to include the talented left-winger Rob Rensenbrink, who had not been schooled in the ways of Total Football. And in defence, his plans were hampered by the absence of the Ajax great Hulshoff, struck down by a serious knee injury. Rather than replace him with another specialist centre-back, however, Michels opted instead to deploy the Ajax midfielder Arie Haan alongside the Feyenoord full-back Wim Rijsbergen in the centre of defence.

The thinking is clear: seek to develop the ball from the back with the more sophisticated ball-playing and more intense pressing skills of a midfielder who was adept at playing multiple positions anyway. The counterargument was that Hulshoff's absence would mean less protection for a vulnerable defence should it be put under sustained pressure. The intention, though, was to proactively press sufficiently that the defence shouldn't come under such pressure, with all cogs in the wheel primed to play their part in the perpetual forward momentum of the team.

This thinking extended to the goalkeeper too. Jan van Beveren, the PSV goalkeeper, was the finest Dutch stopper at the time but injury had seen him lose his place during the qualifiers. He was fit again by the World Cup, but when Michels had wanted him to prove his fitness in a friendly, Van Beveren only countenanced playing one half to avoid hampering his recovery. Michels took umbrage, citing a lack of character. As a result, the best Dutch goalkeeper of his generation was sent from the squad, his chance of a World Cup place gone. Schrijvers would go as an understudy, but Michels, with no little influence from Cruyff, entrusted the main goalkeeping duties to an untested 33-year-old from FC Amsterdam.

Jan Jongbloed had first played for the national team back in 1962 as a fresh-faced 21-year-old, with a brief, disappointing substitute appearance in a 4-1 defeat. His next cap came 12 years later in the 4-1 win over Argentina just weeks ahead of the 1974 World Cup. Jongbloed wasn't overly renowned for the traditional goalkeeping attributes of shot-stopping and commanding his back line. What he brought instead was his ball-playing skills and ability to keep the ball in motion, linking with those in front of him.

Michels and Cruyff were clear, and again clearly ahead of their time when you consider the role of the goalkeeper in modern football, that these skills outweighed any deficiencies in Jongbloed's game: that his overall contribution to the fluency of the team was more valuable. This unlikely, and unexpected, member of the glorious Dutch would go on to play in two World Cup finals.

Some of the tactical tweaks may have been forced on the Dutch, but they served to push the team further into Total Football. The injury to Hulshoff and the issues with Van Beveren led to these sophisticated, futuristic adaptations. Ball-playing defenders and sweeper-keepers are regular sights nowadays but are no modern innovation: crafted by the Dutch in 1974. Would they have been so fluid had some of these changes not been forced? It's tempting to consider how things may have turned out had either Hulshoff or Van Beveren played in the World Cup, but equally, perhaps their presence would have taken something of the fluidity away: the forced changes pushing the totality of Total Football further as to be truly groundbreaking.

The Feyenoord contingent in the squad were led by the magnificent talents of the tactically adept Willem van Hanegem, and the stylish defender Wim Jansen, while PSV were represented by the twins René and Willy van de Kerkhof. But the heart of the squad was Ajax-schooled. The names roll off the tongue, conjuring up images of orange-clad cool in your mind's eye: Krol, Suurbier, Haan, Neeskens, Rep, and, of course, Cruyff himself.

As the 1974 World Cup progressed, the Dutch attracted increasing adoration, gradually elevating themselves above the crowd, moving from being one of a glut of potential winners towards being outright favourites with each game they played. Hindsight may make us believe that the Dutch were always destined for greatness in 1974, but coming into the tournament that had been less clear. The hosts, and European champions, West Germany were the overwhelming favourites, while David Lacey in *The Guardian* noted at that time that, other than a handful of weaker teams, 'There is remarkably little to choose between the other 12 countries.' Those perceptions would quickly alter once the world was hit by the elegant orange blur, captivating and enchanting with each performance.

The Total Football they produced was even symbolised by the numbers they wore on their shirts, with the squad numbered in alphabetical order rather than based on position. This may have been an administrative point rather than a footballing one, but it was apt given position mattered little in the Dutch style. There was one exception, though, as Cruyff wore his favoured number 14, marking him out as different from the rest. With only two stripes on his sleeves rather than the Adidas three due to contractual disputes, Cruyff stood out as a maverick even in a team of nonconformists. His importance was beyond doubt: while Michels could organise the team off the field, it was Cruyff who was the on-field organiser, issuing instructions and adapting during the game.

In the opening group, Uruguay were the first to face the Dutch onslaught. The South Americans struggled against the incessant movement, with Cruyff's meanderings triggering the movement of the other nine outfield players throughout. Uruguay, startled and rigid, struggled to get out of their own half at times, such was the intensity of the opposition. The Netherlands won 2-0, Rep scoring both, but it could have been five or six, such was the dominance. If ever a game represented the new world order, this was it. The traditional ways appeared backwards, the new approach invigorating and intoxicating by contrast. In a World Cup where even the Brazilians had abandoned style and beauty, the Dutch espoused everything that was good and inspiring about football.

Michels replaced Rensenbrink with Keizer for the next game with Sweden – a player with a troubled relationship with Cruyff. Whether that was the reason for a stodgier performance is inconclusive, but this was a more laboured performance by the Dutch in a goalless draw best remembered for one moment of pure magic that would become the defining image of the brilliance of Cruyff and this team. It was a moment of flawed beauty too, however, symbolising more than simply the ability of the Dutch.

Midway through the first half the ball was fed to Cruyff on the left with his back to goal. He executed the most astonishing body feint, dragging the ball back with his instep, instantly turning through 180 degrees to leave the Swedish full-back Jan Olsson grasping at thin air, confounded and confused. Cruyff raced to the byline but his cross led to nothing, the wondrous moment devastatingly effective in its instant, but ultimately delivering nothing of quantitative substance.

The beauty of the Cruyff turn made it an irrelevance that it didn't lead to a goal, however. It's remembered for its aesthetic and symbolic qualities, not the eventual outcome. Its symbolism extends far beyond that single moment, or even that game. Equally, what at first appears an individual rather than collective moment of brilliance doesn't tell the full story. The ball found Cruyff via a midfielder popping up on the right wing, and another midfielder nominally in the defence stepping up to keep the move flowing. Even Cruyff was positioned on the left, more naturally the domain of Keizer on that day, or Rensenbrink on others.

As such, this flash of brilliance is emblematic of the whole concept and destiny of this great team: in a moment representing the exquisite beauty they were able to create, and the lasting memory their actions cast over the footballing world. But so, too, it represents beauty winning out in our minds over victory or, in that particular moment, over scoring a goal. One single moment echoing the ultimate destiny of this team: a wondrous, magical lasting legacy, but no ultimate victory. The moment, just like this Dutch team, is remembered despite not delivering its ultimate goal.

With Rensenbrink restored to the team, Bulgaria were swatted aside with arrogant, almost effortless ease in the final group match. The rampant Dutch won 4-1, but as against Uruguay, if anyone was flattered by the scoreline it was the beleaguered opposition. Cruyff's nonchalantly curled cross for the substitute, Theo de Jong, to head in the fourth was as graceful as it was natural, rounding off a superlative display from the Dutch who surged into the second stage, now considered a real prospect for overall victory.

The Dutch reputation was enhanced yet further in their second-round group which began with irresistible wins over Argentina and East Germany. The 4-0 victory over Argentina was particularly destructive with Cruyff in imperious form. He scored twice and set up another for Rep, each in their own way highlighting the exquisite joy of this Dutch team. The first saw Cruyff controlling a lazily looping Van Hanegem ball into the box with one delightful touch, before rounding the goalkeeper with the next, and rolling the ball into the now empty net. It was simple but ruthlessly effective and delightfully stunning.

After Krol had slammed in a second, Cruyff inspired the third, supplying a pinpoint cross for Rep who headed in before Cruyff volleyed in the fourth himself from a tight angle. If what had gone before in the opening round had served notice that the Netherlands were real contenders, then this performance confirmed it. The already stylish had now become the sublime, as they racked up the memorable moments: a vast array of clips that would remain etched in the minds of those who saw them and those who have appreciated their magnificence from the distance of a few decades.

Rensenbrink and Neeskens scored the goals which saw off East Germany, as the seemingly inexorable march towards the final continued. All that separated the Dutch from the showpiece match were the defending champions, Brazil. The final was within reach for both, each having beaten Argentina and East Germany, but anyone anticipating a clash for the ages of grace and panache were to be sorely disappointed. The Brazilian beauty of 1970 may as well have been a lifetime ago rather than just four years, such was the contrast in their approach in 1974; more grit than grace.

Dutch glamour was dragged down by the more robust slant of the 1974 Brazilians, but they gave as good as they got. It jarred both stylistically and visually, with both teams playing in their change kit – Brazil in blue, the Netherlands in white – the anticipated magic looking wrong from the outset. This physical skirmish was punctuated by two moments of Dutch splendour. Neeskens scored the first, sliding and stretching to reach Cruyff's pass and loop a shot beyond the Brazilian keeper into the net. Cruyff added the second with another iconic strike, flinging himself acrobatically to hit a flying volley into the goal, sending the Dutch into their first World Cup Final.

Waiting for them were a rejuvenated West Germany. Where the Netherlands were winning plaudits, West Germany, by contrast, had been far less impressive. A loss to East Germany had left them second in their group, their fortunes conflicting with the ease and grace of the Dutch. While that slip-up had meant they were kept apart from the Dutch in the second stage, they had faced a magnificent Poland team inspired by Grzegorz Lato, Andrzej Szarmach and Kazimierz Deyna. Stylistically, the ideal final would have been the Netherlands versus Poland; these were the two most impressive teams of the World Cup, the two who had lit it up. If us football romantics could have had our way, Poland would have overcome West Germany in their decisive de facto semi-final.

Had the rain not poured and the pitch not deteriorated into a quagmire, perhaps they would have done, as Poland's sleek technical elegance may well have prospered more on a dry day than on a pitch that made such artistry impossible. In another world, Poland would have made it through, and this chapter may have been about them instead. But West Germany won 1-0 with a late strike by Gerd Müller and reached their date with destiny in the final in Munich.

The Germans' patchy form, however, meant that it was the visitors, not the hosts, who were the favourites on the eve of the final, reversing the pre-tournament perceptions. West Germany weren't short on talent, though, far from it. Entering an era of Bayern Munich domination in the

European Cup, that they had taken over from Ajax at the pinnacle of the club game added a level of intrigue. The core of that team – Franz Beckenbauer, Müller, Sepp Maier, Paul Breitner, Uli Hoeneß – also made up the core of this West Germany team.

They had won the European Championship in 1972 in some style, the guile of Günter Netzer adding a degree of swagger that had been missing from the 1974 team up to this point. Netzer's style and outlook perhaps made him more akin to the Dutch team of 1974, his free-spirited ideals and performances bringing a dose of the unexpected. He was in the 1974 squad but had been limited to a 20-minute cameo in the defeat to East Germany; a player seemingly past his peak, symbolic of a team just beyond their prime. West Germany had been supreme in 1972, playing with a style and substance that seemed on the wane by 1974.

Little wonder the Dutch were supremely confident ahead of the final, then. But were they too confident? One theory on their demise is based on a burgeoning arrogance and complacency which developed through the tournament and peaked following the victory over Brazil. And with the fact that Ajax had thumped Bayern 4-0 a year before, to many within the Dutch squad there seemed little reason to doubt their coronation would be sealed come the final.

Preparation became lax, standing in stark contrast to the thorough and professional approach of the Germans. With the foot off the gas, Dutch focus slipped, culminating in the incident published by German tabloid *Bild* of players cavorting in their hotel pool with local girls. Attempts to portray this as a smear by the Germans are short-sighted according to David Winner, who argued that the *Bild* story was not only accurate, but a very mild reflection of the indiscipline now rife within the squad.

There had been other incidents during the tournament such as Michels returning to Spain to help Barcelona through their Spanish Cup Final, enhancing the feeling that by this stage it was the players running the show. This mattered little when they kept winning, but the seeds of complacency were sewn. The Dutch went into the final convinced they would win, to the extent that playing the game seemed almost an irrelevance. The focus and desire that had brought them this far was slipping, leaving them underestimating the task ahead, defeating themselves to some extent.

The Dutch had what the legendary writer Hugh McIlvanney expressed in his preview of the final in *The Observer* as 'a deep conviction that they have the talent, the courage and the collective maturity to lay emphatic hold on the championship'. It was a conviction shared by so many thrilled by their exploits. 'Yet, for some of us,' he added, 'those echoes of events that took place so many seasons ago tend to form ice clubs in the blood.' The pain of the 1954 Hungarians, so clearly the best team of an entire era, letting victory elude them against an underdog West Germany, haunted McIlvanney's thoughts.

Dutch certainty was absolute, though. When they then took the lead in the final in only the second minute, this was embedded yet further. It had been a magnificent opening, the Dutch kicking off and playing the ball around lazily, before Cruyff, the deepest Dutch outfield player, suddenly surged forwards all the way into the German box. A panicked Hoeneß brought him down, conceding a penalty which Neeskens, as adept as anyone before or since from the spot, slammed into the net. The Dutch had crafted a goal in the World Cup Final without their opponents so much as touching the ball in the match so far. Every preconceived notion of how the final would play out seemed vindicated and confirmed.

Dutch on-field assurance now led to another oft-cited criticism of them in this final. Some players themselves have discussed how there was a feeling of wanting to humiliate the Germans, to demonstrate Dutch superiority and control. For some, the identity of the opposition mattered not, but to others, that it was the Germans was cause for such thoughts to emerge. For Van Hanegem, having witnessed his father, sister and two brothers die in the war, there was always that undertone to it all, a need for some form of revenge, however misguided. The mere fact of it being West Germany facing the Dutch had seen references to the Second World War to come to the fore in the build-up.

Dutch intensity did indeed drop off, though any noticeable attempts at humiliation were gained because the Dutch were significantly better at retaining the ball, which they did with minimum fuss but without purpose. They failed to go for the jugular, content to play the ball around and keep it from the Germans. The Dutch seemingly forgot about trying to score more, happy to show their ability to maintain possession at will: a humiliation held at arm's length.

'Perhaps they thought they could win the World Cup without allowing Germany to play in the final,' wrote David Lacey in *The Guardian* of the misguided slowing rhythm of the Dutch. Whatever the reasons, the Netherlands failed to build on their startling opening, and by the 25th minute West Germany were level with a penalty of their own. Bernd Holzenbein was challenged by Wim Jansen in the box, and while Jansen's leg was dangling dangerously close to contact, the extent of the German's swallow dive and dramatic fall convinced the referee it was a foul. Breitner,

West Germany's own attacking full-back, converted to level the scores. The Germans did what the Dutch had failed to do and took advantage of the momentum shift in their favour. By half-time they had taken the lead with a decisive turn and shot from arch poacher Gerd Müller past a static Jongbloed.

The Netherlands were now trailing, having appeared set to dominate, and yet their quality ought still to have won through. The second half saw wave after wave of Dutch attacks with Cruyff's influence growing by the minute. Maier in the German goal had the game of his life, keeping the frequent efforts at bay, though the Dutch finishing lacked its usual clinical nature. For all the pressure, the ball simply wouldn't go in, an equaliser remaining agonisingly elusive, Rep spurning the clearest opportunity 15 minutes from the end. For all the Dutch domination, it was actually West Germany who came the closest to adding to the score, Müller having a goal incorrectly ruled out for offside.

The final few minutes had seen Dutch desperation cause them to resort to a more direct approach, as last-gasp panic left the Dutch abandoning their usual style and playing like all the rest for a few fleeting minutes. It seemed inappropriate, these revolutionaries reduced to mere mortals, symbolising the end of the dream.

Müller's twisting turn for the winning goal just before half-time was effective and decisive, but lacked the ease and elegance of the turn Cruyff had made famous a fortnight before. Both were memorable in their own right, but does this contrast in elegance encapsulate the difference between the two? One, beautiful and graceful, but ultimately leading to no tangible reward; the other clinical, decisive and leading to victory.

The Dutch squad returned home to a hero's welcome, the perception of a successful tournament with a mere blip at the end masking any disappointment. For players and fans alike, the belief that the style they showed and the joy they gave was beyond that achieved by anyone else helped them overcome the irrevocable fact that they lost when they should have won. The enduring pain hidden away by the certainty that what they had done was more worthwhile than victory.

There's no getting away, though, from the fact that ultimately it was a sporting failure: the greatest team of the tournament, and the decade, reaching for glory and falling short. Failure did matter. It mattered to the players and it mattered to a conflicted nation, but what they did achieve and the legacy they left despite the defeat was deeply impactful regardless.

The Netherlands maintained their position as one of the world's finest national teams over the next four years, to a European Championship semi-final in 1976 and on to the 1978 World Cup. With Michels having returned to his day job in Barcelona, the coaching duties were passed on after the 1974 World Cup to George Knobel, who had led Ajax the previous season. They had progressed in convincing style, notably a 7-1 aggregate rout of Belgium in the European Championship quarter-final only to come a cropper against Czechoslovakia in the semi-final after extra time. The style was still the same, but so too was the over-confidence, arrogance even, meaning that success remained elusive. That defeat denied the Dutch the opportunity to take on West Germany in a second successive final and the chance to exorcise their demons.

Come the next World Cup in 1978, the Netherlands, now coached by the Austrian Ernst Happel – the mastermind behind Feyenoord's peak at the start of the decade – travelled to Argentina as one of the favourites once again, but things were undeniably different. That they failed to light up the tournament as they had done so mesmerically in 1974 is no real surprise given the difficulty in maintaining such high levels of performance. The Dutch of 1978 had to battle their way to a second successive final, rather than the inexorable rise of 1974.

There were various reasons for this. The break-up of the great Ajax side of the early 1970s saw more players seek out pastures new, as Cruyff himself had already done. He was joined in Barcelona by Neeskens, who opted to reunite with both Cruyff and Michels. Rep had moved to Bastia in France, Suurbier to Schalke, and Haan had joined Rensenbrink at Anderlecht. The Ajax contingent in first-team contention was now restricted to Krol and Schrijvers. The Total Football so schooled in these players was not only more far-flung, but was no longer the revolutionary game it had been four years earlier. And while many of the names in the Dutch team were the same, those changes that there had been seemed less dynamic, less radical.

More significantly though, a raft of withdrawals damaged the Dutch, pushing them to near breaking point. Van Beveren was still the best Dutch goalkeeper, still excelling at PSV, but would miss out again, Jongbloed and Schrijvers both seeing game time in Argentina. Willy van der Kuijlen was another PSV hero, a magnificently elegant and talented playmaker, whose issues with the Cruyff-led hierarchy caused him to leave the national team. Their absence was harmful enough, but the identity of two other players no longer involved was even more damaging.

Wim van Hanegem, the best player of the 1974 final, pulled out of the squad during the build-up, announcing his withdrawal in a tearful television appearance, primarily citing arguments around the equality of bonuses. These absentees were trailblazers in the grand tradition of stubborn Dutch withdrawals, in a nation where stubbornness seemed an ingrained character trait. But none were as significant as the final absentee.

Cruyff had insisted, following the 1974 final, that he wouldn't travel to another World Cup, and the time away from home it entailed. He had played in the 1978 qualifiers, but his stance on taking part in the finals remained even if the reason behind it changed. As the tournament approached, a concerted campaign in the Dutch media saw the pressure on Cruyff to relent increase. A television station spearheaded a 'Pull Cruyff Over the Line' campaign, but nothing would make him change his mind. Suggestions that he refused in protest at the Argentinian regime were common, but false. Rather, an attempted kidnapping was the decisive factor, when Cruyff and his family were tied up at gunpoint in their family home in Barcelona. They escaped unscathed but the experience, which only came to light decades later, understandably scarred him deeply, and the prospect of being away for a couple of months was unthinkable to him.

Against this tumultuous backdrop, the Dutch struggled in the opening group. They had begun well enough, beating Iran 3-0 thanks to a hat-trick from Rensenbrink, before a goalless draw with Peru and a 3-2 defeat to Scotland had seen the Netherlands come perilously close to being eliminated at the first hurdle. Rep's blistering strike against Scotland had rescued what was on the verge of disaster, with Scotland within reach of the three-goal margin that would have seen them progress ahead of the Dutch. As it was, the Netherlands only emerged from the group on goal difference, well behind the group winners Peru.

Brian Glanville cited an Argentine journalist reflecting on the stuttering performances so far from a team missing Cruyff, which therefore 'resembled a superb machine which lacked the man who invented it'. The second-round group saw a Dutch resurgence, however. Austria were resoundingly beaten 5-1 before a much-anticipated rematch of the 1974 final against West Germany. This time the Germans took the lead early, only for Haan to equalise with a spectacular long shot. West Germany again led in the second half, but a second equaliser eight minutes from time, Willy van de Kerkhof setting up his twin brother René, gave the Dutch a vital draw. While it was no revenge for what happened in 1974, it kept the Dutch in pole position in the group, one win away from another final appearance.

Where the Brazil clash in 1974 had been a semi-final in all but name, now in 1978 the last group match with Italy was just the same. It was Italy who started the more positively, taking the lead midway through the first half in what was a disastrous moment for the Dutch. The Italian forward Roberto Bettega had burst through towards the penalty area and was poised to shoot. In attempting to nick the ball away, Ernie Brandts, the young PSV defender, succeeded only in firing it into an unguarded net, before colliding with the onrushing goalkeeper. Schrijvers, injured in the collision, had to be stretchered off, his World Cup over. Enter Jongbloed once again, having been replaced by Schrijvers following the opening-group phase. The unlikely man entering the sharp end of another World Cup.

Italy dominated much of the proceedings, but could not add to their lead in what was becoming a feisty, physical encounter in echoes of that Brazil match four years earlier. This time the Dutch were largely second best throughout, and ultimately fortunate to win through, thanks to two spectacular second-half goals.

First, following a partial Italian clearance the ball fell to Brandts, the defender finding himself in a forward position in the true spirit of Total Football. He let loose a fierce shot which flew into the top corner, atoning for any fault surrounding Italy's opening goal. And yet that was nothing when compared to the winning strike from Haan which rasped in off the post from nigh on 30 yards out; a goal worthy of winning a place in a World Cup Final.

As in 1974, waiting for the Netherlands in the final were the host nation. In 1974, Cruyff had inspired the elegant evisceration of Argentina, but things were rather different this time around. Without getting into the political accusations that have surrounded this match in the years since, even on a purely footballing front the Netherlands were facing a very tough prospect. The Argentina of César Luis Menotti were an exuberant, potent force, fuelled by the fervour of a desperate, demanding nation. For them, winning was not merely a hope, or even an expectation, it had more the feel of a necessity.

In the raucous volatility of El Monumental in Buenos Aires, as the ticker tape descended and the atmosphere tipped over into frenzied desperation, the Netherlands took to the field alone, forced to wait on the pitch for their opponents for nearly ten minutes. The delay was pure gamesmanship from Argentina, aiming to unsettle their opponents, as were the fierce and sustained protests about the plaster cast on René van de Kerkhof's wrist, which he had worn without objection in previous games. Such were the ferocity of the complaints that the Italian referee relented and demanded Van de Kerkhof add extra, softer bandaging.

Argentina were good enough to win without having to resort to such pettiness, but it's a sign of the sheer desperation felt in the home camp to achieve victory by whatever means that they felt this approach was warranted. Equally, it symbolised the refereeing favouritism overtly displayed towards the hosts in that such obvious ploys were given any credence. The Dutch may have been able to brush off the first delay but this second attempt to get under their skin seemingly succeeded, with Dutch feathers well and truly ruffled. They threatened to walk off the pitch at one point, then flew into reckless tackles as much as the Argentina players once the game finally got under way.

The Dutch had some early chances, though, Rep twice going close only to be denied by Ubaldo Fillol in the Argentina goal, a man without whom Argentina may have been blown away early on by the angered opponents. Instead, Mario Kempes gave Argentina the lead late in the first half, finishing off a fine move by sliding the ball from among the strewn ticker tape and underneath Jongbloed. As in 1974, Jongbloed could certainly have done better with a crucial goal in the final, but on this occasion the Netherlands were able to fight back in spite of suffering the regular frustrations of more Argentinian spoiling tactics: incessant handballs or niggling fouls unpunished beyond a simple, play-interrupting free kick.

Rensenbrink had already gone close, denied by Fillol's feet, before the equaliser eventually came just eight minutes from the end when substitute Dick Nanninga headed in René van de Kerkhof's cross. The style may not have had the sublime fluency of 1974 but the team had fought their way to within touching distance of the ultimate glory. As time ticked on towards the end of the 90 minutes, the Netherlands would come far closer than they did in 1974 to claiming the prize.

Rensenbrink is cursed to be remembered for perhaps World Cup history's clearest 'what if' moment. With the match already in stoppage time, he latched on to a long free kick that had somehow eluded the entire Argentine defence. Under pressure from a defender and the onrushing Fillol, he nudged the ball goalwards from a tight angle. As all of Argentina held its breath, the ball rebounded off the post and was cleared by the panicked home team. In truth, there was barely space between Fillol and the post for the ball to have squeezed through. Had he not hit the post he may well have hit Fillol. We will never know of course, left to suffer the anguish of a sliding-door moment, when fortune briefly flickered with an orange hue only to slam the door shut; the agony of the missed opportunity enhanced tenfold by the fact that the ball smacked against the post.

For Rensenbrink, the man who so nearly won the World Cup for the Netherlands, the agony lived on. 'Sometimes I think it would have been better for me to miss completely,' he reflected years later. 'Then people wouldn't ask me about it. If it was a big chance, I would still suffer from it, but really it was impossible to score.' Such was the favouritism being shown to the hosts, many Dutch contend that had Rensenbrink scored, either it would have been disallowed for some spurious reason, or Argentina would have been awarded an even later penalty.

Instead, the final went to extra time with Argentina scoring twice as the Netherlands suffered the anguish of a second successive World Cup Final loss: two defeats four years apart, both equally agonising in their vastly different ways. The 1978 outcome bears closer resemblance to the

Netherlands' third final loss – a unique feat for a nation yet to win the trophy – in 2010, at least in terms of the missed opportunities in the final. For Rensenbrink in 1978, read Arjen Robben in 2010 and the late chance he had to win the final when put clean through on goal; Robben similarly destined to forever rue the spurned opportunity. It is also similarly overlooked in the Dutch consciousness compared to 1974, as Elko Born explained to me, 'It feels like 1978 was some kind of a coincidence, similar to 2010. We didn't win in the end, but it's no big deal for some reason. Like an anomaly that's not part of the bigger story.'

However, 2010 was so far removed from the 1974 artistry as to be from almost another planet, while 1978 maintains a clear lineage from the original purity of Total Football, even if it was a paler imitation which didn't linger so long in the mind, falling outside the narrative of Cruyff, Van Hanegem and Michels.

The bigger focus of this chapter has been the 1974 Dutch team, for clear reasons. They were the ones who exemplified beauty and grace, and it is they who are in the conversation for the best team to fail to win the World Cup. But for all of that, it was in 1978 that the Dutch actually came closer to winning it, within a few centimetres of doing so. So why is it less celebrated?

It all harks back to the questions posed at the start, of whether glory and victory are really all that matters. If they were, then the 1978 and 2010 Netherlands teams would be those more frequently cited as suffering the agony of missing out on World Cup victory, but, instead, it is to 1974 that we are always drawn. Thoughts of who was the right winner favoured the Dutch in 1974, but less so in those other tournaments. The Dutch had been far from their best in the early stages of the 1978 tournament, whereas 1974 was a collage of memorable moments and images etched into our minds despite the outcome. The pain is still there, but the beauty endures too.

That it all ended with Cruyff, forlornly staring into the distance as the West Germans celebrated and others sought to commiserate with him, provided an appropriate final image of this great team: its inspiration, its leader, lost at the last, contemplating the incomprehensible, and a destiny unfulfilled. He stared past them all as though they were simply in another plane of existence to him: his isolation and pain so clear and so raw. Cruyff has long maintained that the 1974 World Cup was a success for the Dutch because of their legacy of artistry and beauty, and the lasting memories they bestowed. The national team had followed on from the successes of Feyenoord in 1970 and Ajax in 1971, 1972 and 1973, the peak to which it had all been building. It's hard to argue with Cruyff's conclusion, the defeat making the story all the more compelling, even if others have since suggested that playing beautifully ultimately became an excuse for repeated failure.

'In a way it's a coping mechanism for people,' explained Born. 'One way of dealing with that feeling of sorrow is to say, "You know what, it's not actually that important. At least we have our playing style."' It's a thought which has permeated Dutch football culture, from fans to players to managers. Michels had set the tone, and others dutifully followed. 'They frame football in such a way that it's not about winning a game, it's about showing beautiful football. It's a really aesthetic way of looking at football. A result comes but it's not the most important thing,' said Born. Many Dutch managers still talk this way: the effects of the 1974 ideology still influencing Dutch thinking decades later.

This is Cruyff's clear legacy. He maintained there was one perfect way of playing, one ideal, so why change it? 'That's still the basis of what people think,' added Born. 'It wasn't about skills but being smart – outsmarting your opponent. If you drop the romanticism, it's a bit arrogant really to say you've figured out the smartest way to play football and you shouldn't even think about trying something else. Others might try different things, but they just haven't figured it out yet, they're not as smart as us.' Romantic, arrogant, and beautifully flawed.

The 1974 World Cup Final is often cited as the match that would define this Dutch team, but to me that misses the point. Victory may have been a suitable crowning of the finest team in the tournament, that which had inspired, delighted and enthused so many. And yet it is precisely those qualities which have ensured the Dutch of 1974 are remembered more than the victors despite, and in part because of, defeat. Added to the exquisite beauty they produced were those moments that will live on through the ages: the Cruyff turn, the magnificent goals, the incessant, irresistible attacking, the destructive victories, the freedom of play and expression, the perpetual motion, the star quality and embodiment of counterculture cool.

This great team are still defined more by those moments than they are by that final loss. They provided the watermark for beautiful football. Everything that has been beautiful since then is measured against this Dutch team of the 1970s. Victory would have been a suitable reward, but its absence doesn't lessen the impact they had, as they continue to stir the emotions decades on.

Theirs is a legacy impacting far beyond the simple, conventional confines of mere triumph or defeat. They showed there is a value beyond the lifting of a trophy, something ultimately longer lasting than victory: that artistry, beauty, idealism and a truly revolutionary approach were a legacy worth far more. That was their ultimate victory, and their gift to the football world.

7

Brazil 1982

The dream has ended, and it's a shame,
because it was a beautiful dream.

Zico

BRAZIL IN 1982 was a tumultuous place. It was a country
and a people in dire need of some escapism. Almost two
decades of brutal military dictatorship was entering its final
throes amid a nosediving economy and hyperinflation.
The so-called 'Brazilian Miracle' of the 1970s, where the
regime's popularity soared even as they tortured, exiled and
murdered dissidents, and the ideal of building an economic
superpower, was doomed by the 1980s. When prosperity
dwindled, so too did the prevailing mood of the nation.

Football, for all its trivialities, has the delightful knack of
uniting people, providing happiness and joy and the escape
from the grim reality of normal life. In Brazil, this feeling
is heightened and intensified given the degree to which
the beautiful game is ingrained into the nation's culture
and identity. In 1982, to see the likes of Zico, Sócrates and
Falcão astound the world with their play, their reinvention

of Pelé's *jogo bonito*, was a much-needed diversion for a troubled nation. A victory that summer in Spain would have been the perfect boost to the national mood at a time of significant hardship for Brazilians.

Football was the perfect means for Brazil to escape their repressive, troubled reality. The style this team espoused was indicative of the social freedoms being challenged, symbolising the hope of a new era and the gradual sense of emerging liberty. A São Paulo radio commentator was moved, during the 1982 World Cup, to describe the Seleção in lyrical tones, 'Our team is divine and beautiful, our players geniuses.' Brazilians were entranced by the carefree, stylish way their team of 1982 played: a mesmeric rapture in yellow, blue and white that captivated not just the devoted Brazilians but the rest of the world too.

Memories of the glory of 1970 were still fresh in the minds of Brazilians and the watching world, misty-eyed in their adoration for the dazzling yellow of Brazil and their breathtakingly extravagant style of play. The warm glow of that Mexican summer, when Pelé and co stormed to Brazil's third World Cup victory, had created an image of what Brazilian football could be, what it could represent. But it was an image that had been tested over the course of the 1970s, when Brazil's style veered from the sublime to the cynical and conservative.

Mário Zagallo, who had been brought in late in the day to lead the Seleção in their 1970 triumph, also took them into the 1974 World Cup. But with Pelé no longer part of the scene, it was a far more limited side that went to West Germany, and one that would be utterly overshadowed by the brilliance of the Dutch. Cláudio Coutinho had been a member of Zagallo's coaching staff in 1974, and when he took over the national team in 1977 his stated aim of emulating the Dutch style, which had enthralled him so much, was not borne out by the reality.

Coutinho had not been a professional player, but was a military fitness trainer who had helped prepare the great 1970 side for the physical demands of a World Cup at high altitude. He was an appointment in keeping with a country under military rule, but his background belied the style his sides displayed with fitness and team-work trumping flamboyance and individual skill, despite his grand intentions.

Under Coutinho, qualification for the 1978 World Cup was secured comfortably, but a subsequent lack of success against European opposition ahead of that tournament put him under increasing pressure. As the burden of expectation bore down on him, any pretence at an expansive style evaporated, replaced by a regimented conservatism. Fear of failure had taken hold and Coutinho was unable to free himself of its shackles, exemplified by the fact that he didn't select the skills of Sócrates or Falcão for the squad, choosing instead the more robust but limited qualities of others.

Ultimately, Brazil missed the 1978 final only on goal difference but they had struggled against European opposition. Their two most technically gifted forwards, Zico and Reinaldo, were dropped part way through the tournament, emphasising the extent of the departure from the beauty of eight years earlier. After securing a third-placed finish, Coutinho hailed his side as 'the moral tournament champions', but back in Brazil the mood was less forgiving. Frustration at having fallen short, despite reaching the final four for the third World Cup in a row, bubbled over into recriminations with Coutinho's decision-making criticised by both media and the public. A further failure at the Copa América the following year brought an end to his reign. It wasn't that his results had been all that bad, but what he stood for, winning or seeking to win ugly, was what he would ultimately be condemned by.

His replacement, Telê Santana, was everything that Coutinho was not. Santana's appointment would see a return to a coach who was wedded to a more open attacking style, but beyond that, he was perhaps a sign that the tight grip of military control in Brazilian sport, as in Brazilian life, was loosening. 'Brazil had failed in 1974 and 1978 with more tactics than technique,' Fernando Duarte, author of *Shocking Brazil*, told me. 'There was a call for more *arte* than *força* in 1982.' Santana signified a return to past traditions, where style and joy were as rewarding as success. Once described as 'the last incurable romantic of Brazilian football', Santana would become one of the most revered managers in Brazil's history.

He was a coaching idealist, who felt that there was much more to football than simply the result. It was also about how the game is played, about how to strive for victory, about self-expression, art and beauty. Brazil boasted the players who were capable of playing football in such a manner, but lacked the direction and leadership to show them the way, to create the organised freedom that was needed to bring the best out of what was a spectacularly talented generation of players.

It was a return to the traditional way in which Brazilians saw themselves. Santana's appointment exemplified a growing need to rediscover their Brazilianness, and the football they used to play. 'That was articulated by Sócrates and Zico,' Dr Peter Watson explained to me. 'But also manifested in the way the coaches wanted to play – those who had come from the *futebol arte* generation.' Santana may have been destined to retain a place in the hearts and minds

of all Seleção followers, but the early days of his reign were
less auspicious. When the squad reunited in April 1980 the
spirit within the camp was low, but, equally, the mood of
the nation was similarly downbeat. To have the symbol of
the nation, the pride of the people, performing at a low ebb,
and seemingly without joy, mirrored the national mood.
Santana's first task, therefore, was to earn back some respect
for the Seleção, both domestically and internationally.

Following several unimpressive friendly internationals
through 1980, the first real opportunity for Santana's Brazil
came in the Mundialito tournament held in Uruguay at
the start of 1981 to commemorate the 50th anniversary of
the World Cup. The compact competition was contested
by five of the six previous World Cup-winning nations,
with England declining to take part and replaced by the
Netherlands. Brazil reached the final, before losing to
Uruguay, but they hadn't been overly impressive. The only
game they won was against a West German team whose
efforts in this mid-season competition were somewhat less
than full-blooded.

Soon after, in World Cup qualifying, the stuttering form
continued with a narrow 1-0 win away in Venezuela; an
inauspicious start to the campaign that would ultimately
end with Brazil earning a place in World Cup folklore. That
win had only come courtesy of a penalty, and when another
away win was only secured by a single goal in Bolivia, there
was little sign of what was to come little over a year later in
Spain. The return fixtures finally saw Santana's Brazil click
into gear, and more crucially also saw the finest Brazilian
player of that generation really step up to the mark.

Zico had been heralded as a superstar in the making
for some time, excelling in the magnificent Flamengo
side of the early 1980s. Having come through the youth

system at the Rio club, he would lead them to a trio of Brazilian championships and a Rio State title before winning the Copa Libertadores in 1981. That success was followed by victory over a powerful Liverpool side in the Intercontinental Cup Final, with Zico excelling. He was a classic number ten, playing on instinct. Blessed with astonishing skill, his ability to play at a pace beyond the greats of the past elevated him above the crowd. He may have been known as the 'White Pelé' but his was a style of greater rapidity and targeted directness than the man he sought to emulate.

He would be joined in the 1982 team by two of his club colleagues, the full-backs Leandro and Júnior. Both would capture the imagination as much as anyone else on the pitch, thrilling us with the way they attacked and the skill they possessed; the epitome of the outlook of this Brazil. There was an all-star support cast in midfield too, but it was on Zico that the greatest focus of Brazilian hopes would fall. He hit a hat-trick against Bolivia in a 3-1 win, justifying his selection following some less than impressive displays, before Venezuela were dismissed out of hand 5-0 as Brazil eased their way to qualification.

Their place at the World Cup secure, it was on a tour to Europe in May 1981 that Brazil served notice to the wider world of their abilities. Given the insecurities Brazil had previously felt against European opposition in recent World Cups, to win all three tour matches against England, France and West Germany within a mere five days was a clear signal of their restored status. The win over West Germany had been particularly impressive, with this come-from-behind 2-1 victory also seeing the goalkeeper Waldir Peres save two penalties. It was the manner of the performances that was the most striking, however.

Santana had crafted his side into playing a delicate, flowing brand of football that was as effective as it was delightful to watch. The ball spun from player to player in tight midfield triangles, with none seeming to touch the ball more than twice, the perpetual motion being mirrored in the constant movement of players off the ball. Dynamic bursts of pace and a regularly encouraged self-expression led to a fluidity and fluency that would become hard to stop. Beyond even its effectiveness against the more rigid structures of the European game, it was a return to the style that many felt was the Brazilian way, their natural style of play. 'We were adamant that Brazil had to abide by the style that had made it famous,' recalled Zico, invoking the joy and glamour of 1970.

Where there had been a stifling fear of losing, now the Seleção took to the field with a sense of freedom, playing with a visible enjoyment which allowed them to perform at their best. The straitjacket of the Coutinho years had been cast off in style, Santana's team a radical change from what had immediately preceded it. The country embraced them, glorying in the return to the *jogo bonito* that most Brazilians saw as their footballing birthright.

It was a style built on a magnificent midfield with a cast of players far more than a support act to the delightful talents of Zico. The names of those in Brazil's creative core echo through the ages as the personification of all that is beautiful and virtuous in football: Sócrates, Éder, Falcão and Toninho Cerezo. These are names which still captivate those of us fortunate enough to have seen this great team, their mere mention enough to bring the dazzling images of yesteryear readily to mind, stirring the emotions we felt all those years ago when witnessing this Brazilian version of sporting majesty.

Sócrates, a radical free-thinking philosopher, heavy smoker and drinker, had split his formative footballing years between the development teams and first team of Botafogo de Ribeirão Preto in São Paulo and his medical studies. Only once having completed his residency exams did Sócrates fully commit to football, joining São Paulo giants Corinthians soon after. Having been overlooked for the 1978 World Cup, his elegant ability to read the game, sublime skills and creative instincts meant that he couldn't be ignored when it came to 1982, even if his radical views made him something of a loose cannon in a team representing a country under military rule.

Éder would fill the left side of Brazil's attack, the one player most set in his position among these midfield maestros, possessing a magical left foot capable of bending in ferocious shots from all angles. Toninho Cerezo was a stylish central midfielder whose constant motion, ceaseless energy and dazzling skills left many an opponent unable to pin him down. The final man added to the mix was Roberto Falcão, joining Cerezo as nominally defensive elements of the midfield. He had been Brazilian Footballer of the Year in 1978 and 1979, but having moved to Roma in Italy's Serie A, he hadn't played for the Seleção for three years. A deep-lying playmaker, he competed with such infectious athleticism, combined with exemplary technique, that he became a vital component of the side despite not having been a part of the squad until only weeks before the World Cup.

Combined together, this collective lifted themselves to a pantheon only attained by the few, a level where footballing immortality lay. The fluidity instigated and encouraged by this majestic midfield would create a style apparently carefree to the observer, but one that was actually carefully crafted to exploit the talents at Brazil's disposal. When they attacked, the whole team attacked. When it came to defence, things were less sound, but what did that matter if they were so exuberant in attack? And yet, one aspect where this Brazil was lacking was at the very sharp end of the attack.

Santana's preference all along would have been for Reinaldo, one of Brazil's all-time greatest strikers, to lead the line. But the Atlético Mineiro man was injury-prone and when he was struck down once again in early 1982, he was no longer an option. Instead, the young Careca, an explosive but raw attacking talent who had only recently broken into the national team, was chosen in his place. When he too suffered an injury on the eve of the tournament, Brazil were forced to turn to the less refined Serginho, more of a gangly, lumbering nuisance of an attacker than an elegant stylist. As such, he stood out like a sore thumb; a workhorse surrounded by artists and *fantasistas*. His natural, physical approach would also be curtailed by Santana, fearful of his striker's aggression overstepping the mark and getting sent off, which may well have hindered his performances in 1982. He was a prolific scorer in Brazil, however, where his feats for São Paulo were considerable, though achieved in a manner apparently out of kilter with the style of Santana's team.

The squad had intensely prepared for their assault on the World Cup. The players spent several months ahead of the tournament training together to make their sophisticated style appear spontaneous. There was a relaxed, homely feel to the squad camps, however. A far cry from the joyless, restrictive *concentração* of the previous tournaments. Thanks to an almost exclusively home-based squad, there was also a bond between players and fans that was far deeper than exists today. The public could identify with the players who, though touched with genius, were living alongside them.

The extortionate riches of the modern day were still some time away, when most Brazilians of ability are shipped off to Europe at the first glimpse of talent.

As expectation began to grow, the streets were increasingly decorated in yellow and green, huge parties surrounding every game. It became a carnival as all focus fell on to the Seleção and their fortunes. Other considerations, such as the critical state of the country, were cast aside as the nation was captivated and enthralled. While the hype reached fever pitch, the feeling that Brazil were once again set to claim what many felt was their divine right was increasingly shared by the rest of the world. The Spanish World Cup was Brazil's great opportunity to convert their universal appeal into tangible success.

Brazil kicked off their World Cup in Seville's Estadio Ramón Sánchez Pizjuán against the USSR, who had beaten them during the struggles of 1980. Brazil would have to make do without Toninho Cerezo's talents in this opener, serving the last of a three-game suspension for a red card against Bolivia in qualifying. With Falcão coming in to the side, he was joined in midfield by Dirceu, with the right-sided attacker Paulo Isidoro missing out.

This change would lead to a stilted first half from Brazil, at least initially, against what was a strong opponent. With the more static, robust play of Dirceu and Serginho, the fluidity with which this side became synonymous was not initially noticeable. Indeed, it was the men in Soviet red who took the lead. Perhaps it was nerves, perhaps it was a lack of experience on such a stage, with eight of the starting 11 making their first World Cup appearance. Whatever the reason, the opening moments of what would become such an iconic World Cup campaign were not so slick.

As with Serginho, another frequently cited weak link was the goalkeeper. Waldir Peres was a 31-year-old stalwart of the São Paulo club and had been in the squad at the previous two World Cups without playing. He was not one to inspire great confidence in those in front of him, however. With 34 minutes gone in the first half, a speculative shot from distance from Andrei Bal shouldn't have caused too much of a problem, but Peres let the ball slip through his legs and into the net in embarrassing style. This error exemplified what was a nerve-jangling opening from Brazil: the carefully crafted plans seemingly thrown off kilter by the loss of Careca and Cerezo, any creativity locked away underneath the surface.

Far from dispiriting the team, however, this setback served to settle and help the Brazilians find their rhythm. Once they did, the creativity flowed, and the style began to emerge. At half-time, Santana corrected his initial mistake by replacing Dirceu with Isidoro, giving the team more dynamic width on the right-hand side. Brazil's attacking intensity increased, growing in waves of pressure, building to an exhilarating crescendo where goals, frustratingly absent thus far, seemed an inevitability. They left it late, but the beauty of the strikes which won this opening match were worth the wait.

Just 15 minutes remained when Sócrates picked up the ball outside the Soviet box. He sidestepped two defenders, dropping his shoulder to avoid their lunges as they forlornly threw themselves at the stylish Brazilian captain. He fired a vicious shot into the top corner before racing off, arms spread wide and aloft, soaking in the adoration loudly voiced in the stands and from his relieved team-mates. It had taken time to break down the Soviet side, but with this strike, this captain's moment from their inspirational on-field leader, it was as if the wall they had built up in their minds in the stuttering first half had been blown apart. With this one sublime strike, everything seemed to change. Now Brazil were playing with a swagger and style that made a winning goal seem a question of when rather than if. In that moment, one of the most iconic campaigns in World Cup history had been ignited.

What followed was 15 minutes of footballing excellence. The iconic team of 1970 cast a huge shadow over the Brazilian sides that followed, but now there appeared a worthy successor. Brazil's winning goal, which came with just three minutes remaining, followed a sequence of moves which had clear echoes of 1970. The slick passing build-up had moved the ball from halfway to the edge of the Soviet box where Isidoro laid it back, behind the crowded penalty area, to the waiting Falcão, who seemed poised to shoot. Instead, he stepped over the ball, casually allowing it to roll through his legs, wrong-footing the defence as he did so. What Falcão could see, unlike those of us watching from home, was the off-camera Éder charging on to the ball.

Without breaking stride, Éder flicked the ball up before volleying a rasping left-foot shot past the static and confused Rinat Dasayev in the USSR goal, for one of the finest goals of this or any other World Cup. It was a goal to seal a beautiful victory, and to blow away any remaining semblance of nerves that may have lingered following the opening half. Remaining true to their approach, and playing without panic, Brazil had conquered through the sheer magnificence of their play. They had not so much given a glimpse of the beauty they could create as hit the world in the face with the sheer exuberance and wondrous ability at their disposal. The world was captivated, enthralled by the magnificence of it all, the sparkling play coming through in the dazzling images on our screens. In Brazil, public belief in victory was already near absolute.

But what this match had shown, too, was the soft Brazilian underbelly. A World Cup favourite shouldn't concede such a soft goal as the one Brazil had, but in the heady haze imbued by the ultimate style of the victory, this was a fact largely glossed over. When Brazil's next match also saw them fall behind, observers would begin to take note, though those of us who were simply captivated by the beauty of it all just knew they would come through anyway. Our concern was more about just how many and how great the goals would be, not the trifling consideration that they may initially find themselves trailing.

Brazil would enter their second group match against Scotland with Santana opting to partner Falcão with the returning Cerezo in the base of the midfield, creating the iconic Seleção line-up; the side that so many remember with such fondness. It was a combination that had only previously been used for a 20-minute spell late on in a resounding warm-up win over Ireland. It may have been an improvised selection, but it was one which promoted an aesthetic beauty, a seductive vibrancy that led to the sublime becoming the ordinary. This was the team the world would fall in love with.

But it came at a price. Without any obvious right-sided player, the team was now overloaded with talent in the central areas. When playing with such exuberance, perhaps this was of little consequence, but the right wing was now more or less abandoned for the remainder of the World Cup, with the attacking instincts of the right-back Leandro aiming to compensate. The midfield quintet would rotate at will, with Sócrates and Zico sharing stints on the right-hand side, but never quite with the true width a genuine winger would. Did it matter? Certainly not at this stage, as the overwhelming nature of Brazil's attacks swamped their early opponents.

Brazil's players floated around the pitch, creating both space and opportunity seemingly at will. As against the Soviets, though, it took time for them to find their rhythm. Scotland, a side arguably even stronger than the one that had gone to the 1978 World Cup amid such expectation only to implode and fail, were possibly more focused on their upcoming decisive clash with the USSR where it would be winner-takes-all for qualification. But that didn't prevent them from taking the lead through a wonderful shot by defender David Narey.

Legend has it that Narey's colleagues would later tease him for having angered the Brazilians with his goal, kicking the hornets' nest as it were. Once behind, the Brazilian side belatedly again settled, unleashing the swagger once more. Zico scored the equaliser with an astonishing free kick, flying past the befuddled and motionless Alan Rough in Scotland's goal. Shortly after the interval, Brazil took the lead through the defender Oscar before Éder then added a glorious third, chipping an increasingly forlorn Rough. Falcão rounded off the 4-1 win late on.

When this was followed up with an emphatic 4-0 victory in swatting aside New Zealand, Brazil had secured maximum points in the opening round for the first time in three World Cups. The New Zealand coach John Adstead neatly summed up the dilemma for anyone facing the Seleção, 'At any one time in the game the only ones who will remain still would be Waldir Peres and Serginho. All the rest are so mobile they could be anywhere at any time.'

If Brazil had served notice in the latter stages of their opening game, now they were firmly installed as tournament favourites, as the manner with which they swept the opposition aside stood in contrast to how the other tournament favourites had performed so far. Only England could match Brazil's perfect record through the opening round. Theirs, however, had been achieved in a significantly less flamboyant style. Neither were the other tournament favourites performing up to the anticipated level.

West Germany had suffered a shock loss to Algeria, only scraping through their group amid the controversy of the shambolic stitch-up with Austria. France had started badly in an opening loss to England but had recovered to qualify. Hosts Spain had struggled, scraping through on goals scored. Awaiting Brazil in the second-round group – a three-team affair in the one-time-only format of the 1982 World Cup – were two of the other expected favourites: Italy, and the current holders Argentina.

Neither had performed well so far. Italy were yet to even win a match, drawing all three group games and only progressing on goals scored ahead of Cameroon. Argentina had lost to Belgium before recovering to beat El Salvador and Hungary, but had fallen well short of the quality being shown by Brazil. Underperforming favourites had caused a skewing of the tournament groupings across the board in the second phase. It was Brazil's misfortune that, as the only opening stage group winner in this particular group, they were to face two such teams. Off-form perhaps, but with a latent quality that had to be respected.

But it was Brazil alone who had produced such audacious, emphatic displays, rediscovering their true selves after the poor fare served up in the previous two World Cups. They alone who stood above all others as champions-in-waiting, the joyous feelings of 1970 rekindled with a newer interpretation of the beautiful game. As the goals flowed and the performances dazzled, so the expectation continued to escalate. Even the note of caution sounded by one of their former managers, João Saldanha, who had led the side in advance of the 1970 triumph, didn't dampen the spirits. Saldanha posited that Brazil were overcomplicating things, and were therefore leaving themselves open to potentially being caught out by a more organised and efficient side than they had faced so far. A troubling portent perhaps, but in the euphoric glow of boundless optimism, one that barely registered. The dominant feeling was that neither Italy nor Argentina had shown the guile and ability to trouble the free-flowing Brazilians.

Held in the crumbling, yet majestically austere, surroundings of the Estadi de Sarria in Barcelona, home to Espanyol, rather than the far larger stadium across town where another second-round group was scheduled, the most epic of World Cup groups was played out. Brazil had the opportunity to assess their opposition with Argentina and Italy facing each other first. Argentina featured the enigmatic, mercurial talents of one Diego Maradona, a precocious 21-year-old at the time, with a point to prove on the world stage. Having been left out of the victorious 1978 World Cup squad, Maradona had felt slighted, his anger adding to his already burgeoning sense of victimisation: the fuel by which his greatest performances were often powered. However, he was marked out of the game in vicious style by the brutish stopper Claudio Gentile, nullifying the young maestro by fair means and foul.

With Maradona stifled and increasingly frustrated, Italy developed from their initial lack of ambition and gradually grew in confidence, an attitude that had been lacking in their campaign so far, to claim a 2-1 victory. Argentina would now need to beat Brazil in the next match to have any hope of retaining their title. This certainly ensured that Brazilian minds remained focused on the task at hand, with a frustrated Argentina still more than capable of inflicting pain on their near neighbours. It would be the third World Cup in a row that they had faced each other: a local conflict played out on the global stage. Brazil would be anticipating the likely physical challenge coming their way, and wary of the fact that they had fallen behind in two of their three games so far and could ill afford to do so again.

Both sides attacked from the off, with Brazil's fluency apparent from the start, unlike against the USSR and Scotland. While there was plenty of creativity on show from both sides with Luis Galván going close for Argentina, it was Brazil who would steal the initiative in spectacular style. Éder, following a lengthy, sprinted run-up, fired in an astonishingly vicious, swerving free kick from distance which crashed on to the underside of the crossbar. Zico beat Serginho in the race to tap the ball home, while the statuesque Argentinian defence looked on.

With the security of a lead, the colourful patterns being forged on the field by the Brazilians kept Argentina at arm's length in the remainder of the first half. But as the game began to stretch in the second, Maradona began to increasingly threaten, his elusive movement and quick change of pace evading successive Brazilian defenders as Argentina pushed for an equaliser. On one occasion, he was cut down by Júnior inside the Brazilian box, only for Maradona's frustration to bubble over when the referee saw fit to award just a corner.

As Argentine frustration and desperation grew, so Brazil gradually took a tighter stranglehold. Momentum was increasingly in their favour as waves of attack poured forth from any and every direction. Finally, midway through the second half, Argentina's captain Daniel Passarella was dispossessed by Serginho, triggering a delightful passage of play. Éder flicked a sumptuous pass with the outside of his boot to Falcão, appearing on the largely unstaffed Brazilian right. His delicately lofted cross found Serginho all alone at the far post to finish off the move he himself had begun. If Argentina were now reeling, within a few minutes they were finished off in clinical style. Zico picked the ball up in the midfield and surged forwards, threading a perfect pass through the foundering Argentine defence where the rampaging left-back, Júnior, was racing through on goal. He slid the ball under the onrushing Ubaldo Fillol before running to the crowd, screaming in delight.

While the watching thousands roared their approval, Júnior broke into a samba-dancing celebration; the party atmosphere perfectly reflecting the carnival of football these gods in yellow were displaying to the world. Brazilian beauty contrasted to Argentine ugliness, with the frustrations of a failed campaign finally causing Maradona to snap, landing a very deliberate low boot into substitute João Batista's groin. Maradona's inevitable red card symbolised his unfamiliar helplessness; the defending champions and their genius-in-waiting unable to stem the relentless flow of Brazilian bravado. In Maradona's misery, the contrast to Brazil's joyous artistry and exuberant enjoyment was brutally demonstrated.

A late consolation goal for Ramón Díaz, making the final score 3-1, could not detract from the consummate display Brazil had conjured. The performance was so complete from back to front, in contrast to the justified criticisms of the defence in the group games, leaving many now convinced that Brazil were certain winners. Everything was so well composed, so well developed, so good. There were no real moments of weakness, all perceptions of greatness now cemented. All that now separated the Seleção from another semi-final was Italy, an apparently limited, unsure Italy, struggling for both goals and confidence.

And what is more, having secured a bigger win over Argentina than the Italians had, Brazil only required a draw to win through on goal difference. In hindsight, perhaps this was more of a hindrance than a benefit to a side now well used to just cutting loose and expressing themselves. Did the ever-present reminder that they didn't actually need to beat Italy affect Brazilian minds in the build-up and during the game?

Had it been Italy who only needed a draw to progress, there is little doubt what their tactics would have been. The defence would have been packed, shutting Brazil down, stifling any creativity, aiming to close the game out without the need for any significant attacking intent. Italy were a counter-attacking side anyway, and would have relished such a challenge. Such an approach was anathema to Santana and Brazil, however. They would remain true to their ideals, continuing their principled crusade without compromise. And without such ideals, this team simply wouldn't have been the same, either in the moment or in the years of adoration which followed.

Some commentators were already thinking of a semi-final against a Poland team who would be denied some of their best players through suspension. The path to glory was becoming clearer. Could there have been at least a degree of thinking ahead and a feeling that they didn't need to be at their exuberant best to progress if a draw would do? Oscar recalled quite the opposite. No matter that Italy had not come close to Brazil's achievements in the tournament so far, he insisted, 'It was never in our minds that the result was a foregone conclusion.'

If Brazilian minds were clear, Italy had problems. Their task may have been certain, if daunting, but their stuttering, uninspiring progress so far had been dogged by controversy, and the pressure bearing down on the coach Enzo Bearzot's selections was intense. It was all about one man: Paolo Rossi.

Italy had been embroiled in a match-fixing scandal in the preceding years involving multiple Serie A clubs. Rossi, implicated in the disgrace, was initially suspended from football for three years. When this was reduced to two on appeal, he was able to make his return for Juventus just weeks before the 1982 World Cup. Four years earlier in Argentina he had been an emerging international striking talent, but having barely played football in two years he wasn't expected to be a part of the 1982 event. Yet Bearzot not only selected Rossi in the squad, he picked him as his main striker in every match.

Rossi, though, seemed to barely resemble an international striker any more. Off the pace, lacking in confidence and match fitness and seemingly bereft, the clamour for him to be dropped as one dire performance followed another increased in intensity with every passing match. He had failed to score in all four games so far, but still Bearzot remained loyal. Rossi, for all his misfiring misfortune, would play against Brazil. Short of confidence, he was also fearful about what his side were facing. 'They did not look from this planet,' he recalled. 'That Brazil side was the very best I had seen. Those players could have worn blindfolds and they would still have known where each other were. As for me, I felt like I was still learning to play football again after the two-year suspension.'

In his preparation for the match, Santana had asked Falcão, familiar with the Italians thanks to his club career in Rome, for his thoughts on their likely approach. Falcão was clear that Gentile would mark Zico closely, but also expressed concern about the potential threat posed by the left-back Antonio Cabrini who was likely to enjoy the space that Brazil's lack of right-sided width would afford him. His suggestion to both of these points was to move Zico more to the right, both dragging Gentile out of position, while restricting the attacking space available to Cabrini.

Perhaps this would have been a more pragmatic move, the kind of tactical tweak that many would have sought in such a critical game, an effective World Cup quarter-final. Santana, though, opted to keep his side's structure the same. A fault, or a reasonable approach given how free-scoring Brazil had been so far? It seems churlish to criticise when you consider the 13 goals Brazil had scored, compared to the four Italy had achieved. Even if Italy were to breach the Brazilian defence, surely the sheer overwhelming nature of the Seleção attack would ensure Brazil's progression?

That was the prevailing mood both in Brazil and the watching world. In every corner of the globe, this Brazilian side had captured the imagination of millions. The brightness of their play and their shirts both sizzled in the Spanish sunshine as the intensely brilliant images were flashed around the world. This was to be the next step in what now seemed their inevitable coronation, another occasion in which Brazil would delight with their perpetual, graceful motion; an ever-changing kaleidoscope of yellow and blue.

In front of a packed crowd, one of the World Cup's most memorable and epic matches began with a shock to the system. Brazil had begun in their usual attacking manner, but when they lost possession in the fifth minute of the match, the ball was worked to Cabrini in space on Italy's left, filling the vacant space identified by Falcão. He whipped in a cross which was headed home by an unmarked Rossi; the goal poacher finally rediscovering his instincts.

No matter though. Italy may have taken the lead, but Brazil had gone behind before and recovered, so why not this time too? They continued their swarming attacks with abandon and their response was immediate and decisive. Seven minutes after the goal, Sócrates strode into the Italian half and played the ball to Zico. One neat turn and incisive pass later, the ball had cut through the Italian defence and was returned to Sócrates in an impudent one-two. He fired his shot past Dino Zoff at the near post, the paint of the goal line bursting into the air in unison with the ecstatic crowd behind the goal, as if joining in the celebration. It was a flash of brilliance that seemed to suggest that Brazil had overcome their initial jitters once again, and, now they were level, could push on towards the expected victory.

A mere ten minutes later though, a poorly placed pass across the back line by Cerezo fell instead to Rossi. Would he have fired so clinically past Peres had his confidence not been restored by his earlier easy finish? His unerring shot showed a new-found poise and restored Italy's lead. Cerezo was crestfallen. At half-time, he had to be repeatedly reassured before his tears could stop and his focus restored.

The second half saw Brazil continue to surge forwards in repeated waves of attack. The pressure was relentless and its just reward came midway through the half when Falcão picked up the ball in space created by the tireless running of Cerezo, desperate to make amends for his earlier error. Falcão rifled a stinging shot past Zoff, before running off in one of the most iconic, vein-popping celebrations the

World Cup has seen. Scores level once more, Brazil just needed to hold on to secure their place in the semi-final. Far from urging caution, though, the Seleção still pushed on in attack, as if knowing no other way to play, and seeking the winning goal that would erase any doubt about their qualification. Instead, with quarter of an hour to go, the opportunity fell at the other end of the pitch.

Having conceded an unnecessary corner, Brazil packed the box, aiming to nullify any threat. Unable to clear, the ball fell to Marco Tardelli. His scuffed shot bounded towards goal where it reached Rossi. Standing isolated from any Brazilian defenders, but played onside by a tardy defensive line, his only rival for the ball was his fellow Italian Francesco Graziani. Rossi was quickest to react. One easy tap-in later, he had completed his hat-trick and Brazil were behind for a third time.

The final quarter of an hour was a frenzy of desperate Brazil attacks, but it was Italy who should have added another goal, Antognoni's shot incorrectly ruled offside. Brazil took that fortune and crafted one final, last-gasp opportunity to rescue themselves. Éder's cross was headed goalwards by Oscar, only for the 40-year-old Dino Zoff to deny him with a spectacular save. In that moment, a dream died.

The final whistle sounded moments later and one of the greatest, most loved teams in World Cup history had failed. Failed on the scoreboard that is, but through that failure their place in the hearts and minds of so many became assured. The destiny that had seemed an inevitability had been snatched away, replaced by a different, lasting legacy of unfulfilled greatness, stolen in a smash and grab from a team who would now seize their own sense of destiny. Neither Italy nor Rossi looked back from this moment, their new-found confidence now carrying them all the way to World Cup victory.

For Brazil, though, defeat was a shock they had barely conceived as possible. There was disbelief writ large over the players' faces, while the stands were full of stunned, tearful faces. A photo of a sobbing young boy became the symbolic image of this defeat, representing the tears of a nation whose dreams had been shattered. The highs this side had attained were such that the comedown was always going to be painful. An editorial in Rio's *O Globo* captured the mood the following morning, 'Brazil has in its soccer an expression of everything that is good in our temperament therefore that yesterday's defeat will have a psychological impact far greater and deeper than a simple loss would to a fan ... It taught us that the chance to dream is always followed by the need to wake up.'

In the dressing room, amid the devastation of the disappointment, Santana told his players, 'The whole world has been enchanted by you. Be aware of that.' Santana would receive a standing ovation from journalists as he entered the room for the post-match press conference, and again as he left. His side, playing as they did, had entertained and thrilled like few others. They seemed to revel in finding increasingly elaborate ways to score a goal, as if a beautiful goal was worth more than a more mundane effort. And in many ways, it was. The delight their play had given so many has had a lasting effect far beyond what is normal for a team exiting at the quarter-final stage. The legacy of this Brazil side would live on for generations, etched in the mind as the very epitome of footballing artistry.

At the time, however, there were some recriminations. Cerezo's error marked him out for criticism, as did the performances of Peres and Serginho, though, thankfully, without the extremities suffered by the scapegoats from Brazil's 1950 loss. But really, without Rossi hitting the sweet spot that day, Brazil would surely have won that match: undone mostly by one man's hot streak, more so than anything of their own fault. As in 1950, though, the tournament had seen the nation carried on a wave of euphoric optimism, only for defeat to send them crashing back down to earth following what was swiftly dubbed *A Tragedia do Sarria*, the Sarria Tragedy.

The repercussions of defeat would be felt by all subsequent Brazilian national teams. Santana's steadfast adherence to his attacking philosophy, a belief that the beauty of the play was as worthy as victory would have been, came in for some criticism for tactical naivety. A degree of pragmatism, the critics claimed, would have seen Brazil past Italy and on to claim their rightful prize. The romantic in you delights in their stubborn approach, and yet the realist yearns for a touch of pragmatism to have been thrown in to see them through. But that would have been to betray what Santana and his 1982 side held dear. Would we feel the same about them had they won through, but had done so by adjusting to nullify the Italian threat?

It is far more poetic to have gone down in flames, to have never betrayed their ideals. We love them because of this, not in spite of it. We love them for the flaws that made these apparent gods mortal. For the fact that their brilliance was counterbalanced with a soft underbelly, the exuberance matched by their vulnerability. Sure, they could and should have won the World Cup, but that they didn't is both painful and joyous.

Following the defeat of 1982, a change began in the Seleção with pragmatism and European physicality being lauded above aesthetic beauty. That beautiful naivety had been lost, never to return. When Santana returned to lead Brazil in the 1986 World Cup, he oversaw the dying embers of his dream. With an ageing Sócrates, an unfit Zico and an unselected Falcão, his team were good, but no match for the exquisiteness of the 1982 vintage. With Careca available, they did have a genuine cutting edge, which led many to lament what might have been had he been fit in 1982. But the Careca of 1982 was not the same Careca of 1986. A young man of impressive raw talent had developed into a world-class striker by 1986, a level beyond what he had been four years earlier.

By the 1990 World Cup, Brazil's style had changed utterly. The beautiful game, the *futebol arte*, had gone, replaced with a more limited, rigid structure. Even the team who won the 1994 World Cup were more robust than revolutionary, more limited than luxurious, more Dunga than Sócrates. As such, they are not recalled as fondly as the team that fell short in 1982, whose ideals and artistry enchanted the world. Brazilians, for all the success they have enjoyed, still see this as the one that got away. Far more so than the 1950 defeat when Brazil were much closer to victory than they were in 1982: artistry winning out over agony in the collective memory. As noted by Falcão in his book *Brasil 82: O Time que Perdeu a copa e Conquistou o Mundo* (Brazil 82: The team that lost the cup and conquered the world), 'We lost that game but won a place in history.'

Their style had rekindled the *futebol arte* of 1970, unwittingly creating an impossible ideal to live up to. But in terms of Brazilianness, all the characteristics Brazilians saw in themselves were embodied in the 1982 side: the style, freedom and rhythm of the samba transposed to the football field. 'Brazilians like to think this natural skill, flair and imagination is still there,' explained Dr Peter Watson, 'magically emerging untrained from the shanty towns of Brazil. The feeling that greatness can be found in this way.' No team before or since has better characterised this mythical ideal, the way in which Brazilians see themselves and their football. There was nothing cynical about them. They played with a love for the game and you couldn't help but be swept along by the beauty of it. They had that magical ability to make people gaze and wonder, 'What are they going to do next?'

Brazil's 1982 Seleção would be the last time a team would play with such a pure idealistic, artistic approach on the world stage. It was as if it was not just a defeat for Brazil, but a defeat for the delightfully attacking philosophy, the free-spirited abandon that made the world fall in love with them. Zico would describe the loss to Italy as 'the day football died'. An innocence had been lost, an ideal crushed, leaving behind a bitterness and an acceptance that such virtues no longer had a place in the world, the fear of losing replacing the desire to express joy and beauty. The 1982 team were the epitome of that idealistic innocence, of playing the way they believed rather than a way more focused on victory alone.

Perhaps a Brazilian win in 1982 would have held the tide of change back for a few more years, but the tide will always change, the more pragmatic approach would have come anyway. There were other exponents of this more free, artistic approach, even if not quite at Brazil 1982 extremes – the way France won Euro 1984 having also delighted in the latter stages of the 1982 World Cup, the way Denmark played in 1986, or Maradona's astonishing performances that same year – but once we move beyond 1986, the global outlook becomes more scientific.

In more recent decades this has matured into a more modern approach, marrying skill with professionalism. The old ways weren't enough any more. Brazilian football, as in Brazilian society, looked to Europe and sought to replicate and augment what they saw. The tactical sophistication, the training methods, the discipline, all of these factors became more developed. Following the 1994 triumph, the ideal has become to develop an enhanced modern style, still always seeking to set themselves apart from the Europeans. Brazilian football thinking was, 'If we do all the training and discipline, we then also have that flair that makes our football better and more joyous,' as Dr Peter Watson explained. 'That is what they seek to produce now, 1982 having proven that the innocence was lost in terms of a more sobering realisation. They can still have their *futebol arte*, but now it is more just moments of brilliance rather than an all-encompassing ideal.'

That ideal did exist in 1982, though. For many, that team remain one of the finest football sides ever seen: their place in history earned not just for the beautiful game they showed the world, but for the fact that they went unfulfilled. They could lose, but they were not beaten. They live on in the memories of so many, defeat simply adding to the legend and enhancing the allure. They may have lost the match, but they won our hearts.

8

Denmark 1986

*Afterwards we were in shock, because it was
impossible with our team that we could lose
5-1. That is the worst thing about it. You can
lose a match against Spain – anyone can lose
against Spain – but 5-1 is ridiculous. That,
for my taste, was too much.*

Preben Elkjær

PLAYING IN the heat of Mexico in their stylish red-and-white-halved kits, exuding a laid-back nonchalance, an effortless cool, the Denmark team of 1986 were a captivating revelation. They attacked incessantly, with mesmerising speed and faultless technical excellence, enchanting and delighting so many.

But does a team who only progressed to the last 16 of a World Cup belong in a book about the great teams who could have won? Ordinarily, no. But Denmark of 1986 were no ordinary team. While I freely accept they don't sit alongside some of the real best who could have won a World Cup, they were still a revelation; a truly mesmerising combination of technique, flamboyance and physicality. They burned so brightly that perhaps it is appropriate that they didn't do so for long before it all came crashing down in fittingly spectacular style.

FIFA's technical report of the 1986 World Cup said that Denmark 'played the most spectacular football during the tournament'. This was a World Cup that had seen Diego Maradona at his unstoppable peak, and welcomed great teams from France, Brazil and the USSR, but none of those produced a collective that was quite so captivating as Denmark.

As astonishing as the football they produced was the fact that Denmark had never been remotely close to such exalted levels of the game previously. While they didn't exactly come from nowhere, Denmark's rise was a remarkable and rapid one. Similarities can be seen with the Dutch of 1974, of an international team with no track record to speak of taking the World Cup by storm. But where the Dutch success was a natural extension of the strength of their clubs, Denmark's rise was perhaps more extraordinary.

Denmark had never even come particularly close to reaching a World Cup before 1986, with only the 1982 qualifying group even having any real air of respectability about it. That campaign included a 3-1 win over the eventual champions Italy, but Denmark still finished short of the qualifying places. The first signs of what was to come were there though, indicative of a rise in fortune and quality that had been a long time coming, but was the result of some fundamental changes.

Back in the mists of time, Denmark had taken part in some of the early Olympic tournaments, even claiming several medals: a gold and two silvers pre-First World War, but perhaps more significantly a bronze in 1948, a silver in 1960 and a couple of quarter-final appearances, most recently in 1972. What these brushes with respectability reveal is that Danish domestic football was amateur until 1978, meaning the majority of Danish players were eligible for, and could hold their own in, the amateur environs of the Olympic Games. There had also been a semi-final place in the 1964 European Championship, but that apparent overachievement was a startling anomaly gained through nothing more than qualifying wins over Malta, Albania and Luxembourg.

The national team had been exclusively amateur prior to 1971, excluding a few foreign-based players, and harming the national team's strength and prospects as a result. The realisation that Denmark needed a change in outlook if they were to produce a more competitive national team led first to the introduction of professionals at international level, and then, seven years later, in 1978 the introduction of professionalism in domestic football.

None of this is to say that Denmark wasn't already producing quality players, despite effectively forcing them to ply their trade away from their home country. Into the 1970s, in particular, Denmark had exported some fine footballing talent. Most notable in their number was Allan Simonsen, the forward who was a mainstay of the magnificent Borussia Mönchengladbach team of that decade, also starring for Barcelona and, remarkably, Charlton Athletic.

He was for a time one of Europe's greatest, leading his clubs to continental silverware and being named European Footballer of the Year in 1977. That had been a season in which he had led Mönchengladbach to the European Cup Final, scoring in the showpiece match against Liverpool, though his side were beaten. To win such a prestigious individual award would have been a major achievement for any player, of course, but for one coming from the relative footballing backwater of Denmark, it was truly remarkable.

Simonsen had been a stalwart of the 1972 Olympic team, where he would have been joined by Denmark's other great of that era, the defensive midfielder Morten Olsen, had Olsen not signed a professional contract prior to the Olympics. He moved to the Belgian club Cercle Brugge before transferring to the powerful Anderlecht team of the early 1980s, establishing himself as a club legend. Both remained part of the full national team, though, with the rules on professionals relaxed, leading the gradual rise from the depths of the international game.

Both would still be there to enjoy Denmark's arrival at football's top table in the 1980s, providing the experience and practiced proficiency of players who had seen it all. They would be joined by a generation of magnificently talented young players who, like Simonsen and Olsen, had also absorbed the influences learned in other, more advanced football nations.

At Anderlecht, Olsen joined fellow Danish internationals Benny Nielsen and Kenneth Brylle. The Belgian club soon added to their Danish contingent with the defender Henrik Andersen, midfielder Per Frimann, and, most excitingly, the forward-thinking and influential midfielder Frank Arnesen. By then, Arnesen had already been schooled in the mid-1970s Total Football methods of Ajax, where he had spent the first six seasons of his career: a football education of the highest calibre.

Other Danish stars remained at Ajax after Arnesen had moved on from the Dutch capital in 1981. The influential midfielder Søren Lerby had been an Ajax player since the mid-1970s. He was joined in 1981 by the left-sided winger Jesper Olsen and then a year later by fellow midfielder Jan

Mølby. That summer, when the mercurial Johan Cruyff returned to the club where he made his name, this Danish trio were fortunate to spend time being educated by the Dutch legend – 'like a King holding court' as described by Mølby in his autobiography. These international influences were a crucial step in the development of a nation whose domestic structures left them some way behind. The best Danish players benefitted from exposure to the more advanced football methods across Europe, absorbing the influences and the knowledge and bringing it back to the national team.

Also developing in Belgium were the sublime skills of Preben Elkjær, an exceptionally gifted forward graced with blistering pace and magnetic control, who had spent six seasons at Lokeren prior to his move to Italy in 1984. Elkjær's play was less subtle than some of his more intricate colleagues. Occasionally, his was more of an eyes down and head for goal approach. But this was built on his astonishing technical abilities and balance, allowing him to instil a panic and desperation in those tasked with stopping him. He was still graceful and glamorous, but in a more easily relatable way. With Denmark, he would form the most prodigious attacking partnership of the era, dovetailing majestically, with someone whose own sublime talent was more of the other-worldly style, as the jewel in the crown of the newly professionalised domestic system emerged.

Michael Laudrup made his international debut on his 18th birthday in 1982 while playing for Brøndby in the Danish league, though he was soon destined for bigger things in the grandest clubs of Italy and Spain. He would become one of the finest players of his generation, a truly world-class playmaker capable of playing in any number of attacking positions.

The introduction of professionalism in 1978 had been made possible thanks to a sponsorship deal with the Danish brewery giants Carlsberg. The massive injection of funds was dependent on not only the implementation of the professional league, but also more professional standards when it came to the national team. Previously, it had been essentially run as a fun club, a chance for players to party their time away in Copenhagen's nightclubs ahead of internationals, rather than take any of it too seriously. While many aspects of the set-up did indeed become more professional, this laid-back sense of enjoyment took far longer to dissipate. Not in a way that hampered their chances though, far from it. Rather, it was the grounding of the hugely successful era, where enjoyment found its means of expression on the field as well as off it.

There was an international influence in the more professional national team management too. While the players had sought foreign fields to enhance their careers and gain football knowledge, an equally key component behind Denmark's astonishing rise in the 1980s had travelled in the opposite direction. The West German Sepp Piontek had taken over from Kurt Nielsen in 1979 as the first full-time professional coach of the Danish national team, completing the transition from the amateur structures of old.

Piontek brought with him a wealth of experience, gained principally in the West German Bundesliga, but also in the unlikely setting of Haiti where he had served as national manager. Dour and stubborn at times, Piontek also had the humour and self-confidence to fit in with the more relaxed approach of the Danish squad; the flamboyance and self-assured nature of the Danish players contrasting but complemented by the disciplined German.

He may have been bringing an added professionalism but such was the culture, the fun club outlook, that it was no smooth road for Piontek to impose his methods. 'Danes don't like the word discipline,' Piontek noted, fighting against a deeply ingrained culture of amateurism at international level. The players may have been playing at Europe's finest clubs, good professionals in their day jobs, but the national team was seen differently. In time, his doctrine was accepted though, and it was in 1981 that Danish fortunes showed the first clear signs of significant progression. The World Cup qualifying victory over Italy was the standout result, but that was just one of eight victories that year in nine outings.

Those qualifiers had been an important improvement, but had still been ultimately unsuccessful. The following campaign, on the other hand, for the 1984 European Championship, would see Denmark's first major breakthrough. It could have gone awry from the start, Denmark twice trailing at home to England in the opening match of the group, but with just a minute remaining came a moment that served notice of a team on the rise.

When Jesper Olsen jinked and swerved his way to a magical solo goal to equalise, it was the moment that hindsight enables us to see as the birth of the era of 'Danish Dynamite'. It was a thoroughly deserved equaliser – they had gone close several times beforehand – but was still viewed in England as a shameful disappointment in what was Bobby Robson's first match in charge, rather than a deserved goal from a team of huge talent. Indeed, Elkjær had tormented the English defence throughout, and it was only some fine saves from Peter Shilton that kept England in the game.

A year later, following a friendly victory over the World Cup semi-finalists and soon-to-be European champions

France, Denmark won 1-0 at Wembley, thanks to a Simonsen penalty. Qualification was now within reach. Not only that, but they were firmly established as one of Europe's best national teams. What the English media still failed to see, much of the rest of Europe celebrated. For the Danes, the victory at Wembley, achieved with an almost nonchalant ease as they kept the ball away from the home team for almost embarrassing stints of time, was a seminal moment. 'It signalled to a great group of players how much they could achieve,' said Piontek, as an already self-assured group now felt the glow of international success as qualification was soon ensured. It had all been achieved in such style, with such groundbreaking panache by their extraordinary generation of players, that Denmark were voted *World Soccer* magazine's National Team of the Year in 1983, with Piontek as Manager of the Year.

At Euro '84 in France, the Danish Dynamite took to the international stage with the ease of a team more accustomed to tournament finals. If there were still those unwilling or unable to acknowledge the emerging greatness of this Denmark team, the performances in 1984 put paid to that. They could no longer be considered an unknown quantity by those whose eyes had remained closed to the obvious for the preceding few years.

Given the accolades bestowed on Denmark in the year prior to the Euros, they arrived at the tournament as one of the teams fancied to do well, despite some less than dynamic form ahead of the finals. Defeats in warm-up matches ahead of the tournament were repeated in their opening match against the hosts, but the manner of the 1-0 loss to Michel Platini's France was more a source of positivity than doubt, Denmark making a team on the cusp of their own destined greatness work exceptionally hard for their narrow victory. The loss may not have overly harmed Denmark's chances of progression in itself, and was indeed an unfortunate one given how well they had performed, but the loss of Simonsen, victim of a horrendous leg break, was an undoubted setback.

All the more remarkable then, that the subsequent victory over Yugoslavia was so seismic as to potentially be considered above even the earlier Wembley victory as the day that Danish football came of age. The 5-0 defeat they inflicted on a startled Yugoslavia doesn't tell the whole truth of a remarkable match which could easily have seen many more goals – for both teams. Yugoslavia had played their part, creating numerous good chances only for Ole Qvist in the Danish goal to produce a string of remarkable saves to deny them.

Denmark, too, could have easily scored more, having set the tone early with goals from Arnesen and the gritty midfielder Klaus Berggreen. But it was the two final, late goals which really marked out a side on the verge of greatness. By the time Denmark scored their fourth, eight minutes from the end, the attackers were queuing up to take turns to finish it off. Laudrup, a key part of the team already, even aged just 20, ultimately nonchalantly teeing up Elkjær to finish off the move. In recording such a resounding victory, Denmark had given themselves a tremendous opportunity to reach the semi-finals, and in doing so they had unleashed their swaggering, stylish attacking dynamism on to the European stage.

With Laudrup combining to astonishing effect alongside Elkjær and Arnesen, Denmark may have been novices at such an exalted international level but possessed an attacking line-up capable of terrifying any defence. It wasn't simply the ability of these players, all adept at closely controlled dribbling, they also all possessed a devastating change of pace. Thus, the speed at which they could all perform these feats made them unplayable at times.

Denmark went from that remarkable match into an absorbing, dramatic occasion in a winner-takes-all clash with Belgium. They only needed a draw to progress from the group along with France, but when Belgium led 2-0 shortly before half-time that outcome was in severe doubt. Denmark fought back, though, to win 3-2, clinched with a crowning moment of glory to seal their momentous international breakthrough. Elkjær latched on to a headed defensive clearance, controlling it instantly and effortlessly, setting off into the Belgian half, zigzagging his way through the scrambling defence. Flicking the ball over Jean-Marie Pfaff with his finish, he scored a goal worthy of sealing yet another newly crowned finest victory in Danish football history.

It earned them a semi-final place against Spain, a team destined to feature in this tale more than once as Denmark's bête noire. As was Denmark's exhilarating wont, this match produced another epic of all-out attack with Spain compelled to react in kind, given the vigour of the Danish approach. It produced another match for the ages, drawing yet more admirers to those dressed in Danish white on this occasion. This spectacular match finished 1-1, Denmark also hitting the post twice, culminating in the dreaded penalty denouement. Like Spain, Denmark scored all of their first four penalties – though Laudrup was given a reprieve, having missed, only for the referee to order a retake – before Elkjær stepped up to take the final effort. He had scored all six penalties he'd taken that season, but on this day, with the biggest kick of his life, it wasn't to be. His shot cleared the bar, leaving Spain to claim a place in the final.

For Denmark, the tournament may have ended on a despondent sour note, but the impact made by this team can't be understated. They had impressed from first to last with their overwhelming positivity, their ceaseless attacking built from a solid base and their sublime control play. Above all, though, it was the sheer sense of enjoyment which everything about their play exemplified. Like their boisterously exuberant fans watching on, they played with a joyous abandon which was simply intoxicating.

To fall so narrowly short in Euro 1984 was a clear 'what if' moment, and a theme which could be the focus of a chapter in its own right. But for Denmark, and this tale, it was merely the beginning; the hors d'oeuvres before the feast that was to come. Two years on, in the World Cup in Mexico, this team would reach even higher peaks and an even greater disappointment. Yet they would also captivate like never before, enthralling a global audience with their audacious brand of incessant attack.

To get to Mexico, and a first World Cup appearance, Denmark had to negotiate a tricky qualifying group containing a superbly strong USSR team, as well as Switzerland, Ireland and Norway. Denmark lost twice but still came out on top in a far from straightforward campaign for the European semi-finalists. From a tricky opening in a narrow 1-0 win over Norway and a stuttering defeat in Switzerland, the Danes were in a fight throughout. As if unaccustomed or even uncomfortable with their new-found status as European football aristocracy, Denmark seemed to have fallen back on old habits and old mentalities. Gone was the free-flowing magnificence of the French summer of 1984 when Denmark came within a whisker of glory. But quality doesn't fade as rapidly as the fickler natures of form, confidence and comfort. An awkward start it may have been, but this was not the Denmark of old: this was a generation set to reach for the stars.

The year 1984 ended with a thumping 3-0 win over Ireland, but it was in their next match some seven months later, in June 1985, that the true extent of Denmark's majestic magnificence was revealed in spectacular style once again. The home qualifier against the USSR in Copenhagen's Parken Stadium would go down as one of the finest exhibitions of football – from both sides it should be noted – that international football has ever seen.

If this is a match which has escaped your attention until now, I would urge any fan of footballing beauty to hunt out the footage. To watch the action unfold, even at the distance of three and a half decades, is to witness a work of art played out in sporting form. The movement, the intricate passing, the audacious goals, the last-gasp clearances, the free-flowing end-to-end action; it is a relentlessly compelling reminder of just how good football can be.

'For me this will always be *the game*,' said Laudrup, quoted in *Danish Dynamite*. 'A lovely sunny afternoon, a packed national stadium and then the game itself: six goals – which could easily have been ten – one amazing opponent and a match where nothing was decided even when at 4-1 after 67 minutes. I haven't had that feeling before or after.'

Denmark, with the forward combination of Laudrup and Elkjær now arguably the finest strike partnership in world football, ultimately won 4-2 to seize the initiative in the group. But this game goes well beyond a simple two points towards qualification, a strong performance, or a fabulous opponent overcome. Far more than that, this was the day that Denmark arguably reached their pinnacle, the day it clicked more magnificently than it had even in the great days they had already enjoyed over the last few years.

Uruguay captain José Nasazzi (left) shakes hands with his Argentinian counterpart Manuel Ferreira ahead of the final, while the Belgian referee, John Langenus, looks on.

Juan Botasso grabs at thin air as Héctor Castro, hidden from view but with his arms outstretched in celebration, scores the final goal of the 1930 final to seal Uruguay's victory.

The Austrian team ready to make their World Cup debut in 1934 against France. Matthias Sindelar is standing, fifth from the left.

Italy's Enrico Guaita bundles the ball past Austria's Peter Platzer to score the only goal of the controversial 1934 semi-final. Giuseppe Meazza lies in the goalmouth, having already clashed with Platzer.

'You, who we already hail as champions.' Brazil ready to meet their destiny as they open the 1950 World Cup in the Maracanã.

Moacir Barbosa lies stricken, about to enter his personal hell, as he turns to see the ball heading into the net from Alcides Ghiggia's shot. With that, the World Cup was lost.

Ferenc Puskás and Fritz Walter lead their teams out for the 1954 World Cup Final in Bern between Hungary and West Germany.

Puskás scores on his return from injury in the 1954 final. A great start for Hungary and their half-fit talisman. He would later be denied a late equaliser by a controversial offside decision.

Eusébio celebrates scoring in the group match against Brazil in 1966, helping secure a victory to make all of Portugal believe that anything was possible.

Jogo das Lágrimas, *the game of tears. Eusébio leaves the 1966 World Cup following the narrow semi-final loss to England at Wembley.*

Johan Cruyff is chopped down in the opening moments of the 1974 final. Netherlands scored from the resulting penalty, taking the lead before their West German opponents had even touched the ball.

By half-time in the 1974 final the tension is showing. 2-1 down after having appeared set to dominate, Cruyff's frustration led to him receiving a yellow card from referee Jack Taylor as the teams left the field. Wim van Hanegem is following Cruyff off the pitch.

A party on the pitch and in the stands as Brazil celebrates Socrates' equaliser in the spectacular clash with Italy in 1982.

Zico, Brazil's enigmatic star, was at the peak of his powers in the 1982 World Cup. Against Italy, he was tracked everywhere by the uncompromising spoiler Claudio Gentile.

Before it all went wrong. Jesper Olsen gives Denmark the lead against Spain, before his later error allowed Spain to equalise.

Spain's Emilio Butragueño takes on the Danish defence in the astonishing tie in the last 16 of the 1986 World Cup. Butragueño scored four to end the dream of this magnificent Denmark side.

Roberto Baggio about to enter World Cup folklore, completing his wondrous goal against Czechoslovakia in 1990. It was a moment to herald the arrival of a new hero, sending Italian belief soaring when the doubts had begun to creep in.

The moment that belief began to drain away. Argentina's Claudio Caniggia scores the equaliser past Walter Zenga in the fateful 1990 semi-final in Naples.

Roberto Donadoni's world crumbles around him, as Argentina's Sergio Goycochea celebrates saving the first of two Italian penalty misses in the 1990 semi-final.

Yugoslavia's Dragan Stojković, here scoring his majestic goal against Spain in 1990, was chief among a stunning generation of talent. A generation whose World Cup hopes were not denied on the football field, but were instead denied by history.

Dennis Bergkamp takes the first of his three majestic touches, on the way to scoring his perfect goal for the Netherlands against Argentina in the 1998 quarter-final. Argentinian defender Roberto Ayala was close at hand but was a mere bystander to this piece of footballing perfection.

Phillip Cocu walks back to his team-mates, head bowed in disappointment after his penalty miss in the 1998 semi-final between the Netherlands and Brazil. Defeat was now just moments away.

Argentina's saviour. Lionel Messi, far left, scores his late, decisive winner in the 2014 group match with Iran.

Argentina went close a number of times in the 2014 final against West Germany, creating the chances to mean victory could have been theirs. Messi was guilty of wasting one such chance, firing wide when Manuel Neuer's goal beckoned.

'What you saw from Laudrup and Elkjær against the Soviet Union really was not normal,' said Piontek, and he was right. Those two masters of the ball played as if from another world, each scoring two, but dominating so much beyond those simple statistics; footballing deities gracing the game with their miraculous abilities. What this led to was an understanding in Denmark and beyond that the great victories they had already achieved at Wembley and in Euro '84 were no flash in the pan. This Denmark were the real deal, and a delighted nation now fully understood that. Those previous highs were no fairy tale after all, but the steps on the path to a greatness that Denmark now seemed capable of. This was the day when Denmark truly understood they had a team which was among the very best in the world.

For all the belief now coursing through Danish minds, they still stuttered their way through to the World Cup. This seminal victory was followed by a 1-0 defeat in Moscow in September 1985, and a goalless draw at home to Switzerland a month later when several good opportunities were spurned. A week after that disappointing performance they then trailed 1-0 in Norway at half-time in the penultimate qualifier, with the prospect of failing to reach the World Cup now suddenly threatening to become a painful reality. Then, as if flicking a switch, Denmark scored five in a pulsating second half, before coming from behind again in Ireland to win 4-1 to ensure qualification.

These troubles hint at a concerning lack of consistency, something of an erratic boom-or-bust tendency, which would come back to haunt Denmark the following summer in Mexico. It was nothing new – they had lost heavily just prior to Euro '84 and went on to perform magnificently when it mattered – but it was becoming a recurring theme. It belied the fear that the fun-loving, light-hearted perspective that Denmark lived by and represented would ultimately prevent them from attaining the heights their abilities deserved. The positivity following qualification, though, was overwhelming. A first World Cup, a team among the world's finest, players who truly belonged to the elite, was dreamland for Denmark: a rhapsody in red played in a contagiously irresistible style in which absolutely anything seemed possible.

Laudrup referred to this team as 'Europe's answer to Brazil', while many others preferred the comparison with the Dutch of 1974, taking the Total Football ethos of ceaseless movement and use of space and enhancing it with such speed as to produce a style that was simply spellbinding. Rob Smyth, co-author of *Danish Dynamite*, described them as, 'Like a fast-forwarded version of that Holland side. No team has ever had such a collection of jet-heeled dribblers.' They played out from the back in a manner that was truly ahead of its time. Nowadays, it may be the norm, but in the mid-1980s, defenders were there to defend primarily, not to instigate attacks. Morten Olsen played increasingly deep, and was such a calm, stabilising presence that he directed proceedings from the back starting the moves which others then glittered with gold.

For all Denmark were new to the World Cup, they were no inexperienced novices. Olsen and Simonsen had already reached the peaks in club football which Elkjær and Laudrup were now ascending to. Now playing in Italy, Elkjær had inspired Verona to the Serie A title in 1985, while Laudrup also won Serie A in 1986 with Juventus. So too, Olsen had won a title with Anderlecht, as had Lerby with Bayern Munich and Arnesen with Ajax. They were a team of serial winners in their prime.

Denmark were cool off the pitch too. They had a refreshingly laid-back attitude that lacked the more brazen flamboyance or hard-nosed arrogance of the 1970s Dutch side. This Denmark team embodied the light-hearted, self-deprecating, joyful outlook of the country they represented. Your heart couldn't fail to warm to this gang of highly skilled impresarios from some of Europe's biggest clubs, whose abilities and exploits never seemed to take away from an everyman quality. The previous amateur outlook in the Danish set-up was yet to fade. They enjoyed a beer and a smoke and the simple pleasure of enjoying their time together, rather than worrying about the more serious tasks of international duty. Decked out in one of the most iconic, striking kits in World Cup history, designed by the Danish sportswear giant Hummel, this team looked cool, acted cool and played cool. Those who watched them with a sense of wonder and bewilderment couldn't help but fall in love.

And there is a key factor here for those of us watching on from the UK and being captivated by their efforts in the World Cup. Having been unable to watch Euro '84, thanks to the short-sighted decision of UK broadcasters not to show all but two matches of that tournament live, Mexico 1986 represented the first real opportunity to enjoy this Denmark team fully. The bright images of the Danes, beamed back from across the Atlantic, dazzled in every sense.

Given their lack of any World Cup pedigree whatsoever, Denmark were among the lowest seeds for the draw: a fact which left them in an extremely tough group along with West Germany, Scotland and Uruguay. It was a group which prompted the Uruguayan coach, Omar Borras, to first coin the phrase 'Group of Death'. New boys they may have been, but Denmark were deservedly being talked about as outsiders for the tournament, even with this difficult beginning.

They opened against Scotland in what would prove to be their toughest match of the group. They had to fight for their win, secured around the hour mark, thanks to an Elkjær goal forged more from the relentless determination of the scorer than the intricate play of others. He picked up a pass from Arnesen at the edge of the Scotland box and forced his way past Willie Miller before bundling the ball in off the far post. It was more determination than dexterity, contrasting with many of the chances that had gone begging in that opening game. Prior to the goal, Laudrup and Arnesen had both gone close following fine moves, but so too had Nicholas, Gough and McLeish for Scotland. Chances continued at both ends with Scotland's Roy Aitken being denied a perfectly legitimate equaliser, the officials wrongly deeming him offside before he too fired in off the post.

That the game ended only 1-0 was remarkable, but it had been an absorbing World Cup debut for Denmark which was duly celebrated by the many colourful and flamboyant Danish followers in the stands. Denmark may not have fully hit their stride, but the signs were there – the ease of movement, the quick passing, the simplicity with which they carved through the defence at times – that Denmark were warming up to produce something very special. Up next were Uruguay, and if the Scotland game had been a closely fought, hard-earned victory when things could easily have been different, the Uruguay match saw one of the most remarkable eviscerations of a strong opponent you could imagine in a World Cup.

A clear recollection from my youth is getting up early before school and watching as much as possible of the game from the night before as I could, but soon found that there was little room for fast-forwarding the video, given the relentless Danish onslaught. Fast-forward is an appropriate term for Denmark on that day, as they seemed to be playing in that manner, so quick and incisive was their play. I was captivated by this performance, as Denmark ran rings around and through Uruguay, seemingly at will. Denmark were simply sensational.

Yes, Uruguay had a man sent off early on, not for the last time in that tournament, and perhaps that mitigation is a reason why this performance could be partially overlooked in terms of truly great World Cup performances. But make no mistake about it, this was as crushing a victory as the 6-1 scoreline suggests. Denmark were already utterly superior prior to the red card and merely enhanced this superiority after it. They had already taken the lead through Elkjær – the first of a hat-trick that day – before Miguel Bossio picked up his second yellow card in only the 19th minute and was sent off, but nobody could have lived with Denmark on the form they produced that day.

Indeed, for Elkjær to score a hat-trick and to have a significant hand in two other goals, and yet still be overshadowed when it came to the plaudits afterwards, tells its own story. Laudrup scored the Danes' elegant third goal early in the second half, speeding and shimmying past and around several Uruguayan defenders in a fabulous run, shifting both his weight and speed with an effortless grace. He surged past the helpless goalkeeper before side-footing the ball into the net for one of the goals of the tournament. 'The boy's a genius,' exclaimed John Helm, commentating on ITV's coverage of the match, and who could fail to agree? Another spectacular Laudrup run set up Elkjær's second, while both his third and Jesper Olsen's strike for

Denmark's sixth exuded the nonchalant confidence of sporting superiority.

Laudrup grabbed the headlines but Elkjær had put in another stunning performance too; a mixture of opportunistic strikes, fine finishes and expert assists. Equally, the performances of Lerby, Arnesen and Jesper Olsen made plain that there was an awful lot more to this team than its two stars up front. Collectively, Denmark were now the most eye-catching of the teams in the first week of the tournament; the first to really light it up with a performance to make everyone sit up and take notice. They were the most impressive of the European contenders at this stage certainly, if not the most impressive of all contenders.

This was a status which they could seal in their final group game if they could overcome West Germany, the runners-up from four years earlier. With both teams already through to the next round, this could have been something of a non-event, but that would be to ignore what this game meant to Denmark. They had never beaten their large neighbours to the south in a meaningful match, and were utterly motivated to do so. In a collective decision, they opted against resting players before a second-round match just five days later, with Piontek only choosing to leave out Berggreen and Ivan Nielsen, both of whom were one yellow card away from suspension. A goalkeeping change was made too, bringing in Lars Høgh in place of Troels Rasmussen.

The players were desperate to show their capabilities against a team and nation that was always felt to be looking down on them. Added to the previous successes over England and the USSR, the Euro success and more, this was also the chance to beat a real superpower of the world game. For Piontek, a German of course, the opportunity to show his worth to a homeland which hadn't given him the opportunities he felt he deserved was equally irresistible. What there was not was any consideration to seeking an easier tie in the next round by losing to West Germany. Hindsight has thrown a greater light on this, drawing many of those involved into a debate about what Denmark ought to have done with the benefit of knowing what was soon to happen. But given the significance of the opposition and the momentum they were gathering, any thoughts of not going all out for victory were barely a consideration at the time.

'The truth is,' recalled the midfielder Jan Mølby, 'we felt we could take them all.' Confidence was soaring, and when Denmark duly beat West Germany 2-0, with another sublime performance in another open game, Mølby's statement seemed valid. Both teams attacked throughout but the Danes showed the greater quality, possessed the greater cutting edge, and outplayed their traditionally more illustrious opponents.

Victory was secured via a Jesper Olsen penalty, casually sending the German goalkeeper the wrong way, and a goal from substitute striker John Eriksen who had replaced Elkjær at half-time. This victory meant that Denmark would face Spain in the last 16; their nemesis from the Euro'84 semi-final. West Germany, as group runners-up, were rewarded with a tie against surprise group winners Morocco. This disparity, of course, feeds the narrative that Denmark were naive to not seek out the easier path through the tournament, but any such thoughts fail to address the seriousness with which the Germans took the Denmark match too, and the simple fact of how well Denmark were playing.

They were the tournament's top scorers and joined Brazil as the only team with a 100 per cent record from the group stage. Denmark had achieved this with such a stunning swagger too, meaning that they were utterly confident no matter who they were facing. They simply believed they were better than the opposition, regardless of reputations. What had not gone so well for Denmark, however, was the final few minutes of the victory over West Germany. While we will get to what went wrong against Spain, it is easy to argue that the latter stages against the Germans is where it started to go awry.

It should have been a moment of celebration, with a historic victory confirmed and a debut World Cup appearance going astonishingly well. Instead, Arnesen uncharacteristically lashed out, having been fouled by Lothar Matthäus, and was sent off, making this key midfielder unavailable for the Spain match. Arnesen had already been booked for dissent when protesting a penalty award he should have got, but didn't. Both that incident, and the Matthäus one in which he saw red literally and figuratively, were the outward expression of a more personal frustration. He had played as if on the edge throughout, unusually aggressive and slightly detached. The reason, only revealed later, was that his wife was suffering suspected meningitis, which leads to the question of whether he should have been playing at all that day. Play he did, but what was now certain was that he would not be playing against Spain in the last 16.

They would miss Arnesen, certainly, but that was just one factor in several reasons for what went wrong against Spain in Querétaro. Jesper Olsen had played in all of Denmark's matches so far, either from the start or from the bench, and he would again start this time, becoming the key figure around whom the story played out in the first half. It had begun so well, Denmark showing the level of dominance to which we had all by now become accustomed. They took the lead through another languidly elegant penalty from Olsen, casually converting as if it were the easiest thing in the world.

At this stage, it all seemed set to follow the expected pattern. It always seemed to be an open game, leading to chances at both ends, but with Denmark's other-worldly talent seeing them through to victory. That's what football romantics like me expected and hoped would happen, but, instead, it all changed just before half-time.

Olsen received the ball from a goal kick having dropped deep on the right-hand side, closely tracked by Spanish forward Julio Salinas. Olsen jinked past his opponent but then opted to pass the ball back to his goalkeeper. Inexplicably, he did so without looking, sending the ball back across the penalty area to where he thought Høgh was positioned. But Høgh wasn't there, Spain's clinical striker Emilio Butragueño was. He delightedly tapped the ball into an unguarded net.

'But Jesper, Jesper, Jesper, that's lethal,' lamented Svend Gehrs on Danish TV commentary, his voice trailing away in resignation. From complete control, Denmark had contrived to let Spain back in. The clichéd tale told here is that Denmark simply fell apart after this, recklessly chasing the game when it was still very much in the balance, leaving themselves exposed as a result. That would come later, but initially, at least, the symbolism of this moment was not that it was the end of the dream, merely that it was a brief setback. Denmark began the second half as they did the first: in total control, playing as neatly as ever, Elkjær going close to restoring Denmark's lead on more than one occasion. It was only once Spain scored again that it really fell apart.

Butragueño headed Spain in front before the hour mark, and now Denmark's reaction was not that of a team

233

who believed their tried and trusted methods would bear fruit if they stuck to them. Instead, panic seemed to set in. Piontek immediately took off a defender to bring on an extra forward, John Eriksen. Denmark overcommitted themselves, their formation becoming horribly lopsided in favour of the attack, leaving the defence to be picked apart at will. Butragueño finished with four goals while Spain finished with five. More than once, he was all alone, one-on-one with Høgh, with barely a defender in sight. It was a cruel injustice that so great a team was beaten so heavily, but it was largely of their own doing. They may have gone a goal down, but it was surely far too early to throw such caution to the wind when they were still largely superior, were creating chances, and looked likely to score if they just kept going.

Had the Olsen error laid the seeds of the panic, which the second goal then reinforced? It's impossible to know. Denmark were used to playing in open games; the openness suited the Danes and their style, of course, but that was always within the structures of a system designed to cope, where the defence was never really the first thought but neither was it neglected. In the latter stages of this game, sadly it was neglected and, as a result, the most bewildering, captivating team of the tournament was gone, falling to their Spanish nemesis once again when victory should have been theirs for the taking.

'At 2-1 and 3-1 it became an all-or-nothing game,' recalled Elkjær, 'and then we were open and too easy to counter-attack.' And yet, given Denmark had crafted the better of the opportunities before this, it should never have become this case of all-or-nothing. Elkjær's pain at the margin of defeat is clear, describing it as 'ridiculous', and he was right. It was. For those of us fast asleep in the UK as this was going on, waking up to find the game had ended 5-1 led to only one conclusion coming to mind: Denmark had surely stormed their way through to the quarter-finals in typically magnificent style. To discover it was the other way around was as astonishing as it was devastating.

Olsen became the scapegoat, such as there was one, as there was less of the pained soul-searching that other, more established countries lapse into at such times. 'I shouldn't have played that pass. It's just one of those things you can't change,' was how he reflected on it years later. It is still talked about in Denmark – a serious mistake is still referred to as 'a real Jesper Olsen' – but really the feeling the squad left with was of a successful tournament that ended sooner than it needed to, but in which there was no disgrace.

The laid-back attitude which had helped them get this far had now potentially worked against them. Piontek noted that there may have been a lapse in their frame of mind when it came to the need to win. He felt the intense satisfaction at how it had gone in the group stage perhaps caused the feeling to grow that they had already done well and could now relax, that if they went out now it was still a success, rendering them unable to see it through against Spain. I'm not sure I agree, given the desperate recklessness of the second half, but certainly it eased the pain of defeat when compared to several others in this book.

Football lovers were denied one of the great quarter-finals, and what could have neatly brought this story full circle. The wondrous clash between Denmark and the USSR in the qualifiers was set to be repeated in the last eight, between two teams playing with such style. For both protagonists and footballing purists alike, that intriguing possibility would be cruelly denied, both surprisingly beaten in the last 16.

The Soviet side, in their iconic kit with the bold CCCP emblazoned across the front, had topped their group having beaten Canada, drawn with the highly fancied France, and resoundingly thrashed Hungary. They were the very epitome of communist collectivism, shaped by the mercurial and pioneering coach Valeriy Lobanovskyi into a Soviet version of Total Football. Lobanovskyi had taken over not long prior to the World Cup, basing his team for Mexico on the hugely talented Dynamo Kyiv he also led, notably with the talented striker Igor Belanov.

The mauling his side gave Hungary served notice of their spectacular credentials, but, as with Denmark, it all went wrong in a last-16 clash with Belgium where they were beaten 4-3 in controversial circumstances, despite dominating the play. Belgium's first two goals, both equalising a Soviet lead, came from offside positions. The second of which, from Jan Ceulemans late in the game, was several yards offside, with the goalscorer glancing around in disbelief, unsure whether to celebrate or not. Belgium won through in extra time, scoring twice on the counter-attack as the Soviets pressed for their deserved winner.

It could have been a magnificent quarter-final between Denmark and the USSR, with a place in a semi-final against Maradona and Argentina awaiting the winner. After the artistry of the qualifying match between the two, to be denied a repeat on the grandest stage adds an additional element of frustration to this tale. Both had lit up the group stages and both had a tale of woe from their ultimate elimination.

It's all hypothetical of course, but who is to say that the brilliance of Maradona would have overcome the all-out attacking team of the Danish Dynamite? Equally, there is plenty of reason to think that the USSR had the talent to test both Denmark and Argentina had they not been denied in their own cruel twist of fate. Either fictional scenario would have been glorious. The sadness is that we will never know. It is the Danish tale that resonates the most for me though: the style of their performances, that swagger and cool, makes you wonder what they could have achieved if fate had smiled more favourably on them.

Instead, we are left with our lament at the demise of an incredible team who had burned so brightly in Mexico, only to quickly fade. And so too did the fortunes of the Danish national team in the next few years. Elkjær suffered injuries, while the team suffered a poor European Championship in 1988 and then failed to qualify for the 1990 World Cup. The great irony came when a lesser incarnation won the 1992 European Championship in remarkable circumstances, making the leap that the great team of the 1980s could not. Spain maintained their nemesis status in Danish perception; having beaten Denmark in Euro'84 and the 1986 World Cup, they beat them again in Euro'88 and in a decisive 1994 World Cup qualifier. But it was the 1986 defeat that left the most scars.

And yet for a team which fell at the last 16 to still be remembered so fondly so many years later is the greatest compliment which can be paid this fantastic Denmark side. To have captured the hearts of so many, so quickly, and to maintain that hold for decades, despite such a spectacular exit, is astonishing. But they were no ordinary team. The Denmark of 1986 were so irresistibly good, almost pure in an endearing but recklessly naive way, that the thoughts of 'what if' are just as applicable to them as they are to the other great teams who missed out on glory by a far narrower margin. The fabulous book *Danish Dynamite* captures their essence magnificently, 'The fact that their story had a bittersweet tang and a doomed innocence only accentuates their alternative appeal. The best stories in life are the ones where those involved don't get the girl, the happy ending or even the Jules Rimet Trophy.'

They truly were good enough to have won it all, but their destiny was instead akin to the crazed rock star who lived fast and died young. Their cult appeal exists in part because of the way it ended; it is certainly enhanced because of the way it ended. There is a painful poetry in the magnificence of both their rise and their fall that appeals to hopeless football romantics like me. Had they won the World Cup, it would have been done in astonishing style, but that they didn't even come close and yet are remembered so fondly, the legend living on so intensely, shows just how good they were. It is not only the winners and those who are narrowly, unluckily beaten when glory is on the line who are so well remembered. Sometimes the real greats are knocked out even earlier, claiming their place in our hearts nonetheless.

9

Italy 1990

Don't wake me up. Let me enjoy the dream.

Salvatore Schillaci

'NOTTI MAGICHE,' went the lyrics to the Italian soundtrack of their home World Cup. 'Magic nights, chasing a goal under the sky of an Italian summer.' While we in the UK were enchanted by Pavarotti and 'Nessun Dorma', all of Italy was absorbed by the gravelly sounds of Gianna Nannini and Edoardo Bennato's 'Un'estate Italiana': the musical accompaniment to those magic Italian World Cup nights when everything not only seemed possible, but felt inevitable.

It had felt inevitable to those of us watching from afar, too, captivated by the drama of this World Cup. For all of England's exploits, the sense that we were building towards an Italy v West Germany final seemed the most likely, and the right, outcome. The Italian story was the one that resonated the most: a beautiful tragedy of operatic proportions, soaked in drama and tension as explosive talents burst on to the scene and unlikely icons stepped up to push a desperate nation towards its World Cup destiny.

To most Italians, seeing the Azzurri lift the World Cup in 1990 was a given. This was no idle, boastful conviction based on complacency, delusion or an inflated sense of Italian worth. Italy, in 1990, was the centre of the football universe.

Serie A was Europe's dominant league, with its clubs at the pinnacle of their powers, attracting the world's finest players to Milan, Turin, Rome and beyond. There had been an Italian clean sweep of the European club trophies just prior to the World Cup. The imported talents of Gullit, Van Basten and Rijkaard at Milan, Matthäus, Klinsmann and Brehme at Inter, and Careca and Diego Maradona at Napoli made the Italian league the best in the world, with a broad depth of talent across several teams. In an age of restrictions on foreign players, only the best could make the move to Italy. The rest of the squads were all Italian, learning from the very best. To play in such exalted company, these domestic players had to be special.

The strength of Italian football also enhanced the feeling of nationhood within the country. 'They were a young nation in need of something to identify with,' Richard Hall, the chief correspondent for *Football Italia*, explained to me. 'And the rise of its football league into continental dominance fed the feeling of just what football means to Italy.' Added to that, hosting in what at the time were futuristic, modern stadia built specifically for the tournament, the World Cup was in the right place at the right time. As FIFA's official film put it, 'Italy had become the spiritual home of the modern game.' Not only was anticipation bubbling over, but so was the expectation on what was the most visible international symbol of the Italian nation.

On this theme, John Foot, in his all-encompassing book on Italian football, *Calcio*, cites a study carried out in Italy in 1990 when various intellectuals were asked what it was that held Italians together. A significant number cited the national football team, a sense visibly confirmed during the tournament when Italian flags, normally a rare sight, appeared all over the country, hanging from windows, on rooftops, and, of course, in the stands of the Stadio Olimpico. Each match Italy played saw cities come to a standstill amid riotous explosions of flag-waving joy. It was a World Cup in the perfect place at the perfect time. 'Coming in on a high, the culmination of having the best league, brought the nation together: a country with a strong north-south divide uniting around a Sicilian,' added Hall. Nobody was considering defeat. Carried away on a wave of emotion, all of Italy felt they were destined to win.

Having lifted the World Cup somewhat unexpectedly in 1982, battling their way against the odds to peak at just the right time, the joyous national celebration inadvertently exacerbated the subsequent decline of the Italian national team. The coach at the time, Enzo Bearzot, would later reflect that the 1982 victory had almost forced him to keep a team of World Cup winners together, rather than seek to rebuild. As a result, the 1984 European Championship qualifying campaign was a disaster and the 1986 World Cup a disappointment too, making Italy's decline clear to all.

When Bearzot moved on, his replacement was the last of Italy's traditional boot-room managers, Azeglio Vicini. Having coached the under-21 side since 1978, he had recently led a new crop of talented players to the final of the 1986 European Under-21 Championship, losing only on penalties to Spain. With the emergence of this new generation, the exuberance of youth stood poised to take over the baton from the stagnated stalwarts lingering from 1982.

There was the goalkeeper Walter Zenga, Riccardo Ferri in defence, and a midfield including Giuseppe Giannini, Fernando De Napoli, Nicola Berti and Roberto Donadoni. In attack, there were the fabulous talents of Gianluca Vialli and Roberto Mancini. In bringing these players through into the senior side, Vicini's new generation energised not just the national team but the hopes of a nation. Many of this group were a part of the 1988 European Championship side which greatly restored Italian pride. In reaching the semi-finals, Italy went unbeaten through a tough group stage playing some fine football, before losing out to a strong USSR. Any disappointment was tempered by the comforting knowledge that Italy were back at the level they yearned to be at, with a squad developing together. With a home World Cup now rapidly approaching, this collective would form the backbone of the 1990 squad.

Amid soaring expectations, Italy, hosting a World Cup in what was so clearly the hub of world football, was not simply expected to win by their hopeful nation. The feeling was more one of a near certainty, an assumption: World Cup victory was considered almost inevitable.

Italy's squad, as glamorous a collection of players as you could hope to see, provided a significant weight of evidence to this assertion with a phenomenal depth of talent. The defensive line had evolved from the traditional man-marking approach into a hybrid between that and the more zonal system favoured by Arrigo Sacchi at Milan. Ahead of Zenga, now the firm first choice between the Italian posts, were his Inter Milan team-mates, Ferri and Giuseppe Bergomi, with the elegant skills of Franco Baresi as the libero in behind them. Midfield playmaking was the realm of Roma's young star, Giannini, whose suitability was the source of much tournament conjecture. His abilities and range of passing weren't in question so much as his ability to direct the creativity of a team who rarely committed too many numbers forward.

The Milanese influence continued with Carlo Ancelotti and Donadoni, who would thrust forwards from the right-hand side, while the young Paolo Maldini was on the left with a more defensive focus. De Napoli sat in behind, alongside Ancelotti, to provide a solid base. This much of the side was consistent and, a few quibbles over creativity or of the more specific man-marking skills of Pietro Vierchowod aside, was generally agreed as being the ideal line-up. But it was up front where the real questions lay, and where the accusations of Vicini's indecisiveness would manifest themselves.

His two preferred strikers were Vialli and Mancini, the Sampdoria pair who knew each other's game so well, and who had come through Vicini's under-21 squad together. Vialli was the standout world-class striker in Italy as well as a key emotional leader within the team. He had suffered an injury-hampered season with Sampdoria, though, meaning he came into the tournament slightly off his peak. Mancini, having been a key part of the 1988 team, would make the squad in 1990 but wouldn't see a minute of action; the unspoken implication being that he was increasingly seen as an arrogant distraction whose outbursts were the actions of a prima donna, not someone willing to play his role within the squad.

Vicini, though, was not clear on his alternative striking options. Instead of being decisive, he hedged his bets and called up almost everyone. Six forwards in all were chosen for the 1990 squad. He selected the new golden boy of Italian football, Roberto Baggio. Then 23 years old, Baggio arrived at the World Cup amid the furore stirred up by his recent transfer from Fiorentina to Juventus for a world-record £11m fee. Indeed, the Italian pre-tournament training camp at Coverciano, not far from Florence, was besieged by irate Fiorentina fans determined to make known their feelings on Baggio's move. But this was a player with the talent to unlock the tightest of defences, perhaps not as a starter from day one but someone whom Vicini could turn to when needed.

Vicini also picked a target man, the tall and powerful Aldo Serena, for when Italy needed to resort to a dash of pure brawn. Then there was Salvatore 'Toto' Schillaci, fresh from his debut Serie A season with Juventus. While he had done well with the Old Lady, his selection was something of a wild-card choice given his relative inexperience at this level. Yet, while Schillaci's World Cup would lead to development of the myth of him having come from nowhere to be included in the squad as the final choice, his selection was understandable given his form that year, even if he was untried at international level. Schillaci was, after Baggio, the second-highest Italian goalscorer in the league, after all.

The same could not be said of Vicini's final striking selection. Napoli's Andrea Carnevale was something of an odd man out in this company, his abilities a level below his striking colleagues. And yet, when Italy walked out at Rome's Stadio Olimpico for their opening World Cup match against Austria, it was Carnevale who partnered Vialli up front.

The group-stage draw had been kind to Italy. As well as Austria, they would face Czechoslovakia and complete outsiders the United States in what was regarded as an ideal, comfortable opening to the tournament for the hosts.

What is more, with all of their group games to be played in Rome, they had the assurance of a huge and vociferous backing each time they played. The atmosphere sizzled on Italy's opening night; the crowd almost hidden by the sheer volume of Italian flags being vigorously waved. On a stiflingly hot evening, all of Italy hoped for, and indeed expected, a win.

Numerous chances came Italy's way, the players in blue swarming all over their bewildered Austrian opponents. But when it came to adding the final punch, Italy were found wanting. With Baggio left on the bench, it was down to Giannini and Donadoni to act as the team's creative fulcrum, and indeed the build-up play was impressive and incessant. The shots reigned in on the Austrian goal but the neon-clad goalkeeper, Klaus Lindenberger, flung himself from one side to the other, acrobatically saving everything that came his way. Other chances were simply wasted with lacklustre finishing. Vicini would later say that he had picked Carnevale to 'give him confidence', but instead his confidence eroded as each chance came and went and the already edgy atmosphere became increasingly jittery. Carnevale, scooping an easy chance over the bar from close range, wasn't the only one to prove wasteful: Vialli, Ancelotti, Giannini and Donadoni all missed good chances too.

What was meant to be a celebratory evening was now threatening to become a disastrous frustration. With 16 minutes remaining, Vicini turned to the bench where two forwards had been selected – Baggio and Schillaci. With Italy desperate for the breakthrough, surprisingly it was to Schillaci that Vicini turned rather than Baggio.

Schillaci was coming off a successful campaign with Juventus, but that had been his only season in Italy's top flight. Growing up in a tough, poor neighbourhood in Palermo, and having dropped out of school early, he was used to fighting against the odds to succeed. His professional career had begun with Serie B's Messina, and it was only at the age of 24 that he had reached Serie A, making him by some distance the least-experienced member of Italy's squad. He had only made his international debut in March 1990 but he was now entering the cauldron of Italy's opening World Cup match, tasked with scoring the goal to give his nation the deliverance they demanded. He was an instinctive, unpredictable striker. Not for him the slick, delicate touches of some of his colleagues. Schillaci was more about explosive pace and an impulsive instinct for goal.

His first touch in the World Cup, four minutes after coming on, would elevate this outsider to national hero status. Vialli's fantastically vicious cross found Schillaci, rising between two misplaced defenders, to firmly head home. As the net bulged in satisfying relief, Schillaci wheeled away in shock as much as delight, the world catching its first glimpse of the wild eyes that would become the image of this World Cup summer. Schillaci would later admit that he had been utterly terrified coming on, afraid that he, like Carnevale, would miss a key chance and be blamed for Italy's failure to win. As he was mobbed by his delirious team-mates, his relief spread through the whole team, around the stadium and all across the nation as Italy saw out a 1-0 win.

The relief was enhanced by the prospect of a goal fest against the United States in their next group match; a team of semi-professionals in their first World Cup in 40 years who had already been thrashed 5-1 by Czechoslovakia. Against Italy, in the bear pit of Rome, surely it was a case of just how many Italy would score, with no repeat of the late desperation of the Austria match? Indeed, Italy scored early with Giannini, the Prince of Rome as he was named by his adoring Roma fans, scoring after just 13 minutes. But the expected goal glut failed to materialise despite Italy initially looking as though their speed of thought and movement would lead to a comfortable victory.

Italy were frustrated in front of goal but also frustrated by the physicality of the Americans, who hassled and harried their more illustrious opponents throughout, visibly unsettling them. Vialli had the chance to make it 2-0 from the penalty spot but his effort was lacklustre in the extreme. The midfield, too, had seemingly lost its rhythm, the balance affected by the loss of Ancelotti, injured in the Austria game, while any creativity the side was producing was floundering on a blunt, unproductive strike force. It was another 1-0 win but another frustrating one. Qualification for the knockout rounds was now confirmed but Italy were no nearer resolving their issues. Carnevale had again been replaced during the match by Schillaci, though the USA had achieved what no other team would do in this World Cup: preventing Schillaci from scoring.

Carnevale would not appear again in the tournament, while Vialli, too, would drop out of the line-up with a foot injury, albeit one that the medical staff couldn't locate. Against Czechoslovakia in the final group match, Schillaci would make his first competitive start for his country, while alongside him all of Italy was demanding Baggio, whose potential thus far had done little more than provoke debate as he sat unused. And it was Baggio they got.

The world-record price tag and the controversy his move to Juventus had stirred up had seemingly left Vicini feeling that, for all Baggio's talents, he was not yet ready to be unleashed on the World Cup. And yet he was a man whose every touch seemed to provoke something positive, as it had in inspiring Fiorentina's remarkable UEFA Cup run, and whose every goal seemed spectacular in one way or another.

It was a vital match for Italy's hopes, too, needing to win to ensure finishing top of the group and to remain in Rome for the next two rounds. But the presence of both Italy's new hero and Italy's greatest hope in the side made for a more positive night. Giannini was spreading the ball around with assured abandon, while Donadoni's intricate skills were coming increasingly to the fore, his close control and ability to find space leaving his opponents trailing in his wake. Schillaci scored again early on to ease any nerves, heading in a high looping ball following Giannini's mishit shot. The new hero had delivered, but this night would be all about Baggio. He had already gone close more than once in the first half, but this was a mere prelude to what was to come.

Twelve minutes from time, Baggio played a one-two near the halfway line with Giannini before embarking on a gliding, bewitching, direct run, leaving defenders stumbling over themselves in an attempt to read his body movement. It ended when he sent the Czech goalkeeper, Jan Stejskal, the wrong way to score the best goal of the tournament. 'I just kept going and going,' was Baggio's own summation in a *Mundial* magazine interview. 'It was very special.' Italy had been looking for a hero to define their tournament, and now they had two.

For all Schillaci's clinical finishing, it was the Baggio goal that Italy needed the most. It made Italy believe again when belief was waning. Baggio's goal set the tournament alight. This elegant player becoming the symbol of the exuberant flamboyance that was on display in the stands and in the streets, and now on the pitch too, emblematic of the emergent new generation: fresh, exciting and intoxicating.

It had been Italy's best display by far. Following their initial stumbles, Baggio's moment now fuelled the nation's mood and its desire for glory. Where previously the anxiety had seemingly taken hold, now, through Baggio, there was real belief again. It was a belief that could see past the fact that Czechoslovakia had a perfectly valid equaliser ruled out for a non-existent offside. Where the opening games, riddled with nerves, had sown doubt, now confidence and positivity reigned. Through Baggio and Schillaci, Italy could sense their path to victory.

'Italy in delirium with Schillaci – Baggio. How beautiful you are,' hailed *La Gazzetta dello Sport* the next morning, capturing the mood perfectly. Amid this increasing optimism, Italy moved into the knockout rounds, crucially continuing their residency of Rome's Stadio Olimpico.

Uruguay, those tough and, at times, cynical battlers, were the opposition. They came into the match with a limited squad, but a lot of quality up front, led by the languid, elegant playmaker Enzo Francescoli. But neither he nor his colleagues were in particularly impressive form, and were not expected to pose a significant threat to Italy's dominant back line. Indeed, Italy had made it this far without having conceded a goal, and barely even conceding a shot.

There was hope, too, that the attacking issues were resolving themselves by one means or another, as Schillaci and Baggio retained their places following their goalscoring heroics. Uruguay, strangely lethargic, seemed content to try to maintain possession without attempting much by way of attacking; an approach which suited the Italians with their high-energy, slick patterns as De Napoli and Giannini dominated the midfield. There was no panic at the lack of an early goal this time, rather the confidence of a nation in their new heroes maintained the impression that the breakthrough would come soon enough. Baggio had stirred the emotions, the iconic talisman proving to the world what all Italians already knew. While Schillaci, the weight of an expectant nation now resting on his shoulders, provided a comfort, and served to enhance the sense of destiny given his unlikely starring role. Midway through the second half, having only minutes earlier missed a good opportunity, Schillaci scored the best of his six goals in this tournament to once again raise the roof.

It was a goal of stunning simplicity, but one that was brutally explosive. Baggio met Zenga's goal kick with a delicate flick to Serena, recently arrived off the bench, who touched a precise ball through the legs of a Uruguayan defender to Schillaci. Before any opposition players could reach him, he unleashed a ferocious, dipping drive with such speed that it bulged the net barely before anyone had time to register what had happened. It flashed over the outstretched arm of Fernando Alvez, the Uruguayan goalkeeper, then dipped sufficiently to duck under the crossbar. 'It was an instinctive thing,' said Schillaci, as the rapidity of his decision to shoot left Alvez out of position and unable to fully react.

As the net bulged, so too did Schillaci's wild eyes, before he was swamped again by his team-mates. *La Gazzetta dello Sport* the next day would declare, 'Toto, the fable continues.' Through their new hero, Italy were on their way once again. Serena added a second late on, heading in Giannini's crossed free kick on his 30th birthday, to seal the 2-0 victory. The stands of the Stadio Olimpico were mirrored in the streets of Rome once again: a sea of red, white and green and continuous, delirious noise echoing long into the night to hail the Azzurri's serene progress. But where Uruguay had proved a relatively compliant opponent, the team waiting for them in the quarter-final were the polar opposite.

Italy may by now have been on a ten-match run without conceding a goal, but such was their concern at facing Jack Charlton's robust Ireland, and specifically the aerial threat they posed, that Vicini felt obligated to adjust his defence. The unlikely menace of Tony Cascarino, Niall Quinn and John Aldridge meant that Vicini moved Paolo Maldini into the centre of defence for his additional height, with Bergomi also switched to right-back to keep tabs on Kevin Sheedy. Are these the actions of a team supremely confident in their own abilities, particularly defensively? But with the now-familiar names up front, however, such defensive trivialities didn't affect the national optimism.

As noted by Pete Davies in *All Played Out*, as the teams were announced, 'The naming of the new God Schillaci brought forth a boiling surge of apocalyptic noise – the place was beautiful and terrible.' Already raucous, the atmosphere bubbled over into a desperate, agitated state of frenzy. Flags were being waved everywhere, to the extent that the stands appeared to be one amorphous frantic mass of red, white and green, expressing their love and their longing for victory in a wall of colour and noise.

As the game began, however, it appeared that Vicini had been right to be concerned about the power of the unapologetic Irish. Italy were a step quicker and clearly the more comfortable on the ball, but in the early stages of this game it wasn't Italy who created the best opportunities. In fact, Quinn came closest of all to opening the scoring with a towering header towards the top corner, only to see Zenga leap across goal at an unlikely altitude to grab the ball, clutching it safely to his body as he crashed back to Earth.

It was the first significant save that Zenga had been forced to make since the USA game. Amid this frenzy, it left both the stadium and the nation screaming in agony as one.

Quality won out on the day, however. Having gone close through a Maldini header, and then seeing a Baggio effort ruled out for offside, Italy's new hero delivered once again. In a tournament of fine margins, this match was decided by a slice of fortune and another dose of Sicilian precision. The ball was pinged beautifully between Giannini and Baggio, the beating hearts of Italian creativity, before being played through to Donadoni, back in the side following an injury lay-off. His stinging shot was only parried by a stumbling Pat Bonner, whose misfortune was Italy's joy.

The ball fell straight to the eager feet of Schillaci who threaded a shot between Bonner and the scrambling defenders and into the far corner of the net. It was a fortunate goal, but they all count just the same. The familiar sight of Schillaci's wild celebrations followed as the rejoicing roar reverberated around a relieved nation. What did not follow, however, were any further goals. Schillaci came the closest, firing a free kick off the underside of the bar, only to see it bounce clear. Another Schillaci strike was incorrectly ruled out for offside late on. But no matter, the Italian bandwagon rolled relentlessly on towards their apparent destiny.

And yet Ireland had clearly rattled the Italians, having nullified their threat for long periods. Vicini's substitutions tell their own tale: the creativity of Giannini and Baggio replaced by the more defensive Ancelotti, returning from injury, and the physical Serena, respectively. Italy had scrapped their way to victory, relying on the scoring instincts of Schillaci to see them through. And therein lay the biggest fear for the Azzurri. While the press were hailing Schillaci as the new Paolo Rossi – in homage to the exploits of the hero who came in from the cold to take Italy to the 1982 World Cup – and delighting in his ability to deliver, the reliance on him was becoming worryingly apparent.

'Please don't wake me up' was the headline in *La Gazzetta dello Sport* following Schillaci's latest decisive intervention. The view that he could do no wrong was becoming entrenched. The outsider, the last striker in the initial pecking order, had now become indispensable. There was no longer any debate about which striker should be playing: Schillaci was undroppable and untouchable. But his presence had caused an adjustment in the balance of the team, altering the focus of an attack that had been developed over the preceding years.

While he was scoring, there was surely no issue with this. After all, banking on an in-form striker is a perfectly reasonable thing to do. As the goals kept raining in, as Schillaci kept on saving the day, why worry about it? Vicini's original plans had laid out a variety of routes to goal and methods of approach play. Through Giannini and now Baggio, there ought to be sufficient guile to carve out numerous opportunities for those at the sharp end of the attack, and with the more subtle and adaptable skills of Vialli and Mancini, Italy would have had the strikers to best suit this approach. But as Schillaci's goals became the dominant feature, so the play adjusted to suit his style almost to a fault. This was fine while the goals lasted, but what if they didn't?

These narrow victories were only an occasional twist of fate or bounce of the ball away from going the other way and leaving Italy in a fight for their life. What if they faced a side with the ability to fight back from a narrow Italian lead? What if they faced a side with a talisman of their own and a coach who knew how to get more from his team than the talents available should dictate? While the euphoria resonated from the quarter-final through to the midweek semi-final, optimism was still everywhere in Italy, but was now tinged with something else. If there was a nagging doubt about the reliance on Schillaci, there was a real fear about who they faced next: Diego Maradona.

It wasn't necessarily that they must now face the defending champions Argentina that was the concern as such. After all, when Argentina had eliminated Brazil in the round of 16, all of Italy rejoiced at the removal of a tricky potential semi-final opponent. That Argentina then clung on to a goalless draw and snuck past Yugoslavia on penalties in the quarter-final merely served to reinforce the view that they were no huge threat to the destiny Italy still felt was theirs. And it wasn't that Maradona, who had dominated their 1986 tournament victory so completely, was at anything approaching his best. It also wasn't specifically that they were leaving the security and familiarity of Rome's Stadio Olimpico for the first time in the tournament to play the semi-final in Naples.

But add these factors together, and Italy began to feel the nerves as the watching nation became increasingly terrified. That they were not simply facing Maradona, but were facing Maradona in his adopted home, his Naples, would give the diminutive genius all the opportunity he needed to stoke the flames ahead of the semi-final.

'The Italians are asking Neapolitans to be Italian for a day,' he declared in the days before the game. 'Yet for the other 364 days of a year, they forget all about Naples. The people do not forget this.' On the eve of the match, he went even further in quotes carried in *La Gazzetta dello Sport*, 'The only thing I don't like is that now everyone's asking Naples to feel Italian. But for the rest of Italy,

Naples has always been forgotten, and been slapped in the face.'

This was no mere rabble-rousing ahead of a crucial match. Maradona had embraced Naples and its people like no other: he knew them, he understood them, he was one of them. Far beyond inspiring Napoli to their only two Italian titles in 1987 and again in 1990, he had become a part of the very soul of the city and its people, and they loved him unconditionally. And what is more, the comments he made were exposing a brutal truth. The anxious Italian nation knew deep down that Diego was right. He declared, 'Naples is not Italy,' encapsulating the north-south divide, and the way its people were treated by a nation that permanently looked down on them. He knew just how to disrupt Italy's wave of euphoria and patriotism.

Italy had grown used to their home comforts playing in Rome. The familiarity bred throughout the tournament thus far had added to the team's belief. It was their house, their arena, and the Roman crowd were unfailingly enthusiastic, providing that additional surge of energy, confidence and colour. Even the team's journey from their nearby base to the Rome stadium was always lined with well-wishers shouting their support. But now, they were making the journey to Naples instead, and the contrast was unsettling to the Azzurri. Where earlier in the tournament the Neapolitan streets had been full of Italian flags, on the day of the semi-final there were significantly fewer. Maradona may not have caused his adopted home to cheer for Argentina instead of Italy, but in reverence to their hero their support was a less intrusive one, almost a more even-handed one. The contrast to the fervour and infernal intensity of Rome was stark, and the Argentinians would feed on the increasing Italian insecurity.

A sign in the stands that night read 'Italia nei cori, Diego nei cuori', meaning 'Italy in our songs, Diego in our hearts'. The crowd wasn't solely Neapolitan, of course, and the Italians from elsewhere gave Argentina and Maradona the treatment they'd become used to in Italy. Their anthem was booed, but less vociferously as had been the case elsewhere. Maradona visibly bristled at this, adding more fuel to his fire, but it was clearly not as brutally partisan as before. Maradona's Neapolitans were clearly conflicted, leading to a more muted, more surreal atmosphere.

For Italy, nerves may have abounded but this was tempered by the fact that this was not a vintage Argentina side they were facing. Argentina had battled and bruised their way to the semi-final, losing several players to suspension as they went, and lacked the quality that had helped them to glory in 1986. Italian anxiety was not eased by the fact that Vicini decided this was the night to break up the Schillaci-Baggio partnership, with the return of Vialli to the starting line-up. He jettisoned the explosive exuberance of Baggio; a return to the experienced over the raw but spectacular. But it was a move that broke the dynamic that had brought Italy this far.

Vialli had been Vicini's original first choice. His tournament had begun under the shadow of injury, and had then seen him usurped by the new hero, Schillaci. His penalty miss against the United States had encapsulated Vialli's tournament: opportunity presenting itself but not taken. The furore surrounding the mysterious injury that had kept him out of action ever since added to the sense of disappointment. But there was always that feeling that he may just come good if given the opportunity again. Class is permanent after all. In the furnace of a semi-final, with the hopes of an expectant nation at stake, he would get that chance. With Schillaci undroppable, the fact that Baggio had to make way was a source of great angst to the Italians: a turn away from the new, young dynamism that had energised both team and fans.

As poor as Argentina had been up to this point, they began the semi-final positively, Jorge Burruchaga forcing an early save. They were getting stuck in too: there were five free kicks in the first few minutes as Argentina sought to disrupt from the off. But it was Italy who would make the early breakthrough. Only 17 minutes were on the clock when the tension was eased in a now-familiar manner following Italy's first attacking play of any real note. Schillaci had begun the move, feeding Giannini who surged into the box in a bustling, slightly maniacal manner. He lifted the ball over a defender and headed it to Vialli who fired off a powerful shot. Sergio Goycochea in Argentina's goal was, like Schillaci, an unlikely star of the tournament. He was a match for Vialli's effort but could only parry the ball back into play where it fell to Schillaci.

One instinctive swing of his right leg later, Italy were in front. He connected with the ball halfway up his shin, but his scuffed effort still rippled the net. It was a fortunate finish to a fine move, but there was a feeling of inevitability about it. Schillaci had delivered once more, and surely, even at this early stage, Italy were on course for victory. Argentina were a level below the Italians and their unbreachable defence. How could they possibly muster the guile to fight their way back from such an early setback?

Italy, though, seemed caught in two minds – to stick or to twist – and became hindered by their indecision as anxiety spread. For Argentina, there was no such issue. They made an attacking adjustment at half-time, yet the sense remained that the security provided by the best defence in the tournament would see Italy through. But if there was ever a sight to terrify the Italians, it was a rejuvenated Maradona beginning to have more of an effect on the match. Vicini's pre-match plan for the Argentine maestro had been for either Bergomi or Ferri to pick him up depending on whose zone he moved into, rather than instruct either to man-mark him. Ostensibly, this was an understandable approach, as the understanding between his two centre-backs had served the side well so far and Maradona was a shadow of the player he had been. For this reason, Vicini ignored the vociferous calls for him to pick Vierchowod, a man-marking stalwart, specifically to deal with Maradona's threat.

But it became increasingly apparent that this plan was not working. Maradona was frightening the Italian defence with the mere prospect of having to take him on one-on-one. De Napoli was dropping further back to provide additional defensive support, while Maradona was increasingly exploiting the spaces. The growing air of tension soon turned into outright panic. Midway through the second half, all of Italy's nightmares began to come true as Maradona eluded his many markers to play in Julio Olarticoechea down the left-hand side of Argentina's attack. His cross looped towards the edge of the six-yard box, where Claudio Caniggia leapt to reach a ball he seemingly had no right to win, marginally ahead of Ferri.

Crucially, Zenga had come charging out, assuming Caniggia was unlikely to reach it, aiming to mop up the imminent danger. Indeed, Caniggia barely made contact with the ball, but his gentle nudge was all it took. This flick of his golden locks was sufficient to divert the ball beyond Zenga's outstretched hands to nestle in the back of the Italian net.

As Caniggia was mobbed in Argentinian delight, the TV cameras showing the replay focused in on Maradona trotting through the goalmouth, arms raised in triumph, his mouth wide open in joy and celebration. In the background, the Italian players look bemused, stunned and devastated. Much like the watching nation.

Belief began to drain from players and supporters alike, as though it had only been a brittle belief all along, and now the puncture inflicted by Argentina threatened to become a rupture. Zenga's aura of invincibility drained away too. So imperious and indomitable up to now, the mask had slipped, exposing a reality far frailer than the Italian fans had imagined.

The recriminations later in the day would focus on the fact that the Italians had failed to capitalise on a more dominant opening period, and that an air of complacency set in given the solidity of their defence. But as Argentina improved, Italy, missing the influence of the partially fit Ancelotti, left on the bench in the semi-final, sat deeper and deeper and the moment, when it came, had been building. Having been pegged back, Italy failed to rouse themselves sufficiently in the remaining minutes of normal time. Vicini belatedly brought Baggio on, hoping the new starlet's skills could find a way to drag Italy back on track. But in doing so, he removed Giannini, blunting another aspect of Italy's attack.

In also replacing Vialli with Serena, there was the indication that the plan B of brute strength was being called for. Two plans in one, effectively, and neither of them worked as Italy failed to regain the lead in either the remainder of normal time or the resultant extra time. Baggio came the closest, forcing Goycochea into a magnificent save from a near perfect free kick, but as Argentina dug in and played for penalties there became an inevitability about how this game would be decided.

There would be no Schillaci on the list of five penalty takers for Italy, however. The man with the golden touch in front of goal had strained a groin muscle late in the game. Better, he felt, to let someone in a better condition take one. Those who did step up were facing an opponent in Goycochea who had already performed penalty heroics in Argentina's quarter-final shoot-out victory over Yugoslavia. His confidence was high, while the Italians had the jitters. Nevertheless, Baresi, Baggio and De Agostini all held their nerve to score with Italy's first three well-taken efforts. So too did the first three Argentinians.

Donadoni, that elegant, curly-haired font of creativity, was the next to take the lonely walk for Italy. While he was far from the first to look like the nerves were crushing his belief, he was the first to suffer the ignominy of missing. His side-footed shot wasn't far enough into the corner – a sure sign of someone shooting without confidence, not wanting to risk aiming for the corner and missing – and Goycochea flew to his left to save. Donadoni sunk to the floor and briefly buried his head in his hands, the despair felt by millions of Italians etched in the agony on his face.

And then came Maradona. It had to be Maradona. With Italy teetering on the brink, he seized the dagger that Goycochea had already plunged into Italian hearts and twisted it, leaving all of Italy clinging on to their faint hopes of survival. He stepped up and rolled the ball slowly, nonchalantly into the net, fooling Zenga into diving the wrong way. It wasn't yet the fatal wound to Italy's hopes, but it felt like it.

When Aldo Serena then took Italy's fifth and final kick, his nerves betrayed a desperate nation who could see the fading of the light, knowing the *coup de grâce* was about to be delivered in this gladiatorial arena. The weight of a nation's hopes and dreams sitting squarely on his shoulders caused Serena's legs to turn to jelly on his long walk to the penalty spot. He struck it firmly enough, but as with Donadoni, it lacked the real conviction that true confidence would have brought.

Serena was a seasoned goalscorer – indeed, he was Serie A top scorer only a year previously – but this was another matter. He would later reveal that he had not wanted to take a penalty, but his hand had been forced by Vicini as nobody else had volunteered. Serena's shot was always too close to Goycochea, who almost landed on top of the ball, his delight at the saveable penalty, heading his way as he dived, apparent on his face. He blocked the ball with ease, snuffing out any lingering Italian dreams. 'The world just collapsed around me,' said Serena, and with it so did Italy's apparent destiny.

All of Italy cried with Serena, Donadoni and the rest. The trauma of Naples, the accursed Diego in his home, the lost opportunity to see out their destiny back in Rome against the West Germans would leave scars that would linger and last. Confidence and certainty destroyed, replaced by emptiness and doubt. Once the players had mustered the energy to leave the field, they sat in silence in the dressing room for some time. A few cried, all were forlorn.

In the media the next day, there were numerous headlines along the lines of 'End of a Dream', while *La Gazzetta dello Sport* simply emblazoned its front page with the word 'NO'. Having enjoyed the ride for weeks when victory had seemed inevitable, the heartbreaking sense of loss was all the harder to take. But while Argentina had raised their game and shown there was more to them than most observers had thought, putting in their best performance of the tournament, so Italy had been exposed for being less than we had all thought.

When the cracks appeared, the belief had seeped away with Caniggia's goal, and the crushing weight of expectation proved too heavy a burden. Donadoni seemed to embody this, as Richard Hall noted, 'Look at his face as he's playing in the rest of this tournament and he's so full of life, full of confidence. And after the goal, and not just at the penalty, everything just drains out of him. By the time it gets to his penalty he looks ill. That Caniggia goal made everyone go, "Oh, okay, maybe this isn't going to be the perfect story." It's almost like in that moment they became fallible.'

Where home advantage had initially spurred the Azzurri on, seeing them through on a surge of emotion, now the opposing edge of that particular sword left Italy unable to rouse themselves, unable to prevent their dreams being stolen away by a master craftsman. When the place in the final was on the line, Argentina were guided by a manager who had been there and done it before. Carlos Bilardo was one of the world's finest, having steered Argentina to victory in 1986. In contrast, Vicini had been found out by some of his baffling decisions and not only in this match. His indecision regarding Italy's attacking options hampered the team throughout the tournament, and doubly so in this match.

Further evidence of his lack of strong leadership and understanding of how to get the best from his squad can be seen when looking ahead to the failed Euro '92 qualifying campaign following this World Cup. That disappointment made it appear the successes of 1990 had come along by fluke, rather than any considered plan. When things came right for Vicini, he just stuck with it before seemingly panicking when the semi-final came along, reverting away from his winning formula and back to an indecisive, ill-thought-out hybrid.

In Euro '92 qualifying Italy lost out to the USSR, who had been abject in 1990 and were very much on the decline, and also to a Norway team on the rise. The sheer quality of the Italian players should have led to a strong showing, but Vicini's plans seemed to exacerbate the fallout from 1990, whose shadow was cast long. For the key protagonists of 1990, the hangover took years to get over, 1992 almost being sacrificed as a result. Following the emotional highs and ultimate lows of 1990, there was almost bound to be a drop-off, the exhilaration and despair of that summer making it impossible to lift themselves. Perhaps the squad should have been refreshed to mitigate this, or perhaps a new coach should have been brought in to give a new direction and make a fresh start?

On the playing side, the two players who suffered most following the dramatic semi-final were Zenga and Maradona. The Argentinian captain was effectively run out of Italy after that summer, surviving one more season at Napoli but doing so under a cloud, with the way the authorities and the Italian public looked at him completely changing following the World Cup.

For Zenga, that one mistake leading to Caniggia's goal came to define his career, so much so that he is still suffering for it. He should be remembered as one of the best goalkeepers of his generation, but instead he is vilified, despite not conceding until that game. 'Whenever I talk to Italians about this World Cup, it's always about Zenga,' noted Richard Hall. 'The penalty takers who missed don't get this grief. Of anyone, he would love to live that moment again and change what he did.'

That we never got to see the two best teams of the tournament, Italy and West Germany, face each other was a major disappointment. There had been an omnipresent rumble in the background, this apparent certainty that to win the tournament, the Germans had to be overcome. It had all seemed so inevitable that this great clash of the titans would decide the fate of the golden trophy. For the Italians, their lingering presence in the other half of the draw was an ever-present fear, but also an enticing finale to their home party. To overcome the Germans back in Rome would justify and validate the perceived procession to Italian glory that the whole nation yearned for, and had expected.

To those of us watching, the disappointment is that we were denied what could have been a great final and instead were served up arguably the worst in World Cup history. That an immeasurably disappointing team in Argentina had denied Italy left a sour taste, as did the dawning reality that it should never have come to that. Italy shouldn't have allowed themselves to be dumped out by Diego and his motley crew. That they did was a sad lament not only for them, but for football in general. As Pete Davies put it in *All Played Out*, 'For non-Italians it was depressing as hell. A beauty of a team had failed, and an ugly dog of a team had gone through.'

For Italians, multiply this a thousandfold. Italy was the centre of the footballing world in 1990: for this tournament, for the eminence of its game, the dominance of its league, and the sophistication of its play. It was meant to be their tournament, their coronation, their destiny. They were the right team in the right place at the right time, but with the wrong result.

It's easy to look back with nostalgic eyes, but there were many cracks below the surface: the development of large stadia in unnecessary locations such as Bari, creating soulless, unloved arenas such as Turin's Stadio Delle Alpi at great expense, or the haphazard preparations and organisation. 'It's so frustrating for Italians,' added Richard Hall, 'because on the face of it, it looked perfect. None of these cracks showed during the tournament. Everything seemed to come off, everything felt right, and they felt lucky. Italia '90 captures everything that you love about Italian football. It had this amazing, beautiful look to it, but underneath it's just absolutely rotten.'

And yet Schillaci and Baggio had made believers of us all, only for it all to end amid the tears and trauma of Naples. For Schillaci, small consolation came with the tournament's Golden Boot, secured with a penalty – oh, the irony – against England in the third-place play-off, but his moment in the sun was soon done. Having scored six times in that Italian summer, he only ever struck once more for his country, his star having shone so brightly but briefly on those *notti magiche*.

It has been described in the host country as an impossible failure: a great generation of Italian players would never lift the golden trophy. It would be denied them in even more painful circumstances four years later when, in the Pasadena sunshine, Baresi and Baggio both missed in the penalty shoot-out in the final itself. They came closer to gaining World Cup glory in 1994 off the back of Baggio's bewitching brilliance, almost single-handedly dragging an incoherent Italy to the final. That was a closer brush with glory certainly, but the sheer overwhelming intensity of Italy in 1990 remains a more captivating story of expectancy and dreams destroyed. That is a feeling echoed in Italy too.

Because it was at home, because Italian football was on such a high, and because they were carried along on a magnificent ride, even now Italia '90 remains huge in Italy. Not only did they ride the wave of emotion, fuelled by Schillaci's unlikely exploits, towards their destiny, but it also saw Baggio become a nation's idol thanks to that amazing goal. For all Baggio did in 1994, it is that moment in 1990 that is looked back on most fondly, all feeding the nostalgic allure.

'They do put that team on a pedestal,' explained Richard Hall, 'because realistically, if Zenga doesn't come for that ball, if that moment doesn't happen, anyone [Italian] I speak to, Italy wins that World Cup. Maybe that euphoria gets them over the line.' We'll never know, of course, but it would have been a compelling final. West Germany were strong but the more captivating story was the Italian one. It was their tournament in their home, and the painful manner in which the expected coronation was wrenched from them cut deep, and ruined the narrative that had seemed set for so many.

This World Cup was meant to be theirs, one that they had seemingly been anointed for, one that all of Italy had firmly believed was a given amid the rising delirium. When the fickle hands of fate decreed otherwise, Italian destiny was cruelly denied and the finale to the World Cup of 1990 was all the poorer as a result. Those magical nights of the Italian summer had captured us perhaps more on an emotional level than an aesthetic one, but the Azzurri, in a gloriously exuberant drama, enchanted so many as they carried us along their doomed path towards that beautifully tragic conclusion.

10

Yugoslavia 1994

The team were far better than the country.

Ivica Osim

'LOTS OF people have been killed. The country was destroyed. Sometimes there are things more important than football.'

These were the words of the Yugoslav national team coach Ivica Osim reflecting on a country descending into tragedy and chaos. Against that backdrop, Yugoslavia's banishment from the 1992 European Championship and the subsequent World Cup in 1994 are indeed trivial matters. But the team that was denied their opportunity as a result would arguably have been one of the finest international teams of the decade, with a spectacularly talented generation capable of challenging the very best.

This is perhaps stretching the concept of teams that could or should have won the World Cup somewhat. It is the ultimate 'what if', however, for a team described in gushing tones even though it never got to reach its peak, leaving potential unfulfilled. This reimagined sporting history can't ignore the fact that it also requires a reimagined political history, one that sees the country still existing in some form. We have to close our eyes and, discounting the brutal, tragic realities of what the former Yugoslavia had become in 1994, visualise what could have been one of the world's greatest football teams: one, sadly, that never existed.

Such an alternate view of football history could have focused on a hypothetical England in the pre-war World Cups, or in 1958, had the Munich disaster not robbed them of Duncan Edwards and reduced the impact of Bobby Charlton. Another could have been Italy in 1950 without the Superga disaster claiming the lives of *Il Grande Torino*. Compelling tales in their own ways, but lacking the resonance that recency provides.

Equally, the 1994 World Cup threw up several other hard-luck stories of teams who were expected to perform well only to fail, or who came close to glory. There was the Colombia side who qualified so spectacularly and were hailed as potential winners by Pelé, only for various pressures to cause an implosion during the World Cup and genuine tragedy in the aftermath. There was the intoxicating tale from eastern Europe of a hugely exciting Romania team which narrowly missed the semi-finals, and there were great stories with Nigeria, Bulgaria and Sweden. And then there was Italy.

No other country at that time had lost a World Cup Final in a penalty shoot-out, and when Roberto Baggio missed that fateful kick to hand the World Cup to Brazil, a real 'what if' moment was cast in stone. The Italy team of 1994 had several fascinating subplots and were dragged to the final by the genius of Baggio. They were not a great team, though, exceeding expectations to some extent given the calamitous nature of their tournament at times.

Baggio and Baresi will have been left bereft and unfulfilled certainly, but the team overall? Not really. And nothing like the unfulfilled potential of Yugoslavia.

The Yugoslavia side of the 1990s that never was has been described as the greatest team the world never had. Just how true that is, is impossible to judge. Unlike other teams featured in this book, there was no footballing misfortune which denied this team its tilt at greatness, no moment when defeat was plucked from the jaws of victory. But there was an emerging array of talent that sat among the finest in the world, which makes the speculation, as unreal as it unfortunately has to be, all the more compelling.

In stark contrast to the country as a whole, as the 1990s began, Yugoslav football was reaching an all-time high. Red Star Belgrade were at the pinnacle of the European club game with a team featuring players from across the Yugoslav federation, while the national team was backing up its strong performance at the 1990 World Cup with an impressive qualification for the 1992 European Championship.

It was a sporting rise built on solid foundations, with many of the key protagonists having progressed through the national youth-level teams together, culminating in winning the 1987 World Youth Championship. The names reel off the tongue as a who's who of footballing excellence: Stojković, Savićević, Prosinečki, Boban, Šuker, Katanec, Mihajlović, Mijatović, Jarni, Bokšić. That another superlative description of this generation hailed them as the Brazilians of Europe tells its own story; this was a collection of breathtaking ability, the majority with youth on their side. But Yugoslavia was a crumbling country, whose foundations were proving anything but solid, as old fractures began to rupture in devastating style.

The seeds of the nation's downfall had been a long time coming, and can be traced back to the death of Yugoslav president Josip Broz Tito in 1980; a moment which could be viewed with the benefit of hindsight as the beginning of the end for Yugoslavia. Economic and political crises followed in the 1980s and, with the glue that had held the multi-ethnic nation together now gone, the fragile collaboration of states increasingly showed the strain: historic divisions that had always been there coming to the foreground again. What was becoming an inevitable collapse was exacerbated when Slobodan Milošević took power in 1989 and resentment at Serbian control grew.

As the pieces were falling into place for the devastating war that was to come, Yugoslav sport was in the midst of a golden age. In basketball, Yugoslavia's other most popular sport, another great generation was achieving success internationally, with several players making the move to the NBA in the USA. Water polo success was almost a given, as were the exploits of Monica Seles in tennis. Football was no exception to this roll of honour.

There is a rich history of national team success, in reaching the latter stages of tournaments at least. Twice Yugoslavia had been European Championship runners-up, in 1960 and 1968, coming tantalisingly close to victory on both occasions, while they had twice finished fourth at the World Cup in the dim and distant past of 1930 and 1962. Never less than technically excellent, the national team through the 1980s was not of the same quality, however, and had struggled. A poor World Cup in 1982 was followed by an abject performance at the 1984 European Championship as the team were brutally taken apart. The presence of a teenage Dragan Stojković in that squad was a first glimpse of what was to come, with the player destined to be one of the greatest ever to emerge from Yugoslavia soon joined by a host of similarly talented young players.

Stojković, a highly skilful attacking midfielder with an elegance of vision and technique, may have already been fast-tracked to the senior team, but those players two or three years younger than him were about to reach international glory at youth level. The team which travelled to Chile for the 1987 World Youth Championship contained many players who would become central to the last Yugoslavia teams, and, indeed, to the national teams of the nations who emerged from the eventual break-up.

Yugoslavia didn't even send their strongest team available, with the captain, Aleksandar Đorđević, banned for four matches having been sent off in the final qualifier, and so not selected. At least four possible starting players were injured, while three others – Siniša Mihajlović, Vladimir Jugović and Alen Bokšić – were also left at home, the federation deciding they would gain more in terms of development by staying with their clubs and playing league football. As a result, expectations were low, although the squad list still contained several players destined for successful senior careers. In defence, there was Branko Brnović, Robert Jarni, Igor Štimac and Goran Petrić. The midfield could boast Zvonimir Boban and Robert Prosinečki, while up front was equally impressive with Predrag Mijatović and Davor Šuker.

Yugoslavia won their group with ease, with a style of play so fluid and effective that belief increased with each impressive performance. Prior to the quarter-final with Brazil, Red Star tried to prize Prosinečki, their teenage star, back home to play for his club in a UEFA Cup tie, only for a player protest and an intervention from FIFA supremo João Havelange to keep him at the tournament. He responded in the best way possible, scoring a last-minute winner with a fine curling free kick, hit into the top corner with barely a run-up, to beat the Brazilians. It would later be voted the goal of the tournament. Prosinečki would become the undisputed star of the tournament, with his ability to see opportunities and space that others couldn't, and the composure under pressure that comes with ease to the game's greats, elevating him above the crowd.

'It was a turning point for all of us,' recalled Mijatović in a documentary about this team, of this hugely impressive come-from-behind victory. Mijatović had earlier scored Yugoslavia's equaliser with a delightful header from a Boban free kick, but it was Prosinečki's exquisite winner that prompted the delirious celebrations which followed this quarter-final success. East Germany were then beaten 2-1 in the semi-final, before an assured performance in the final against West Germany saw Yugoslavia ultimately prevail on penalties despite missing both Prosinečki and Mijatović through suspension. Boban had scored in the match and then despatched the decisive penalty to hand Yugoslavia a world title that nobody had expected at the outset.

History has lent an air of myth about this 1987 youth team given what the future had in store for Yugoslavia, but while it is easy to get carried away with what they may have been able to achieve as senior internationals, it is clear that the eulogising is largely justified. They played with a technical elegance and creative sophistication that was beyond their ages. Prosinečki edged out Boban to the player of the tournament award, with Šuker as top scorer. It was a roll of honour that told the clear story of this success. Yugoslavia were dominant, a cut above the rest, and surely destined for greatness. Indeed, the core of this team would remain at the top of the European game for much of the mid to late 1990s.

That they had unearthed a generation of such talent was cause for great optimism, particularly when set against what the senior national team were doing at the same time. Just 17 days after the trophy had been lifted in Chile, the full national team were ripped apart by England, suffering a 4-1 drubbing in Belgrade in a European qualifier. The time for the new generation to come through and mix with the more established players was at hand.

Coach Osim began the 1990 World Cup qualifiers with a core of experienced players, but gradually the youngsters were given their chance. Even taking into account the unofficial squad quotas, which Osim dutifully adhered to, discreetly ensuring representation from all republics in the national team, the talent was sufficiently spread around as to lessen the impact of such censure. Prosinečki, Šuker and Boban were the most prominent of the newcomers, but there was opportunity, too, for the likes of Bokšić, Brnović, Jarni and Mijatović.

Adding this new generation to what was a strong, if underperforming, core, enabled Yugoslavia to qualify with ease. The beguiling Stojković was the inspiration, naturally, but the experience was also provided by the likes of Dejan Savićević, Darko Pančev, Srečko Katanec and the veterans Zlatko Vujović and Safet Sušić. The creative and attacking talent is astounding when listed out, and from the moment that Stojković scored a late winner to beat France towards the end of 1988, Yugoslavia dominated their qualifying group.

While World Cup qualification was assured, the country was becoming increasingly embroiled in national tensions. Just a month before the World Cup, when Dinamo Zagreb hosted Red Star Belgrade in May 1990, the political landscape was deeply volatile. Played just weeks ahead of Croatia's first multi-party elections in more than 50 years, as was also the case in the other Yugoslav states, the tinderbox only required a small spark to ignite. With nationalism on the rise, urged on by long-standing ethnic and religious divisions, many in Croatia favoured independence. The visit of Red Star and their hooligan element, strong supporters of Serbian nationalism, made a clash with their Croatian counterparts almost inevitable.

While there were many skirmishes around the stadium, it escalated into a riot once inside. The occasion is most famous for a kick by Boban, Dinamo captain at the time, at a policeman who had been dishing out some heavy punishment to a Dinamo fan. While the legend of the kick that started a war isn't accurate, the moment served as a symbol of Croatian defiance and of the desire to fight for independence from Serbian domination. 'Here I was, a public figure prepared to risk his life, career, and everything that fame could have brought, for one ideal, one cause: the Croatian cause,' was Boban's poetic explanation. It was a moment that would cost Boban any hope of going to the 1990 World Cup.

Just three weeks later, Yugoslavia played their final preparatory friendly ahead of the World Cup in that same Stadion Maksimir in Zagreb against the Netherlands. The Yugoslav anthem was booed by the crowd: the team representing a dying entity in a city and republic in which the calls for independence were the most vociferous. This was far from a positive send-off to the World Cup from their home crowd, many of whom openly supported the Dutch throughout. Yugoslavia had become a place that many were not happy to belong to, and weren't represented by.

Given this backdrop, perhaps it is little wonder that, once in Italy, Yugoslavia's World Cup began with a heavy defeat to the champions-in-waiting, West Germany. But in beating Colombia and the United Arab Emirates, Yugoslavia secured progress from the group with a style of elegantly technical football that began to show what they were capable of. This set up a clash with Spain in the first knockout round where the whole team put in a sensational performance, and the individual display from Stojković marking him out as a true star of the World Cup.

Osim would describe the victory over Spain as the best of his time in charge of Yugoslavia. Stojković scored two fabulous goals, the first of which displayed the exquisite touch and technique which would earn him a move to Marseille soon after. Controlling a flicked-on cross with such poise and sufficient disguise to fool an onrushing Spanish defender who slid right past him, Stojković then fired into the far corner. His second was wondrous too: a cleverly bent free kick around the Spanish wall to send Yugoslavia to the quarter-finals. It was an emergence on to the world stage of a strong collective spirit in contrast to the chaos at home, producing a harmonious and stylish football team, with more than a dash of star quality at its peak.

As if to emphasise the turmoil back home, Yugoslavia would have to face Argentina in the quarter-final without the influential Katanec. A Slovenian with a Croatian mother, Katanec had received threats that if he played his family would be harmed. Yugoslavia dominated throughout, in spite of playing the vast majority of the match, including extra time, a man down following a first-half red card for defender Refik Šabanadžović. The numerical handicap was barely noticeable as Yugoslavia's remaining players outplayed their illustrious counterparts.

Prosinečki, described in Brian Glanville's *The Story of the World Cup* as, 'splendidly creative in midfield' and the 'heir apparent' to Stojković, dovetailed majestically with his more senior team-mate, making Yugoslavia's numerical disadvantage appear immaterial. While the opportunities were more fleeting following the red card, they still led Argentina on a merry dance with their slick dominance of the ball in midfield, still probed effectively on the wings, still made the South Americans dance to their tune.

This makes it easy to argue that Argentina were only able to contain their clearly superior opponents thanks to their advantage in manpower. A full Yugoslav complement would surely have made the breakthrough in either normal or extra time, something that Argentina barely threatened to do at any stage. 'If you can play like that with ten men against Argentina, of course you are able to do more,' was Stojković's assessment in an interview with the website *In Bed With Maradona*. To then lose the penalty shoot-out despite Argentina missing two of their kicks, Maradona included, is a bitter pill to swallow. That Stojković set the tone in missing the first penalty was deeply unfortunate for a player who had made such an impact on the tournament.

As fondly as some recall the 1990 side in the former Yugoslavia, there is also the feeling that their ultimate defeat was representative of a pattern. 'Yugoslav football was mostly about getting close to achieving amazing stuff, but still failing,' Serbian journalist Nebojša Marković explained to me, citing those past World Cup and European Championship near misses, multiple lost Olympic finals and close calls for Yugoslav clubs in Europe.

And yet Yugoslavia were clearly a team on the rise, even as the country was in freefall. With many of the emerging generation awaiting their opportunity on the fringes of the team – the explosive attacking talents of Pančev and Savićević were largely frustrated at their limited opportunities in Italy – and others still yet to progress to the senior ranks, there was a squad poised to make significant inroads in the coming tournaments. Youth hadn't been given enough of a chance in 1990, but all would have been central come 1992 or 1994. What greatness may await them down the line?

This new-found confidence and assurance, gained from what ought to have been a semi-final appearance in 1990, was mirrored at club level too. While the country continued on its path to destruction, the Yugoslav First League survived the impact of Boban's boot to play another full season in 1990/91. Again, it was won by Red Star in what was a very strong league featuring the best of the six republics. At this final peak of Yugoslav football, as if scaling the heights before the inevitable imminent plummet, Red Star, with their team containing players from across the various republics, achieved the finest success in their history. In winning the 1991 European Cup they finally reversed the trend of ultimate tournament disappointment for Yugoslav football.

If their performance in the final itself was distinctly underwhelming, beating Marseille on penalties after an insipid, defensive goalless draw, the manner of their progress to the final was stunningly impressive. The semi-final victory over Bayern Munich was the pick of the bunch, following on from comfortable wins over all who had stood in their way in the earlier rounds. A 2-1 first-leg victory in Munich heralded Red Star's arrival as a real force in European football. With goals coming from Pančev and Savićević, Red Star could boast arguably the most lethal strike force in Europe at the time. Both players would frequently cite the other as the best strike partner they ever played with, complementing each other perfectly.

Pančev was the more clinical finisher of the two, while the explosive guile of Savićević, whose abilities would make him a hero of AC Milan in the coming years, was the perfect accompaniment. Pulling the strings behind them were two players both of mixed Croatian-Serb parentage, one who would become a symbol of Croatian footballing creativity, and the other of Serbian sporting strength. The beguiling flair of Prosinečki made him the elegant schemer in the Red Star midfield, providing the opportunities for the strikers. While much less refined, but equally vital, was the force of nature that was the left-sided midfielder and sometime defender, Siniša Mihajlović. Possessing boundless energy, and a robust presence in the heart of the team, he was also capable of shooting with such force that he would become something of a free-kick expert through his career.

Mihajlović's finest hour came in the return leg of the semi-final with Bayern, when he was key to both of Red Star's goals. The first was a trademark free kick rattled in from distance, while the second provided a last-gasp equaliser to win a tie which had been heading for extra time, when his cross was turned into the net via a heavy deflection from Bayern's Klaus Augenthaler.

Red Star were more defensive in the final against Marseille, which is a shame in many ways, as it is that match which cemented Red Star's international legacy given the wider exposure it brought. Fear of Marseille's counter-attacking ability was the reason for their negative approach on the day, but had they played their more natural game, with the talent at their disposal, victory may well still have come, and in finer style.

Their victory would be the final football act of the Yugoslavia of old. The 1990/91 season was the dying ember of a burnt-out ideal. In September 1990, a match between

Hajduk Split and FK Partizan saw more violence around a clash between a Croatian and Serbian club. Nationalist parties were coming to the fore across all republics, with Bosnia joining the call for independence being loudly heard in Croatia and Slovenia. Serb nationalists, meanwhile, were intent on maintaining a Serbian-dominated Yugoslavia. By the time of Red Star's European Cup success, the country was already at war as the Croatian War of Independence had broken out. On 25 June 1991, both Croatia and Slovenia declared independence, an action that triggered the Ten-Day War on the Slovenian border.

On the football front, the First League played on in 1991/92 but now without clubs from the newly independent Slovenia and Croatia. The Bosnian War would soon mean that Bosnian clubs wouldn't finish the season, with both the Croatian and Bosnia wars lasting for several years. Macedonia broke away soon after, leaving Serbia (including Kosovo and Vojvodina) and Montenegro remaining under the label of Yugoslavia.

The national football team that had begun the qualification process for the 1992 European Championship represented a larger entity than the one which finished the qualifiers. By the time Yugoslavia had secured their place in the finals, they were already shorn of any Slovenian, Croatian, Bosnian or Macedonian players. Katanec was the principal Slovenian player to no longer be available to Yugoslavia, as was Pančev from Macedonia and Hadžibegić from Bosnia, while the list of Croatians who may have been a part of the 1992 squad is a lengthy one: Prosinečki, Boban, Šuker, Jarni, Bokšić, to name just a few.

Even without these players in their final few qualifiers, Yugoslavia secured the top place in their qualifying group ahead of Denmark and were expected to perform well in the tournament in Sweden. They were still led through qualifying by the Bosnian Osim, but he resigned from his position on 23 May 1992, with his family in Sarajevo suffering in the bombardment. 'My country doesn't deserve to play in the European Championship,' he said. 'On the scale of human suffering, I cannot reconcile events at home with my position as national manager.'

One week later, on 30 May, the United Nations passed a resolution imposing sanctions on the combatants in the Yugoslav Wars, including ending participation in sporting events. The European Championship finals were just 11 days away but Yugoslavia would not be taking part. While calls were made to the Danish federation, as runners-up in the qualifying group, to take Yugoslavia's place, other calls were made to the Yugoslavian training camp in Sweden where the players were well into their preparations. One such call was to the captain, Dragan Stojković.

'It was the worst day of my life,' he recalled. 'We had been training, we were already at the hotel in Sweden, and now we had to go home. We had to go back to reality.' While we can wonder at the naivety of Stojković not seeing what was on the cards when it came to Yugoslavia's expulsion, in pure sporting terms it robbed the tournament of what would still have been a very strong side despite the loss of the players from the independent republics. It is far too simplistic to imagine they would have won purely because their replacements, Denmark, actually did go on and win the European title. It's far less of a stretch, though, to imagine that a Yugoslavia which had not been torn apart, and was still the whole it had been in 1990, would have been one of the favourites to win Euro '92. 'Maybe we would have been champions and maybe not,' said Stojković. 'But we would have played a very important role.'

Many in the former Yugoslavia do take this step in imagining victory denied in 1992, given not just Denmark's success but also that of Red Star the year before. Yugoslav participation was close enough to being a reality as to allow people to relate to it. But this was already a vastly different Yugoslavia to the one that had begun the qualifying. This was not the 1990 side with two years of progression under their belts. It was a much-reduced entity. The United Nations sanctions would keep Yugoslavia out of the 1994 World Cup and the 1996 European Championship as well, while the independent Croatians would make their mark in England in 1996 in some style before even greater exploits at the 1998 World Cup.

Here we enter the realms of speculation, but in a parallel universe where the Yugoslav Wars had never happened and the country had remained as one, what may have happened in the 1994 World Cup? While people in the former Yugoslavia may have been able to picture a 1992 European Championship victory, 1994 is less discussed given the country as they knew it was long gone, in contrast to the new national identities being forged. This view hasn't changed particularly, with thoughts of the war remaining fresh. But for the football players, it was a lost competition that fell in the prime years for many.

Yugoslavia were drawn into the 1994 World Cup qualifiers, which had been made in late 1991, well before the UN sanctions were imposed. The qualifying group they would have been in was ultimately won by Greece ahead of Russia – another newly independent nation – but neither were particularly strong.

Russia were the seeded team, having themselves replaced the USSR side, but it is inconceivable to think that a complete Yugoslavia would have done anything but dominate this group, qualifying for the World Cup comfortably.

But what of the team who would have travelled to the USA in this parallel universe? The year 1994 could potentially have been the sweet spot for this collection of hugely talented individuals. The 1990 World Cup had come too early for some of the emerging stars who remained on the fringes, but by 1994 many of those who had excelled in the World Youth Championship in 1987, or with Red Star in the early 1990s, were now at their peak. Undoubtedly, Yugoslavia would have been one of the strongest teams at that World Cup.

That Greece and Russia, the two teams who benefitted in terms of Yugoslavia's exclusion, were abysmal at the World Cup just enhances the thought that Yugoslavia would have brought far more to the tournament. One of those two would surely not have qualified had Yugoslavia participated, but beyond that Yugoslavia would have brought a team with talent beyond the reach of many who did perform well in the USA. They would also not have been as reliant on one or two great individuals, as were the two teams who ultimately progressed all the way to the final that year.

Brazil and Italy played out a drab goalless draw in the final in Pasadena, settled in Brazil's favour in a penalty shoot-out. This was far from a vintage Brazilian team, however: the 1982 greats, they were not. It was a more pragmatic, stodgy Brazil, almost jarring to those of us brought up on the silky brilliance of the early 1980s. They did possess a phenomenal striker in Romário, ably assisted by his strike partner Bebeto, but beyond that, they were more about solidity than great play. Their Italian counterparts were similarly reliant on the brilliance of Roberto Baggio to almost single-handedly drag them through in a string of wondrous performances, taking Italy to a final that had seemed well beyond them at several stages in the tournament. In short, neither team were so great as to be beyond a team as talented as Yugoslavia could have been.

Let's just envisage what the team may have looked like. In goal, there could have been Dražen Ladić, who went on to represent Croatia at both Euro '96 and the 1998 World Cup, or his experienced Croatian counterpart Tomislav Ivković, who had played in the 1990 World Cup. In defence, the Serbian Siniša Mihajlović, then playing in Serie A with Roma, could be joined by Croatians Robert Jarni and Slaven Bilić, Bosnian Refik Šabanadžović, or the Serbian Miroslav Đukić and Montenegrin Branko Brnović. Strong defenders, perhaps not as illustrious as some of their more attacking colleagues, but nevertheless a depth of defensive strength more than a match for many on view in the 1994 World Cup.

Progressing forwards, the talent becomes increasingly impressive. Playing in Italy's Serie A at the time were AC Milan's Montenegrin attacking midfielder Dejan Savićević and Croatian Zvonimir Boban. Both were key parts of the Milan team that was at its loftiest peak, having destroyed Johan Cruyff's Barcelona Dream Team at the 1994 Champions League Final in a devastatingly dynamic 4-0 victory. Savićević and Boban were crucial cogs in that sleek Milan wheel, at the top of their game in the summer of 1994. Also in Italy was another hero of Red Star's 1991 triumph in the early days of a long career in Italy's top flight, the Serbian attacking midfielder Vladimir Jugović at Sampdoria. The experienced Slovenian Katanec was nearing the end of his career also at Sampdoria. Also from the all-conquering Red Star, and still in his prime now at Marseille, was the Serbian hero of 1990, Dragan Stojković, while the Croatian Robert Prosinečki was with Real

Madrid, though arguably not quite fulfilling the potential he so clearly had.

If that list of midfield talent wasn't enough, when it came to the strikers, the imaginary Yugoslavia of 1994 had four who could all lay claim to being among the finest around. Playing in Italy were the Macedonian Darko Pančev at Inter and the Croatian Alen Bokšić at Lazio. In Spain the Croatian Davor Šuker was grabbing goals aplenty with Sevilla, while the Montenegrin Predrag Mijatović was doing likewise with Valencia. Both would go on to great things with Real Madrid in the years that followed. While Pančev wasn't having the best of times with Inter in this period, any downturn in form for him would be more than compensated by the talents of the other three strikers, as well as the incredible creative talents behind them.

This would have been a squad of hugely impressive strength in depth, and a startling amount of attacking creativity and finishing prowess. Quite how to blend them together into a workable unit is a whole other question and challenge. It's not as simple as just gathering a collection of great players and hoping they fit together, of course. But regardless of who would be in or out of the starting line-up, the depth of talent was phenomenal.

To imagine that they would have been capable of taking on the best on offer at the 1994 World Cup is no great leap of faith. This was a team more than capable of competing with the ultimately successful, but rigid and limited Brazilians. The creative spark that Yugoslavia possessed could have lit up the tournament in a way that only individual players, rather than teams, actually did in that American summer. They possessed individual star quality too, copious amounts of it, in fact, but they also would have had a more wide-ranging spread of talent across the team that could well have elevated this team above all others in 1994.

We will never know, of course. But just imagine Savićević, Prosinečki and Stojković dictating the play, with Boban keeping things neatly in order in the midfield, Jarni and Mihajlović storming up from defence on the wings, and the scoring talents of Mijatović, Bokšić, Šuker or Pančev finishing the chances off. What an intoxicating brand of football this team could have produced were they to have had the opportunity.

Leaving this imaginary world aside, back in reality, Yugoslavia remained barred from participation in the 1996 European Championship. Croatia reached their first tournament that year, though, producing some scintillating play, with Šuker announcing himself as a star with some delightful goals firing his team as far as the quarter-finals. They went further still in the 1998 World Cup, riding the wave of emotion and national pride to a semi-final before narrowly losing out to the ultimate victors, France. That they finished third in a debut World Cup, with Šuker claiming the Golden Boot as the tournament's top scorer, tells quite a story. Yugoslavia, what remained of it, were also at the 1998 World Cup. They reached the first knockout round, but the mind wanders to what could have been achieved had Mijatović, Mihajlović, Stojković and Savićević been added to the talented Croatian squad.

Srečko Katanec once claimed in an interview that, had Yugoslavia remained, they would have 'crushed the world'. Discussing this with me, Nebojša Marković argues, 'It's easy to say things like that since there is no accountability for it. But the sentiment is probably somewhat right – that team would have been really strong. Just take a look at the players and the peak years they would have been in, and then take a look at how the 1994 World Cup went and what kinds of teams managed to go deep into the tournament.'

A counter-view was suggested by Slaven Bilić, claiming that the Croatian side of that era was so good in its own right that it couldn't have been improved by adding others from the former Yugoslavia. His thoughts perhaps betray the extent to which nationalism and nationalist sentiments, sporting or otherwise, had become so important. Had he accepted that a Yugoslavia team in the mid-1990s would have been stronger than a team of Croatians, his words would have been acknowledging that Croatia would have been stronger with the addition of some Serbians and Montenegrins. 'And that was a big no-no in Croatia, especially in those years at the end of the 1990s,' added Marković. 'I think it's simple maths though, saying that the imagined Yugoslavia would have been clearly stronger. But for that Yugoslav team to work, you would have to have a scenario where the war between Yugoslav republics never happened, and the situation in the still operating Yugoslavia was at least somewhat normal.'

There is the question of squad harmony too: all of these disparate nationalities and ethnicities coming from a region that had been on a knife-edge for some time. If we are imagining a Yugoslavia that still teetered on the brink for several more years, then perhaps a comparison to 1990 is appropriate in terms of how a team representing a troubled nation and made up of players from across the republics blended together in harmony.

'In the team there were no problems,' recalled Stojković of the 1990 squad. 'We had Prosinečki from Croatia, Pančev from Macedonia, Sušić from Bosnia, Katanec from Slovenia, me from Serbia, Savićević from Montenegro. We never had these kinds of problems and we never discussed or joked about it.' This view may be a rose-tinted one in part, but most reports suggest any contention was more about club rivalry than nationality and nationalism. Whether that would have lasted had Yugoslavia remained intact into the mid-1990s is a whole different matter, of course.

The tragedy of Yugoslavia clearly goes way beyond a trivial sporting one, but the sporting shame is that we never got to see what this star-studded crop of players could have achieved together. While it's not possible to say that they would have won the 1994 World Cup, we can say with some certainty that they would have been among the favourites. And it's arguable that they would have been capable of beating all comers that summer if they played with the style and ability which we know they had.

Unlike other teams to feature in this book, this Yugoslavia team were not denied by football misfortune, mistakes at crucial moments, or by being beaten by a team that was better on one fateful day. Instead, Yugoslavia and these great players were denied by history. Not only was glory denied, but so was the opportunity to even compete for glory.

The greatest international team that never was? Quite possibly so.

11

Netherlands 1998

It's difficult, because we're not really a killer team. What I say about myself could be the same for the Dutch team as well. If we were a killer team, we might forget to play the football we're good at. You never know where that will end.

Dennis Bergkamp

IT'S NOT just the frequently flamboyant football that makes the Dutch stand out. It's the style, the swagger, the gloriously bright orange shirts. It's the often outspokenly strong characters at the heart of the squads who have both defined and destroyed Dutch national sides over the years. But as one great generation ceded to another in the early 1990s, the newly dominant character was much more measured. The grandest statements of Dennis Bergkamp were saved for when on the pitch in the heat of battle. Inspired by him, the wondrous talents of the Dutch in the 1990s rose again to push for the summit of the world game, playing an entertaining style that was both robust and graceful.

Bergkamp's perennial search for footballing perfection would see him lead his country to the edge of greatness. Perfection, fleeting and momentary, would indeed come. But perfection, unattainable to most, is a transitory ideal, as impermanent as it is idealistic. Bergkamp seemingly sought this ideal throughout his playing days, but momentary perfection alone can't lead a nation to World Cup glory. For the Netherlands, another chapter of their endless search for the trophy would be written. It remained an elusive goal, but through Bergkamp, the Netherlands reached heights of unimaginable beauty, yet the end result remained as frustrating as the Dutch stories of before.

Following the peak of 1988 and the great team of Ruud Gullit, Marco van Basten, Frank Rijkaard and Ronald Koeman, Dutch football had fluctuated between near greatness and disappointment. While the 1988 *oranje* had returned to the scene of the Netherlands' most heartbreaking moment from 14 years prior, Munich's Olimpiastadion, and emerged victorious in the European Championship, the teams that followed hadn't quite been able to live up to that glory.

Blighted by infighting, inflated egos and mismanagement, that same generation flattered to deceive before imploding at the 1990 World Cup. Two years later, the Netherlands were among the favourites to win the 1992 European Championship. This ought to have been a sweet spot for the Dutch. The stars of 1988 were arguably at their peak four years later. Gullit, Van Basten and Rijkaard were key to the dominant AC Milan team who had just gone unbeaten in winning Serie A, while Koeman arrived at the tournament having scored the winning goal in Barcelona's first European Cup triumph. Added to these was an experienced domestic-based core from PSV, and the first shoots of a new generation emerging at Ajax.

Chief among them was the 23-year-old Bergkamp; the player who would become central to the Dutch story for the rest of the 1990s. Back in 1992 he was the next great hope of Dutch football, but his arrival on the scene was initially to complement rather than replace the other stars. All of which made the team of 1992 the most talented in the tournament. And yet, despite playing the most exhilarating football of any in the competition, with Bergkamp scoring three in four games, when it came to the semi-final, complacency seemed to set in. Faced with a Denmark team on a wave of carefree optimism, the Dutch struggled to impose their clear superiority, and what had seemed set to be a successful defence of their European title instead became a tale of crushing disappointment and missed opportunity. It wouldn't be the last.

By the time of the 1994 World Cup, they had neither Gullit nor Van Basten any more. While injury cruelly cut short the playing days of the wondrous Van Basten, Gullit's absence was more self-inflicted. He had clashed repeatedly with the coach, Dick Advocaat, throughout the previous year, primarily about the role he was being asked to play, shunted out wide on the right rather than more central to proceedings. The emergence of the dynamic Marc Overmars in that same right-sided role saw Gullit ostracised further. After being substituted in favour of Overmars in a qualifier against England at Wembley in April 1993, Gullit vowed never to play for the national team again. A year later, in the build-up to the World Cup, he was persuaded to change his mind, but the bitter feud between star player and coach hadn't eased at all. He only played one pre-tournament friendly before the fractures fissured again and he walked out on the team, never to return.

In his absence, the *oranje*, now firmly led by the talents of Bergkamp, reached the quarter-final having stuttered their way through the group stages. Narrow, nervy wins over Saudi Arabia and Morocco sat either side of a defeat to Belgium before they belatedly hit their stride in a comprehensive knockout victory over Ireland. In the last eight they ran into a limited Brazil side who were on their way to World Cup glory. The clashes in the World Cup with Brazil form a key part of the story of the Dutch, harking back to the 1974 tournament and the Cruyff-inspired win on the way to the final. It was the Dutch who were frequently the more swashbuckling and extravagant in these key meetings, though come the 1990s, it was Brazil who would prevail.

The 1994 quarter-final was a frustrating one for the Dutch, seemingly unable or unwilling to seize the initiative until the situation had become desperate. In the second half Brazil had taken control, as much through a dropping of the level of intensity by the Dutch as by any particular Brazilian brilliance. Trailing 2-0, the Dutch belatedly decided to show the world what they could do. Shocked into action, the deficit was cut within a minute, Bergkamp scoring after a burst into the box. Where there had been hesitancy, now suddenly there was cohesion and fluency as the Dutch play clicked into gear, playing the best football of either team in the match. Bergkamp weaved his way elegantly between the Brazilian lines, while Koeman increasingly stepped up from the back to direct the forward surges of his team.

Brazil, a week away from becoming world champions, couldn't contain them. When Aron Winter made it 2-2 soon after, following a corner won through more

Bergkamp brilliance, there seemed only one likely winner. A spectacularly swerving late Brazilian free kick from Branco put paid to that, however, leaving the Netherlands eliminated and unfulfilled.

By fighting back from a two-goal deficit, the Dutch had shown what they could do. And yet the frustration must be that they seemingly didn't have sufficient belief in themselves prior to being forced into action – not a usual Dutch footballing failing. When left with no option but to force the pace and assert themselves, they showed they had what it took to hurt Brazil. Had they played with such vigour sooner, perhaps the outcome could have been different, but really this was a team starting a new cycle, building towards the World Cup four years down the line: France 1998.

If Bergkamp had marked his World Cup debut with frequent glimpses of the effusive elegance of his play, his club career was stuck in a bit of a rut in the middle of a two-year spell at Inter Milan. A move to Arsenal in 1995 rekindled the freedom and joy he had previously known at Ajax, which was enhanced a year later with the arrival of Arsène Wenger in north London. The elegant, almost idealistic beauty of Bergkamp's play at this time wasn't solely an attempt to achieve the aesthetically pleasing. It was more often simply the result of his imagination and quick thinking; doing the extraordinary with the ball was simply the outcome of a mind seeing the possibilities that others couldn't.

He may have lacked the killer instinct of a true goalscorer, something he readily accepted, but his view of the game led him to produce some of the most iconic goals of the era. Think of the Premier League goals he scored for Arsenal when completing his hat-trick against

Leicester City in 1997, or against Newcastle United in 2002. Both required a deftness of touch equal to the degree of imagination being displayed. In the 1998 World Cup he would create another masterpiece of technical majesty, but more of that later.

Bergkamp was the figurehead of Dutch football, but there were many more strings to their bow. With a core of young stars coming through in Amsterdam in a hugely successful Ajax side, the Dutch talent pool looked primed to push the Netherlands to the forefront once again. The Ajax team led by Louis van Gaal had won the Champions League in 1994/95 using a sophisticated, intelligent style of play that had been ingrained in every player coming through the youth set-up at the club, with players comfortable in multiple positions. The whole team moved in specifically planned set patterns: precise passes played with a crisp, clinical speed, shuffling around the pitch with an entrenched, stylish synchronicity.

Its effect was astonishing. Ajax dominated domestically, but it was victory over AC Milan that heralded the arrival of a generation of wonderful Dutch players. From Edwin van der Sar in goal to Michael Reiziger and Frank de Boer in defence, the youthful back line was enhanced by the experienced additions of Danny Blind and Frank Rijkaard, returned from his Milanese sojourn. Ahead of them were the stylish Clarence Seedorf, the relentlessly tenacious pit bull Edgar Davids and the pacy Overmars, with Ronald de Boer and Patrick Kluivert further forward.

The list of names reads like a who's who of Dutch stars of the era. In a first-team squad that only featured three non-Dutch players, the bulk of the side were Dutchmen in their early 20s or still teenagers. They came within a penalty shoot-out of repeating their success in the 1996 Champions

League Final, pipped by Juventus on that occasion, before the team broke up, as players moved to the richer leagues beyond the Netherlands.

A generation emerging together and achieving greatness at club level would naturally have a significant positive impact on the national team. The Dutch side that went to England for the 1996 European Championship was based on this Ajax core. They arrived amid high anticipation, to succeed only in imploding once again when the action began.

After drawing with Scotland in their opening game, the Netherlands beat Switzerland 2-0 to be on the verge of the quarter-finals before the disastrous 4-1 defeat to a rampant England. The internal cracks within the squad were showing, though, and would rapidly become significant fissures as the Dutch dirty laundry was aired in public. Rumours have often suggested a racial split within the squad, largely on the basis of a photograph of a players' lunch which showed black and white players sitting on separate tables. While such claims were overblown and inaccurate, splits in the squad were all too apparent, though not on racial lines. The biggest issues to affect the squad were more to do with the inequality felt by some of the younger players, largely the Ajax core, and their better-rewarded colleagues playing abroad. Some of that same group also felt they were being unjustly overlooked by Hiddink in favour of these more established stars.

The most cited example would be Jordi Cruyff starting every match ahead of Kluivert, with Davids also claiming that Hiddink was far too close to Blind. While most of those feeling slighted were indeed black, several have since corroborated each other confirming that race was not the issue. Kluivert came off the bench to rescue his team with a late consolation against England which edged the Netherlands into the quarter-finals. There they faced France, but with the turmoil of a squad at loggerheads with each other, team spirit was shot to pieces. After a goalless quarter-final, the *oranje* lost on penalties and went home disappointed once again.

The pressure cooker of a tournament bubble had affected the squad, and they returned home to criticism and blame. But within months, when the qualifying campaign for the 1998 World Cup began, Hiddink drew a line under it all, forgetting all that had gone before and focusing solely on qualification for the World Cup.

It was a qualification that began relatively smoothly, thanks to opening with four straight victories including a 7-1 humbling of Wales, but more significantly a 3-0 win away at near neighbours Belgium. As well as the Ajax cabal, the early skirmishes of the 1998 campaign saw the likes of PSV's Jaap Stam and Phillip Cocu coming through to earn international recognition. There was a recall for their club-mate Wim Jonk, who had missed the cut for Euro '96, as well as Celtic's Pierre van Hooijdonk.

The Dutch qualification campaign only hit two stumbling blocks throughout, both courtesy of the same opponent. A 1-0 defeat in Turkey in April 1997 was the sole significant spanner in the works though. By the time Turkey secured a goalless draw in the return match in Amsterdam, that point earned was the one that secured the Netherlands place at the World Cup. Beating Belgium for a second time was the key; the Dutch edging past their local rivals just as they had done in qualifying for the famous 1974 World Cup campaign. While the squad hadn't changed hugely since 1996, the mood certainly had, with positivity replacing the acrimony of two years before, albeit a measured positivity.

In what was to be only the Netherlands' sixth World Cup finals, the *oranje* were paired with Belgium again in the group stage, along with South Korea and Mexico. It ought to have been a fairly comfortable group for a squad as talented as the Dutch, but they opened the tournament in unconvincing style. They weren't the first big team to begin a World Cup slowly and they won't be the last, but the goalless draw with Belgium left the Dutch deeply frustrated. It was a match dominated by stout defending on both sides, with the robust nature of the challenges mirroring the physique of many of the defenders on show. Stam had recently become the world's most expensive defender following his move from PSV Eindhoven to Manchester United shortly before the World Cup, and his combative style was emulated by his Belgian counterpart, the similarly vigorous Mike Verstraeten. Stam and Verstraeten even looked alike – muscular, shaven-headed giants – and both set about this match in the same way, pushing the boundaries of sporting legality with a variety of bone-crunching tackles.

What attacking intent there was on display was coming most frequently from the Dutch, with Overmars in particular causing untold problems on the left side of Belgium's defence. Such was the damage he caused that Belgium replaced their outpaced left-back, Bertrand Crasson, as early as the 21st minute. His replacement, Eric Deflandre, settled on a strategy that kept Overmars at bay: fouling him at every opportunity. With Bergkamp appearing from the bench only midway through the second half, coming on along with Boudewijn Zenden as the Netherlands adjusted from their initially stodgy formation, the Dutch struggled to break down an opponent whose apparent sole intention was to stifle and spoil.

The Netherlands also suffered a late, self-inflicted wound. Kluivert had a frustrating evening which was added to by the Belgian defender Lorenzo Staelens, who provoked the striker by taunting him on his high-profile troubles. Kluivert had not long been cleared of rape, and had also been in court in recent years following a fatal car crash. His reaction, a low elbow into Staelens's arm and side, was far from vicious, or even painful, but once Staelens tumbled to the ground holding his face there was only one inevitable outcome. The red card duly arrived and a night of Dutch frustration was complete.

While that opener may have been bruising and unsatisfying, a more compliant opponent in their next match made for a more productive occasion. South Korea didn't, or couldn't, replicate the Belgian spoiling tactics, allowing the *oranje* to cut loose in an effervescent display, high in tempo and quality. As if slighted by the inability to show their worth in the opening game, they stormed to an emphatic 5-0 victory, serving notice that this Dutch vintage possessed the players and style to create the beauty with which Dutch football has long been associated.

Davids and Bergkamp both came into the starting line-up, producing a more pleasing synergy all round. The Koreans, startled and powerless in the face of the orange storm heading their way, had packed the defence in an effort to hold the tide back, but the sheer quality of the Dutch made that a thankless task. Picking the finest goal of the five the Dutch scored is equally problematic. Cocu, Bergkamp and Ronald de Boer all scored wonderful goals in the rout, but beyond the individual delights it was the cohesion of the collective which impressed the most. Inferior opposition it may have been, but this was a first real glimpse of what this team were capable of.

Such performances boost the confidence, and for a team with a fragile recent history, it was a welcome one. This positivity took them into a 2-0 lead in their final group match, outclassing their Mexican opponents with clinical ease and Bergkamp at the heart of it all. With such graceful speed of attack and finish, the Netherlands had continued just where they had left off against South Korea. Slick, quick passing was the order of the day, and the Mexicans simply couldn't cope. The two-goal lead ought to have become three or four, before things became scrappy late on. There had been plenty of evidence of the strengths of this Dutch side, but in allowing the Mexicans to salvage a point with two late goals, some defensive frailties were also exposed.

Nevertheless, the *oranje* had won their group. In a tournament which so far had revealed several strong teams but none of them overly dominant, the Netherlands, with their attacking flair and depth of talent, took their place among the favourites. Even the Brazilians, with a rampant Ronaldo raining the goals in, had contrived to lose to Norway; their own frailties brutally laid bare.

Awaiting the Dutch in the last 16 were Yugoslavia, returning to the tournament following their exile, but now representing a much smaller land and population than had been the case before. Yugoslavia still enjoyed a significant seam of talent running through their side, particularly in attack. They had been unfortunate not to have topped their first-round group with maximum points, having let a two-goal lead over Germany slip late on. In failing to hold on against the Germans, we were denied the enticing prospect of the Netherlands facing Germany in the last 16, where Dutch grace would surely have overcome the ageing German squad.

Nevertheless, it was a highly anticipated clash when Yugoslavia took on the Dutch in Toulouse, in what proved to be a match delicately poised throughout. It really shouldn't have been, though. The Dutch were infinitely superior both in outlook and application, and yet a deserved victory was only clinched at the last. Yugoslavia's defensive tactics signified the threat the Netherlands posed, and the dangerous inventive players who could turn a match in a moment. But in choosing to take a more limited approach, the Yugoslavs not only denied those of us watching the hoped-for spectacle of attacking prowess, but also served to blunt their own forward play. Such was the fear instilled by the sight of the orange wave they faced.

It was a scrappy match in truth, but quality finds a way even in such circumstances. Bergkamp gave the Dutch the lead late in the first half, latching on to a long ball from Frank de Boer and forcibly holding off the challenge of Zoran Mirković before firing past Ivica Kralj. It was almost a trial run of the famously sumptuous goal he would score in the quarter-final a few days later: slightly less elegant perhaps, but symbolic of Bergkamp's increasing dominance of proceedings and indeed of the Dutch team and its fortunes.

It was a dominance the Dutch almost threw away, however. Yugoslavia had equalised early in the second half thanks to some slack Dutch defending allowing a free header on goal, and were then handed a gilt-edged chance to take the lead and potentially close out the victory. Stam was guilty of shirt-pulling, giving Predrag Mijatović one of the few chances he'd had in front of goal in the entire tournament, from the resultant spot kick. Just six weeks earlier, Mijatović had scored the only goal in Real Madrid's historic *séptima* Champions League victory, but in France he had been off the pace and peripheral. When he smashed his penalty against the crossbar, fortune seemed to be smiling on the Dutch. And when Bergkamp escaped a red card just minutes later – having pushed Siniša Mihajlović over before treading on his ribs – there appeared little doubt that fate was on their side.

Grasping their good fortune on both counts, the Dutch stepped up another gear, overwhelming their opponents. They could have sealed victory on any number of occasions before they eventually did, but the decisive strike finally arrived two minutes into stoppage time, just moments after Kralj had stretched to deny an Overmars shot destined for the far corner. When another, fiercer shot was aimed at the corner of Kralj's net, he was unable to stop it. Davids's effort from outside the box may have been aided by a slight deflection and an absence of the attention of any Yugoslav defenders closing him down, but it was a goal worthy of winning such an occasion.

It was no less than the Dutch deserved given their dominant performance and clear greater quality, but it was an incredible relief given the twists of fate that went their way. Beyond that, had Bergkamp been given the red card he probably deserved, he wouldn't have been in the team five days later for one of the most memorable matches in recent World Cup history, and the day that defined his national team legacy.

The Yugoslavia game had revealed the multiple contradictions within this Dutch team. Attacking verve contrasted with defensive frailty, while, within Bergkamp, the fuse that occasionally sparked his red mist saw him cross the boundary of decency, with this most graceful of players committing a graceless act. As Bergkamp himself maintained, if he could change anything about his style it would be to be more ruthless in the box and to reduce the more reckless side of his game. He also questioned, however, whether he would have been the player he was if such changes of character were possible.

For most footballers, Bergkamp's constant search for aesthetic perfection would be a concept that would remain forever out of reach: an unattainable ideal, forever unfulfilled. With three touches of the ball in the space of two seconds in the final moments of the 1998 World Cup quarter-final, Bergkamp would achieve perfection, if only for a fleeting moment in time.

Up against Argentina in the quarter-final, the Dutch were forced to face their demons of yesteryear. It was close to 20 years to the day since the 1978 World Cup Final in Buenos Aires when Rob Rensenbrink had come within the width of a post of winning the World Cup for the Netherlands. They had exorcised their German demons of 1974 in several subsequent key victories, but Argentina represented a wound that had lain bare, festering for two decades. Far from the tense hostility and ticker tape of Buenos Aires in 1978 where forces, both footballing and political, seemed to converge against the Dutch, the energy-sapping afternoon heat in the bright sunshine of Marseille in 1998 would finally provide the chance for redemption; a 'weird and perfect redemptive mirror image' of 1978, as described by David Winner in his seminal book, *Brilliant Orange*.

It was an epic match, fit for the occasion of a World Cup quarter-final. Neither team held anything back, trading punches back and forth throughout. In a game full of invention and deft beauty, it was fitting that it would be decided by a moment of genius, but the magical moment we're building up to wasn't Bergkamp's only moment of brilliance in this match. His assist for the first Dutch goal was as delicate as it was decisive: a moment of such exquisite control that Kluivert's act of scoring the goal was merely the icing on the cake.

The game was only 12 minutes old when Ronald de Boer hit a firm pass to the left of the penalty box where Bergkamp nudged a delicate, perfectly placed header back across goal into the path of Kluivert. It was a beautifully majestic assist, Bergkamp falling backwards in order to cushion the ball to perfection, all sting taken out of it. Kluivert gratefully accepted the gift-wrapped opportunity and touched the ball past Carlos Roa for an early Dutch lead. It was a moment overflowing with the beauty of total control and awareness that few could perform so flawlessly, a moment to demonstrate why he was so revered by team-mates and fans alike. That it would be so utterly overshadowed by what followed from the same player later in the match speaks volumes for the levels Bergkamp reached in this match.

Before the final *coup de grâce*, though, there was a close contest to be fought. Argentina surged back from the disappointment of conceding so early on to fashion a rapid response, Claudio López rounding off a terrific move with a fine finish just five minutes later to level the scores. The Dutch continued to exert their dominance of the ball, though Argentina remained a constant threat throughout, primarily on the break, testing the Dutch defence time and again. Argentina hit the post twice, while the Dutch also hit the woodwork once.

The match remained on a knife-edge with two high-calibre teams pushing each other to the limit. In the final quarter of an hour, that limit was crossed with both sides losing a player to a red card. The Dutch were reduced to ten men first, defender Arthur Numan earning a second booking after going in hard on Diego Simeone in midfield. Initiative belatedly handed to Argentina, they tried to up the ante, but with Stam playing above himself and stifling the on-form striker Gabriel Batistuta, and the perpetual motion of Davids shackling the enigmatic Ariel Ortega, Argentina were kept at bay.

As Argentinian frustration mounted, a late surge into the Dutch box saw Ortega take a tumble in search of a decisive penalty. He was about to be shown a yellow card for diving when, with Van der Sar leaning over him to remonstrate, Ortega jabbed his head into the Dutch goalkeeper's jaw in a reckless act of self-sabotage. The resultant red card restored numerical parity. With just two minutes left on the clock, the match seemed destined for an additional half an hour that most observers were looking forward to with relish. One man had other ideas, however. Within a minute of Ortega's expulsion, Bergkamp's moment had arrived.

Frank de Boer, excellent throughout alongside Stam in defence, stepped out of the back line and, spotting Bergkamp forward as the lone Dutch frontman, sent a magnificent floated pass of astonishing accuracy more than 50 metres into the Argentinian penalty area. As the ball fell from its high arc, for Bergkamp, this was the moment that his search for perfection would reach its beautiful, spectacular zenith.

Within the space of two seconds, Bergkamp's three touches of the ball secured his place in World Cup legend. First, the control. Letting the ball drop over his shoulder, with one deft touch of his instep he killed the pass as it fell from on high in an instant. His next touch took the ball away from the startled Roberto Ayala, flailing ineffectually, a mere bystander as the most beautiful of goals played out around him. Now faced with just Roa, and with greatness beckoning, Bergkamp flicked the ball past the onrushing goalkeeper high into the net. Three touches, two seconds, one magical moment.

Bergkamp had scored one of the finest goals in World Cup history, scaling heights of football beauty that few others can even dream of, sending the Dutch into a World Cup semi-final after one of the most enthralling, entertaining matches of the tournament. Given the context of the moment, for many this goal far outweighs any of Bergkamp's other great strikes, its importance far beyond any other. For sporting greats, time seems to slow down in such moments, allowing the genius to see the possibilities in what is a split-second blur to us mere mortals. For Bergkamp, it was time enough to assess the possibilities, conceive of a plan, and then execute it. This is a plane of greatness far beyond but a select few. That he had misplaced a pass just moments earlier, putting Argentina on the break, only adds to the magnificence for me. Perfection is not something sustained, or long-lasting, but a passing moment in time that has to be seized: as fleeting as it is majestic, as impermanent as it is imperious. Only a player of the calibre of Bergkamp could grab that moment and not allow it to pass.

As the stadium erupted around him, Bergkamp wheeled away in stunned delight, momentarily, instinctively covering his face in his hands in apparent disbelief, before being mobbed by his team-mates. Moments earlier, the Dutch had been hanging on with ten men. Now they were 2-1 up and into the semi-final. Where 20 years earlier Rensenbrink's last-gasp shot against the same opponents had hit the post and the Netherlands' chance was gone, now Bergkamp's late, glorious strike had secured a modicum of revenge.

Beyond the simple confines of this match, this was a moment to encapsulate the Dutch: a beautiful moment to seal a beautiful game. This was the moment denied them by West Germany in 1974 and Argentina in 1978, though sadly not in a final. 'You're in that moment,' said Bergkamp afterwards. 'That's the feeling. After the first two touches … that moment! You give absolutely everything. It's like your life has led up to this moment.' Few players are capable of seizing that moment in such a way, though. This is a level reserved for greatness. 'You never play the perfect game,' he added. 'But the moment itself was, I think, perfect.'

What a way to crown a magnificent match. For all the fine play that had gone before, it was in this moment that a Dutch World Cup victory felt a possibility. With such style, such precision, such sublime artistry, Dutch beauty had slain the Argentine beast; a moment 20 years in the making. Bergkamp, although he wasn't pivotal to all of the action that day, was central to the Netherlands' two goals, both magnificent in their differing ways. Beyond that though, this was the game that confirmed the Dutch were the real deal. In overcoming one of football's superpowers in such a manner, having dominated much of the action with an assertive control through a team brimming with talent, the *oranje* reached the semi-finals with very real prospects of winning the World Cup.

Now in their path were the reigning champions Brazil, the team who had so narrowly knocked the Dutch out of the previous World Cup. Brazil had their own phenomenon in the form of 21-year-old Ronaldo. As described during this tournament by the former Argentina striker Jorge Valdano, Ronaldo was simply on another level at this time, 'He didn't come to France to compete with the players of his generation, but to seek a place among the best of the two millennia – this one and the coming.'

Ronaldo's brilliance had led to an over-reliance on their star man, however, which would be brutally exposed in the final with France. They were a side with a soft underbelly, relying on the brilliance of an individual, admittedly one of the finest of all time, to get them out of scrape after scrape. The caution of Mário Zagallo, the coach who had been in charge during the glorious triumph of 1970 a generation earlier but arguably had a greater influence over the poorer 1974 side, was hindering them. Brazil were eminently beatable, especially if Ronaldo wasn't at his explosive best, as demonstrated by their group-stage defeat to Norway. They had scraped past Scotland in their opener prior to that too, only clicking into gear against Morocco and more spectacularly against Chile in the first knockout round in which Ronaldo was simply unplayable.

But in their quarter-final with Denmark, they were exposed again. Denmark, like the Dutch, were a northern European team possessing inspirational artists – the Laudrup brothers in their case. Unlike the Dutch, though, the depth of their squad was limited, and yet they gave Brazil an almighty scare in a terrific match which ended 3-2 to the South Americans. Even with Ronaldo, there was no reason for the Netherlands to be scared of the Brazilian challenge.

In fact, of the four semi-finalists, the Dutch and the Brazilians were arguably the best positioned to win the World Cup. In the other semi-final, France, for all that hindsight has lent an air of destiny to their journey to ultimate victory, had only sporadically shown glimpses worthy of champions-in-waiting. For them, the knockout rounds so far had been an exercise in dicing with death, and they lacked any punch up front. France's opponents, Croatia, did have that goalscoring punch and had achieved greatly to reach this stage, but the final always felt a step too far for them.

For both Brazil and the Netherlands, however, the tantalising glimpse of golden glory seemed within reach. Both looked capable of grasping that opportunity, both had players gifted with inspirational quality, while both remained beatable too. This semi-final would be a step above the iconic quarter-final of four years earlier, more evenly matched than the de facto semi-final of 1974.

Both teams began the semi-final at Marseille's Stade Vélodrome in tense fashion. The first half saw two sides unwilling to commit to attack, feeling each other out, as the tension of what was at stake seemed to paralyse somewhat. The best chance of the half fell to the Dutch, whose composure on the ball was apparent even amid such tension, with Kluivert's header narrowly clearing the bar. No such caginess in the second half, though, as this slow-burner ignited into a truly epic contest.

Almost immediately, a fine through ball from Rivaldo sliced open a Dutch back line that had kept Brazil in check up to that point. His pass dissected a narrow gap between Cocu and Frank de Boer and fell invitingly at the feet of Ronaldo. Fighting off Cocu's attempts to unsettle him, he controlled the ball with one touch before firing through the legs of the advancing Van der Sar to give Brazil the lead. Earlier Dutch composure now temporarily abandoned them as the men in orange were clearly slightly rattled at this setback.

Missing the injured Overmars on this occasion, a significant loss, the Dutch lacked the pace to test Roberto Carlos defensively. With Dunga providing an obdurate shield in the Brazilian midfield it took the Dutch a while to recover their smooth composure, but they gradually worked their way back into the contest. Apart from a great chance for Ronaldo that Davids snuffed out with an effective defensive toe-poke of the ball away from the striker, the Brazilian threat was largely limited to wildly off-target Roberto Carlos efforts from distance. The Dutch had reasserted control and were unfortunate not to equalise when Kluivert was put through on goal by Van Hooijdonk midway through the half.

Kluivert was not to be denied, however. Only four minutes remained when some tenacious pressing stole the ball, and Cocu released Ronald de Boer in acres of space on the right. His inviting cross gave Kluivert the chance for another clear header as the static Brazilian defence stood in statuesque helplessness. He drove a powerful header firmly past Taffarel into the Brazilian net, securing the equaliser that was the very least the Dutch deserved. For Kluivert, it was just reward for a fine attacking performance in which he had repeatedly dominated the suspect Brazilian defenders, highlighting the flaws that France and Zidane would expose again in the final.

Extra time brought a fightback from Brazil, but one that the Dutch weathered well, the impressive Frank de Boer and Stam repeatedly stifling the threats that their opponents could muster. De Boer was responsible for preventing what could have been one of the great World Cup goals from Ronaldo, putting in a performance which displayed everything that was great about him pre-injury – arguably his last truly great performance.

The Dutch made little headway in extra time themselves, save for a few half-chances, but as the game neared its conclusion the Dutch had arguably put in the better performance but were unable to make that count on the scoreboard. When a penalty shoot-out loomed, all of the Netherlands must have feared the worst. This would be the *oranje*'s third competitive penalty shoot-out and they had lost the previous two: a semi-final in Euro '92, and a quarter-final four years later.

Having scored their first two kicks through Frank de Boer and Bergkamp, given the Dutch history of penalty frailty, it was little surprise when Cocu missed his effort, handing the initiative to the Brazilians. When Ronald de Boer stepped up for the Netherlands' fourth penalty, he had to score to keep the Dutch in it. His hesitant run-up and weak shot belied his nerves, leaving Taffarel with an easy save. The Dutch dream was over once more, the pain refreshed anew.

To add to the frustration, the reality of the night was that the Dutch had been the better team, and ought to have won before their penalty demons became a factor. They had taken on the reigning world champions in a pulsating game, put in a performance worthy of a place in the final, and yet fallen short once again. Brazil, more usually associated with attacking flair and style, had held on thanks to the defensive wall marshalled by the combative Dunga; their defensive display forced upon them by the ever-apparent Dutch threat. With Ronaldo limited to feeding off scraps, the Dutch had contained the primary threat barring that clinical strike with which he had given Brazil the lead.

The most maddening factor, in addition to the failures from the spot, was the fact that the Dutch talisman was largely peripheral to proceedings. Bergkamp had put in his least-impressive performance of the tournament, his space restricted by the pack of defenders that closed him down incessantly. What that did show, though, was that the Dutch were significantly more than a one-man team. With Bergkamp muted, his colleagues came to the fore and so nearly took the Dutch to the final they deserved. And yet it is an unavoidable truth that, had Bergkamp been at his best, the Netherlands would surely have risen to a level which the Brazilians of 1998 could not have coped with.

Combined with the absence of the electric Overmars, the effect of Bergkamp's struggles was to leave the Dutch a touch below their best. That they were still the better team on the day regardless simply emphasises the fact that this was a great generation and a great team, though once again World Cup destiny had been missed. As Hiddink was at pains to point out, one of his side's strengths was that it didn't rely too heavily on one player, as he felt the great team of 1974 had done. There is a painfully bitter irony, therefore, that had their talisman Bergkamp been able to free himself from the shackles in the semi-final, it may have seen them over the line.

Instead, Brazil went on to the final with their French hosts. It could well be argued at this point that Brazil ought to have been the focus of this chapter rather than the Netherlands. After all, had Ronaldo not suffered that infamous fit on the day of the final, they would certainly have given France a better match than they ultimately did, and perhaps prevailed. It's a fair argument. Brazil reached the final in 1998, possessing a cutting edge, but played the biggest of occasions with Ronaldo present in body but not in mind or spirit. That he and many of his 1998 team-mates would complete their own redemption four years later in the 2002 World Cup makes their loss in 1998 less compelling.

The real story, the more romantic one if you will, is of the Netherlands. Where Brazil had one magnificent player who papered over the cracks of a good but not great team, the more beautiful tale to me is the one tinged with orange, the majestic skills of Bergkamp and the talented generation who had emerged together.

As good as Brazil were, raised by the other-worldly talent of Ronaldo, the Dutch were the better team. That they lost the semi-final was the biggest of shames, even if not fully appreciated at the time amid the Ronaldo mania. 'I think people at that time didn't quite realise how good the Netherlands were,' Dutch journalist Elko Born told me. 'They were surprised to hear quotes from Thierry Henry when he mentioned France weren't afraid of Brazil really, but they were afraid to meet the Dutch in the final. But the more time passes, the more it is felt that 1998 was a golden opportunity to win the World Cup. That was such a good team when you look back on it. A couple of missed penalties is not a lot, and who knows what could have happened in the final.'

With Dutch defeat, the watching world missed out on one of the finest players of the era being seen on the grandest of stages, but we were also denied what would have been an intoxicating final. Zidane and Bergkamp, Davids and Deschamps, Overmars and Henry, De Boer and Petit, Stam and Desailly; the potential is compelling. Hindsight makes us view the French victory in the final as predestined, but the Netherlands were comfortably at least a match for them. France had not produced football as free-flowing and glorious as the Dutch. They lacked the *oranje's* cutting edge and they could only dream of achieving the perfection of Bergkamp.

Perhaps, too, the sheer beauty of Bergkamp's goal against Argentina overshadowed the missed opportunity of the tournament as a whole. The joy people felt at that moment is what we look back on when thinking of the Dutch in 1998, far more so than the opportunity they had to win it all. That it came in a moment of redemption 20 years on from losing a final to Argentina enhanced its significance.

Add in the drama of the Brazil match and it's easy to see why the Netherlands' tournament can be looked on fondly, rather than with regret. 'It's such an emotional story already, with such big highs, perhaps that makes you forget about what really happened and the fact that maybe you should have won the World Cup,' added Born.

And yet the fact remains that this 1998 side, like their 1974 forebears, demonstrate the enduring appeal and value placed by the Dutch on their most aesthetically pleasing teams, even if others came closer to victory; 1978 and 2010 both saw the Dutch come closer to winning, but they don't resonate so much and aren't recalled so fondly in the Netherlands and beyond. 'They remain the anomaly, the afterthought to the more pleasing narrative of playing the right way, maintaining your ideals and not compromising,' Born explained. If there is a legacy, though, it may be that the Dutch culture is changing, as the Brazilian outlook did post-1982. It took until after 2010, but the realisation that victory may require a willingness to adapt your philosophy to the circumstances of a match, an opponent, or a tournament has belatedly gained strength in Dutch thinking. But such teams will never be prized in the way those of a purer heart will be.

Pleasing on the eye they may have been but this great Dutch side of the late 1990s, combining such artistry with a formidable midfield base and a strong, if occasionally lapsing, defence, would gain no glory. They would be forever left wondering. The penalty curse would last into the 2000 European Championship where it would reach a painful nadir in almost comical agony in a semi-final loss to Italy in Amsterdam.

That had been the last great chance for this generation. In losing penalty shoot-outs in three successive tournaments, from 1996 through to 2000, the Dutch generation of Bergkamp et al would never have the happy trophy-laden ending their combined talents deserved. Save for the glory of 1988, this has been the Dutch way. That the semi-final defeat in 1998 came when they had the team playing the best football in the tournament added a new tale of devastating disappointment. In possessing the players, the team and the cohesion to go all the way to World Cup glory, it is a disappointment that left a nation once again wondering what might have been, even if those feelings took longer to take hold, masked by the brilliance and fleeting perfection of one player touched by genius.

12

Argentina 2014

*We had the better chances and, well ... we'll
regret the chances we had but couldn't score for
the rest of our lives.*

Lionel Messi

IT WAS all of Brazil's worst nightmare. While minds had
been focused on Neymar and his colleagues, Brazilians
could set aside the ever-present feeling gnawing away in
their thoughts. Writ large by the effervescent and boisterous
Argentinian fans camped out on the Copacabana at the
heart of Rio de Janeiro's World Cup experience, a frightful
prospect was building. Argentina, with the finest player
of his generation, Lionel Messi, in his prime and in their
ranks, winning the World Cup in Brazil was an outcome
many dared not even contemplate.

But even with their own continued progress, Brazil's
path to World Cup victory on home soil, and a chance
to banish those demons of 1950, was leading towards a
terrifying denouement. With each passing knockout round,
as teams fell by the wayside and both halves of the draw

converged, the paths of Brazil and Argentina seemed to be inexorably heading for potentially the most seismic of all South American clashes in the final in Rio's Maracanã. 'The Maracanã ghosts were still strong,' Fernando Duarte, author of *Shocking Brazil*, told me. 'Brazil didn't play a single game there in 2014 – that was not a coincidence.' The final would be at the Maracanã, though. For Brazil, the chance to cast aside the ghosts of 1950 by beating Argentina in a Maracanã final was the stuff of dreams. The idea of losing to them, in that stadium of all places, the worst of all nightmares.

Fate decreed a wholly different nightmare on Brazil in 2014, however. The brutal 7-1 dismantling of the Seleção by a ruthless Germany in the semi-final in the Mineirão in Belo Horizonte inflicted a new humiliation on a desperate, traumatised nation. Now Brazil had a Mineiraço to evoke that old spirit of national shame felt with the Maracanaço of 1950. When Argentina won the other semi-final, a distraught Brazil now faced the unbearable prospect of their South American rivals piling agony on top of misery with Brazil looking on from the sidelines. A tiny minority of Brazilians adhered to the rules of continental solidarity, preferring to see the Europeans, the much-moneyed, all-powerful Europeans, vanquished. For the vast majority, however, with Argentina noisily seeking to assert their own self-proclaimed South American superiority, the prospect of an Argentinian victory in the Maracanã was unthinkable.

The seismic defeat to Germany hadn't caused quite the same introspection as the 1950 loss, given football history had now placed them in a far greater position of strength as five-time world champions, but it did reopen old wounds. The failure to win at home again exposed that same mental fragility criticised after the Maracanaço. The pressure had been intense, increasingly piled on by the press. With so many of the squad playing abroad, coming back to Brazil and winning at home was a big deal for the players, but collectively they had buckled.

What was very different from 1950 was a general dissatisfaction about hosting the World Cup given the cost and the numerous social issues in Brazil. 'There was far more cynicism and criticism about the politicisation of the World Cup than had been the case in 1950. A bit of national doubt,' explained Dr Peter Watson, Latin American Studies Fellow at Leeds University. 'Their social confidence as well as their football confidence was being questioned. That frailty of the football team had started to pervade the Brazilian psyche. Whether we are as good as the Europeans, whether that flair is actually enough any more. As the pressures increased, when those fissures started to surface, then they just exploded all at once.'

Comfort could be sought in the fact that Argentina, and indeed Messi, had not been overly impressive en route to the final. And in facing a Germany side whose confidence was sky-high following their semi-final victory, and had indeed been a better team than Argentina in the tournament, surely Brazil's feared outcome would not come to pass? But what if Messi turned it on in the final? What if, in a tight match thanks to a strong Argentinian defence, a clear chance or two were to fall to Messi or one of his highly rated attacking partners? As Brazil struggled to comprehend what had happened to their Seleção, such a nightmare scenario was all too real, and would ultimately come oh-so close to becoming a reality.

The 2014 World Cup had long been anticipated as being Messi's to dominate. 'The Maradona paradigm was laid out for him,' as described by Jonathan Wilson in *Angels with Dirty Faces*. Messi couldn't dominate in the manner of

Maradona, but he did produce a series of decisive moments to lead his country through, raising the already lofty expectation at every turn. While Brazil desperately feared an Argentinian triumph, for Argentina the chance to win a World Cup in the home of their greatest rivals was an irresistible opportunity. For a nation who saw themselves as superior to Brazil in so many ways, to have the chance to prove it in the home of their rivals, and in front of the world, was irresistible. The prospect of Messi emulating Maradona and leading Argentina to the World Cup, to be hailed as one of the all-time greats, and to do it through his feats in Brazil, was an enticing one.

It was a prospect which had tempted many thousands of sky blue and white-clad Argentinian fans to make the pilgrimage to Rio, dominating the fan parks and beaches. As Argentina progressed, so the number of itinerant Argentinians grew in number and noise. The all-pervasive sound of the latter stages of the tournament was of hordes of Argentinians singing their version of Creedence Clearwater Revival's 'Bad Moon Rising', the lyrics altered to taunt their Brazilian hosts, which became increasingly pertinent as the World Cup neared its climax.

> *Brazil, tell me how it feels*
> *To have your Papa in your home?*
> *I swear even as the years go by*
> *We will never forget*
> *When Diego outplayed you,*
> *When El Cani stuck the needle in you.*
> *You've been crying since Italy until today.*
> *With Messi, you're going to see,*
> *The cup, he's going to bring us.*
> *Maradona is greater than Pelé*

The lyrics are mostly in reference to the match in the last 16 of the 1990 World Cup, when Argentina, a bedraggled ragtag collection of players mostly either past their prime or injured, or both, took all that a clearly superior Brazil could throw at them and stood firm. Then the genius of Maradona, largely hidden up until that point of the tournament, found the reserves within himself to explode into life, dragging his almost crippled body into supreme action. His explosive dribbling terrified the Brazilians, attracting panicked defenders to him like moths to a flame, leaving Claudio Caniggia – the 'Cani' of the song – all alone. Maradona deftly slotted the decisive pass through to Caniggia to score the only goal of the match. Argentina went through and Brazil went home.

The unacknowledged truth of the rivalry ever since, however, was that far from being Brazil's 'Papa' as noted in the lyrics – meaning to consistently get the better of someone – Argentina had been very much in Brazil's shadow, right up to finally winning the Copa América in 2021. La Albiceleste may have frequently had the players, the star names who could set any match ablaze, but often, when it came to the crunch, Argentina had consistently fallen short since the days of Maradona. They'd had Batistuta, Crespo, Ortega, Riquelme, Tevez and Messi – the list of greats is extensive – but none could rid Argentina of the dominance of Brazil. Even when Brazil were at weaker points in those intervening years, they could consistently look down on Argentina, beating their rivals when it mattered and going deeper into tournaments, including twice winning the World Cup since that 1990 trauma.

For Argentina, 2014 represented the opportunity to reverse 20 years of history since their last trophy win at the 1993 Copa América. That tournament victory had included a quarter-final win over Brazil, but since then, for all the wonderful players at their disposal, Argentina were unable to add any more silverware for nearly two decades. Since reaching the final of the World Cup in 1990, Argentina had not gone further than the quarter-finals, and had twice not even reached that stage. They'd even gone out in the group stage in 2002 as Brazil added their fifth world title. Brazil, in contrast, not only won two additional World Cups but also won the Copa América four times.

Even when Argentina reached a Copa América Final again for the first time since their 1993 triumph, it was Brazil who were there to destroy their hopes in the cruellest of ways in the 2004 final. Argentina had been seconds away from victory, leading 2-1 in the closing moments thanks to what had seemed a late winner from César Delgado, only for Adriano to equalise three minutes into added time. Following an extra-time stalemate, Argentina fell apart in the penalty shoot-out. The pair met again in the 2007 Copa América Final, and this time Argentina had stormed their way through the competition in far better style than Brazil had managed. Any hopes of glory were quickly dashed again, however. Brazil led the final after only four minutes, and were given a helping hand thanks to an Argentinian own goal and another of their own to comfortably win 3-0 against an Argentina including the likes of Juan Román Riquelme, Carlos Tevez, Javier Mascherano and, yes, a young Lionel Messi.

At every turn, Argentina were haunted and thwarted by Brazilian success. But now, in 2014 with Messi at his sublime peak, it was the perfect opportunity to change all of that, the chance to get one over Brazil and win the World Cup in Brazil's backyard, to be the 'Papa' once again.

'Argentina has a sense of cultural superiority over Brazil that had emerged in the early 20th century,' explained Dr Peter Watson. 'But they have a lot of doubts about their own footballing superiority. They've failed to win when they don't think they should have done. And now this was the perfect moment to establish that permanent one-upmanship.'

Messi had made his first World Cup appearance in 2006, coming off the bench to score in a group match with Serbia and Montenegro a few days short of his 19th birthday. In the process, he became Argentina's youngest-ever World Cup player and scorer, and indeed the sixth youngest goalscorer in World Cup history. He played in the final group match when many of the first-choice players were rested, and came off the bench again in the last-16 tie with Mexico. But when he was left on the bench for the quarter-final loss to Germany, his exclusion was one of the main criticisms made of the coach, José Pékerman, for Argentina's failing.

Beyond just Messi, this had been a magnificent Argentina team, inspired by the enigmatic Riquelme and a fine supporting cast, who had the talent to go much further than the quarter-final they reached. Their elimination to Germany led to lost heads on the field and recriminations off it with a real opportunity missed, but the optimism for the future was high, thanks to the emergence of the mercurial Messi.

Messi was rapidly developing into one of the world's best, and he quickly became a regular in the starting 11 for Argentina, taking his place in that 2007 Copa América Final with Brazil. But in playing as part of a strike partnership with Tevez, he was forced into a position and a system which didn't suit him. The role he needed was more withdrawn, a position occupied at that time by the lavishly languid Riquelme.

A year later, Messi was more central to the team that won the 2008 Olympic gold medal in Beijing – Argentina's only international title since that 1993 Copa América – where he and Riquelme combined to great effect, with Sergio Agüero and Ángel Di María also coming through to make their mark. Messi would even go head-to-head with the man he had replaced at Barcelona, the Brazilian Ronaldinho, in the semi-final. With Messi dominant, almost taunting the Brazilians with his abilities, Argentina finally bested their great rivals, going on to win the final against Nigeria thanks to a Di María goal set up by Messi.

Until the 2021 Copa América victory, for this Olympic gold to be the high point of Argentina's international record in the post-Maradona age was incredible. Even the victory over Brazil in that Olympic triumph can't be fully held against their rivals as the Olympics are not full internationals, but an under-23 tournament. Messi, and Argentina, still had to deliver when it really mattered.

It also wasn't the signal for any great Argentinian revival led by their new hero, now firmly ensconced as one of the world's best players. The 2010 World Cup saw Maradona in charge of the team, having come in to rescue a troubled qualifying campaign more through sheer force of personality than anything else. In South Africa, the team's tactical naivety was ruthlessly torn apart by a youthful, talented Germany in the quarter-finals. In the 2011 Copa América held in Argentina, the team, now under the stewardship of Sergio Batista, was even worse. Booed off in the group stages, there were frequent arguments between players, and when Argentina were beaten on penalties by Uruguay in the quarter-finals, the recriminations were intense.

Messi was hounded by the Argentinian media for his apparent inability to reproduce his magnificent form for Barcelona when wearing the national colours. Despite the many Champions League successes and the endless stream of Ballons d'Or, Messi struggled to replicate his club form for Argentina, falling short of the heights hit by Maradona in the sky blue and white. Always being viewed in comparison to Maradona, who consistently produced for Argentina when it mattered, Messi's more sporadic contributions frustrated many. This constant need to measure Messi's achievements against those of Maradona is a natural one, given their comparable other-worldly talents, and, of course, their nationality. But it served to make the Argentinian shirt weigh heavily on Messi's shoulders, expected to live up to an impossible ideal, or be damned for failing.

There are many nuances to this, of course, not least how the game has changed since Maradona's day. Equally, though, at Barcelona Messi played in a system and with players suited to help bring the best out of him. At Barcelona he was a cog in the wheel, albeit one capable of magic that no others could replicate, whereas with Argentina there was more of an apparent reliance, born of the Argentinian mythologising of the number ten as something of a magical figure. When it really matters, it is the number ten that Argentinians look to, but equally when it goes wrong, they are the one criticised for not producing the magic.

Such issues caused Messi's relationship with Argentinian fans to be somewhat strained at times, and worlds away from the adoration Maradona was always lauded with. Messi has spent most of his life in Spain, not in Argentina, having left his hometown club, Newell's Old Boys of Rosario, when still a teenager to join the Barcelona youth set-up. The easy, lazy criticism for any performances not meeting the lofty expectations, for explaining why he couldn't do it for Argentina when it mattered, was to decide he lacked Argentinianness, that he was now more Catalan than Argentinian. Argentina's great hope, yes, but some felt he wasn't quite one of them, not as committed. It's a short-sighted view, and far from the truth, of course, though Messi's aloof manner contrasted so much with Maradona's exaggerated expressions of patriotism that it became an easy line of attack.

Given his abilities and astonishing success with Barcelona, Messi was still the figure that all of Argentina looked to. For all of the great players they had produced who hadn't taken Argentina to the sharp end of a World Cup, now here was surely the man to do it. Through Messi, all of Argentina's unrequited dreams of glory could be fulfilled. If he could lead his country to World Cup victory in 2014, in Brazil of all places, Messi would fulfil the destiny his ability and his nationality had mapped out for him in the minds of so many onlookers, emulating the achievements of the player he was forever measured against.

It is a narrow view, of course, to suggest that winning a World Cup is a prerequisite to being acknowledged as a great. Very few are lucky enough to win a World Cup, and the overwhelming majority of those who have are infinitely inferior players to Messi, fortunate to be in the right place at the right time and, crucially, hailing from the right country. But certainly within Argentina, for Messi to emulate Maradona would elevate him to being at least close to the great Diego, allowing him to escape the shadow cast by Maradona and find his own place in the hearts of Argentinians.

Following the disappointment of the 2011 Copa América, Argentina dispensed with the coaching services of Batista and gave the job to Alejandro Sabella. He was tasked with resurrecting La Albiceleste from what had been a relatively disastrous period. Sabella had been a measured and technical attacking midfielder in his playing days, lining up for the Argentinian giants River Plate and Estudiantes, and also having stints in English football with Sheffield United and Leeds United. As a coach, he had initially worked as assistant to Daniel Passarella, including a spell with the national team at the 1998 World Cup. In 2009, he went his own way to become head coach at Estudiantes, leading the La Plata club to a Copa Libertadores victory. Having left his role there in early 2011, he had been set to coach in the UAE before the Argentinian FA came calling.

To try to arrest the slide in the national team's fortunes, Sabella's first action was to declare Messi his captain, bestowing on him a responsibility that wasn't a natural fit in terms of vocal leadership. But Sabella's tactical switches would enable Messi to lead by example, ushering in arguably the finest spell of his international career. Sabella altered Messi's role, moving him to what was nominally a right-sided attacking position, but actually giving his key man the licence to roam wherever he saw fit. This freedom from restriction saw Messi blossom in the national colours. He scored ten goals in 14 games in the qualifying campaign as Argentina stormed their way to the World Cup, Messi pulling the strings of what was a hugely talented squad.

For all the fine attacking quality, Argentina's defence was also a fearsome unit. Backed up by the Sampdoria goalkeeper Sergio Romero, the experience of Ezequiel Garay, Martín Demichelis and Pablo Zabaleta lent a degree of reassurance at the back, with the excellent Mascherano or Fernando Gago providing protection at the base of the midfield. Attacking options were even more impressive with the pace and trickery of Di María on one flank, and Ezequiel Lavezzi on the other, with Messi joined by one or more of the striking talents of Agüero, Gonzalo Higuaín and Rodrigo Palacio.

One excellent striker not a part of Sabella's plans, though, was Tevez: an extremely popular player with Argentinian fans. Like Maradona before him, he fitted the Argentinian *pibe* stereotype, of the cunning street kid made good, fairly closely. Unlike Messi, he had served his time in Argentina and done so with distinction. But Tevez and Messi needed to be in the same spaces, they made the same runs, and they simply couldn't play effectively together. Tevez's popularity also saw some incidents overlooked. He had been dropped by Batista after he'd withdrawn from a squad, citing injury, only to appear for Manchester City days later. Political pressure saw him recalled, but he was dropped again for the final group game in the 2011 Copa América where the team played well and with far greater balance without him. When he came on as a substitute in the semi-final defeat to Uruguay, he was seemingly sulking and disinterested. His miss in the penalty shoot-out was symbolic of this attitude and saw Argentinian public opinion start to shift. When he was suspended by Manchester City later that year for refusing to come off the bench in a Champions League match, that gave Sabella, by then the new national team coach, the excuse to leave him out, the team gelling into a hugely effective unit and system without Tevez.

Having topped the South American qualifiers, suffering only two defeats in the 18-game qualifying marathon, Sabella's methods had successfully crafted a team capable of scoring freely while also remaining solid in defence. In Argentina, ahead of the 2014 World Cup, optimism was high that this generation could finally succeed where so many other hugely talented squads had failed. There was a strong sense of togetherness, which had developed during the steadily improving qualifying campaign, as the troubles of the recent past were replaced with a team that at last looked capable of reaching the heights that its talent warranted.

Drawn into an opening group with Bosnia and Herzegovina, Iran and Nigeria, there was little for Argentina to fear, and an opportunity to ease their way into the tournament. And yet the group gave them all sorts of problems. The first was arguably of their own making. Abandoning the 4-3-3 formation that had proved flexible and successful when used in the majority of the qualifiers, Sabella opted instead for a 5-3-2 approach in the opening game with Bosnia, primarily as a way of risking fewer of his injury-hit forward line.

In the Maracanã, where Argentina's World Cup would reach its ultimate end point a few weeks later, it was Bosnia who played the more impressive, fluid football. Having taken the lead early on through an unfortunate Sead Kolašinac own goal from Messi's whipped cross free kick, Argentina were unable to establish much of a foothold, sitting back, through an inability to get any forward momentum going as much as from the slick but largely unthreatening play of the Bosnians.

The story goes that Messi was one of those urging a change in formation at half-time, back to that which had served them so well previously. Sabella did indeed make the change, resulting in a much more impressive display after the break, leading to the first of many flashes of Messi magic just when Argentina needed them the most. He picked the ball up just inside the Bosnian half, paused for a moment assessing his options, then seemingly decided to go and win the game by himself.

Messi surged forwards and played a delicate one-two with Higuaín, side-stepping two defenders, leaving them prostrate and tangled in his wake. Faced with three more defenders, he bypassed them completely, rifling a shot into the far corner. Inside the stadium the exultation was tinged with relief that their star man looked more than ready for the World Cup challenge, registering his first goal in a World Cup since that debut goal against Serbia and Montenegro eight years earlier. In the space of just six or seven seconds, Messi had ignited Argentina and their boisterous fans, turning what was a match on a knife-edge into a done deal.

Bosnia scored a late goal to make it 2-1, but by then the story had been set. When Argentina needed Messi, when they had been largely second best and struggling, he delivered a wondrous goal to save the day. Against Iran, this feeling would be enhanced as the team struggled for fluency again in the face of an obdurate opponent. The Iranians not only defended brilliantly but also came extremely close to scoring on more than one occasion: a header from Ashkan Dejagah forcing a desperate save from Romero in one particularly close shave for Argentina. La Albiceleste were becoming increasingly frustrated: the party atmosphere being replaced with a growing sense of unease. As the match entered stoppage time still goalless, it seemed that Iran had succeeded in gaining a vital, and hugely impressive, point. But it only takes a moment to change a match, and, once again, Messi delivered.

With only moments remaining, Messi took control just outside the right-hand corner of Iran's penalty area. Faced with the entire Iranian 11 in the narrow space between him and the goal, he shifted the ball on to his left foot and curled a sublimely fierce shot beyond the despairing dive of the excellent Alireza Haghighi, finding the narrow space between his fingertips and the post. As the net bulged, and Messi ran to the crowd, arms stretched wide in celebration, he wore an expression that made it seem all in a day's work for him, as if such moments of majesty were commonplace. It was a wonderful goal in any context, but to do it in such a precarious moment, with the burden of expectation hanging heavy and the stuttering tensions mounting – Maradona himself had already left the stadium in irritation – was stunning. This was a player seizing the moment, deciding to win the game himself when nobody else could.

Again, the narrative was set. Two games, two goals, fleeting moments of Messi magic when his team absolutely needed it. He wasn't taking entire games by the scruff of the neck, but then neither did Maradona in the 1986 group stages. But he was doing what the greats do, and coming up with just what was needed at just the right time. Messi was delivering for Argentina.

A 3-2 win over Nigeria followed in the final group match, with Messi scoring twice more. His first was early on, after Di María had been unfortunate not to score, denied by a terrific save from Vincent Enyeama, Messi lashing in the rebound. His second came from a fabulous free kick, curled into the corner, succeeding where an earlier sighter had only narrowly failed. It was a very open match, with Nigeria chasing the point they would have needed to progress had Iran won against Bosnia in the other fixture. Argentina were twice pegged back in the only real instance of Argentinian defensive weakness in the tournament, save for the scares they had just about repelled against Iran. Marcos Rojo scored the winner with a header from a corner early in the second half, making it 3-2 to Argentina. As

Nigeria soon realised they were set to qualify anyway, the pace of the game slowed, allowing Argentina to see out their third win in a row, while the fans serenaded all and sundry with renditions of their 'Brazil, tell me how it feels' song on an apparently endless loop.

Argentinian fans were taking over Brazil's cities now whenever their team came to town. Indeed, it was around this final group match in Porto Alegre, in Brazil's south, not too far from Argentina, that a hugely popular YouTube clip shows Argentinian fans taking over a food hall in the city, dancing and singing their song, transposing the stadium terraces to a more everyday setting. The party mode was becoming their default setting, inspired by Messi and the moments he was producing to keep Argentina winning. Having come through the group unscathed, but without really fully igniting, their overall performance levels would need to be raised as they progressed into the knockout rounds. But with Messi in fine form, Argentina were in a very strong position to make it to the latter stages.

Against Switzerland in the last 16 in São Paulo, however, it would be a tense occasion with the Swiss arguably having the better of the opportunities, in the first half at least. Both Higuaín and Messi went close early in the second half, with Argentina continuing to grow into the match as it progressed, Di María proving increasingly troublesome for an obdurate Swiss defence. He had already gone close before he finished off a fine move, having been released by Messi. It was a moment of great quality amid an anxious match that remained on a knife-edge throughout. Argentina were fortunate to scrape through, particularly since the Swiss midfielder Blerim Džemaili somehow failed to convert a last-gasp, back-post header which rebounded off both the post and Romero before bundling wide. It was a let-off in a match where Argentina had their moments, but had been largely frustrated and intensely tested.

They would begin their quarter-final, with Belgium, rather more on the front foot, with Higuaín volleying in a fine opener in only the eighth minute, instinctively turning and firing in. The same player came close to making it 2-0 early in the second half, his shot glancing the crossbar after a superb, storming run through a back-pedalling Belgian defence. Belgium's opportunities were largely limited by a fine defensive performance from Argentina, just about holding on for a 1-0 win. But as much as the defence was robust throughout, the attack was limited to sporadic bursts, with Messi foiled on his one clear chance at goal. Argentina had made it through another tough test to continue on to a semi-final with another strong European nation: the Netherlands.

The day after Brazil's humiliation in their own semi-final, the World Cup was enveloped in an odd mood. The Brazilian hosts were stunned, a nation in disbelief at what had just happened to them, though the manner and margin of their defeat meant that denial was one emotion not available to them. There was a sense that Germany were now champions-in-waiting following their 7-1 demolition of Brazil, but there were two other teams still in with a chance even if the second semi-final had an element of after the Lord Mayor's Show about it.

Argentina had never failed to come through a World Cup semi-final victorious, but the 2014 version would not be one of their more comfortable victories in the last four. Their Dutch opponents had been one of the early favourites thanks to some magnificent results in the group stage. Their 5-1 demolition of the reigning champions Spain was an astonishing result of tactical and technical excellence, only surpassed in the ranks of surprises by the German semi-final victory. But the Dutch had laboured a little ever since, in a clear parallel with their Argentinian opponents. Narrow victories over Mexico and Costa Rica, on penalties, made it appear that the Dutch, led by Louis van Gaal, had peaked too soon.

The semi-final was a defensive stalemate with the high-stakes tension pervading everything, providing a sharp contrast to spectacular events of the night before. Messi was shadowed everywhere he went by an ever-present cabal of Dutch players, whose tactics on the night were to stifle and contain, such was the fear and dread that his presence caused. He had gone close with a free kick but was otherwise kept largely at bay. The Dutch came closest through Arjen Robben's surging run into the box in the second half, only to be denied by a quite breathtaking block by Mascherano. He had scrambled and stretched so much that he later revealed he had torn his anus in doing so – yes, really.

Palacio might have scored in extra time with a bit more control of his close-range header, while Messi went on one of his surging runs, shrugging off the repeated close attention of the Dutch defender Ron Vlaar, only for his cross to be weakly fired at goal by Maxi Rodríguez. As the match petered out, the inevitable penalties hove into view. Unlike in their quarter-final shoot-out win, the Netherlands were unable to substitute their goalkeeper. Newcastle United's Tim Krul had come off the bench to completely psych out Costa Rica on that occasion, but now the Dutch had to continue with Jasper Cillessen. He had played well through the match but was considered less effective than Krul when facing penalties.

The tone was set when Romero saved the first Dutch kick from Vlaar, not one of the Netherlands' most obvious penalty takers. In stark contrast, the first Argentinian taker was Messi, very much a practised penalty exponent. When he duly scored, the pressure on the Dutch became too much. Robben scored, but when Sneijder's shot was also saved by Romero the game was up. Rodríguez converted Argentina's fourth successful penalty and La Albiceleste were through to their fifth World Cup Final.

Argentina may have had the best player in the world at the time, but given the style with which Germany had reached the final, it was they who would go into the showpiece match as favourites, demoting Messi to the unusual position of being an underdog on the big occasion. There was considerable World Cup history to the clash of Argentina and Germany too. Not only were the 1986 and 1990 finals contested between the two, with spoils shared, but Germany had also knocked Argentina out of the two tournaments prior to this 2014 meeting. A close encounter in the 2006 quarter-final arguably ought to have gone Argentina's way but a groundswell of momentum for the German hosts on that occasion saw them fight back to earn a penalty shoot-out in which German cool prevailed over some Argentinian lost heads. In 2010 things were far more clear-cut: Germany's young bucks demolishing a tactically deficient Argentina 4-1. The core of that German squad remained the heart of the side that was now on the verge of glory.

For Argentina, they may not have reached the 2014 final with quite the same swagger as the Germans, but they were lifted on their own surge of optimism with the backing of thousands of their partying countrymen in Rio. And what is more, in a Brazil that was humiliated, hurting and embarrassed, they had the chance to rub salt into those raw wounds by winning the World Cup in their bitterest rivals' home. They had finally emerged from the Brazilian shadow that had held sway over Argentina since 1993, or in World Cup terms, since 1990.

To Brazilians, their own humiliation was so profound that perhaps it no longer mattered who won the final. As one report of the time put it, 'If the country has stopped crying, it is because they ran out of tears.' But deep down, the fact that they simply had no grounds to look down on Argentina, in what was supposed to be their own redemption, cut deep. As the hordes of Argentinians on the Copacabana and beyond sang 'Brazil, tell me how it feels' with increasing gusto, the impending Brazilian doom of an Argentinian victory increasingly struck home.

Instead of Brazil, it was Argentina who stood on the edge of history, with the beaten hosts either forced to root for the team that had so humiliated them just days before, or to maintain an increasingly uncomfortable position of South American solidarity. Argentina felt assured back in the comfort of the place they always felt was theirs: being South America's best. Having already become champions over Brazil, going the distance when Brazil couldn't, they would now become champions of the world.

Given the manner of Germany's semi-final victory, there was something of an assumption that Argentina would need to set up very defensively in order to contain them. But this Argentina defence was solid and had not conceded yet through the knockout stages, while prior to that astonishing semi-final, Germany had not been particularly free-scoring, struggling against Algeria before beating France with a set-piece goal. The less emotive analysis of the two finalists would suggest an even contest in which fine margins could make the difference. Having the world's best player on your side can't hurt in that situation, although after his group-stage heroics, Messi had certainly been increasingly shackled as the tournament wore on.

Argentina as a whole had not played particularly well, however. There was an apparent sense of deference to Messi that perhaps held some of his colleagues back at times, though not to the extent it would do so in the years following 2014. But if Argentina were to win through, it may need the likes of Higuaín, Agüero and others to come to the fore when opportunity knocked. They would remain without the injured Di María, Lavezzi retaining his place from the semi-final in his stead, but there was an abundance of attacking flair in Argentinian blue to match that in German white. That Germany would not set out to simply stifle Messi and Argentina, as the Dutch, Belgians and Swiss had all done, but to attack and aim to seize the initiative, may also lead to greater opportunity for Messi and company to exploit. It was an initiative they took, and one that really could have seen them to victory.

The first real chance of the match fell Argentina's way, and what a chance it was. A poor, loose header from German midfielder Toni Kroos sent Higuaín free, bearing down on goal. Perhaps he had too much time; perhaps he would have succeeded if the proximity of German defenders had forced him to rely on instinct? As it was, he seemingly lost his nerve, scuffing his shot wildly wide when he should have given Argentina the lead.

This would be the story of Argentina's night. It looked to be going differently soon afterwards when Messi battled his way free in midfield, releasing Lavezzi in acres of space on Argentina's right. His fine cross was met by Higuaín who side-footed home, only to be correctly flagged offside. This all came in a period of the match when Argentina were the dominant side, putting in a stronger performance than they had managed in their recent matches, certainly more so than in the semi-final. As in these opening minutes, however, their night overall would be defined by the chances they didn't take.

As well as Higuaín's big chance, there was the moment early in the second half when Messi was released into the box at a wide angle by a fine through ball from Lucas Biglia. He may not have been as free as Higuaín had been, but by Messi's lofty standards, to shoot wide when presented with such a glimpse of goal was an opportunity spurned. In extra time, the best chance fell to Palacio, whose attempted lob of Neuer fell narrowly wide when a better first touch may have given him a greater chance to score.

Neuer, as fine a keeper as he was, arguably should not have been on the pitch for much of the second half and extra time due to an incident shortly after half-time, soon after Messi's miss. With Higuaín poised to latch on to a ball at the edge of the German box, Neuer raced out and leapt to punch clear, but in doing so his knee struck Higuaín in the jaw. It wasn't intentionally brutal, like the Harald Schumacher incident against France in 1982, but in taking man and ball so recklessly it should have been a penalty and, under the rules at the time, a red card too. Instead, the Italian referee, Nicola Rizzoli, gave a free kick against Higuaín.

None of this is to imagine that Germany didn't have great chances too – Benedikt Höwedes heading against the post in the first half when he too should have scored being the clearest example – but that Argentina created more such opportunities, more moments when World Cup glory seemed within their grasp. Ultimately, though, it was the one chance that fell the way of Germany substitute Mario Götze, left woefully free in the penalty area, which decided the destiny of the 2014 World Cup. As his volley flew past Romero there were still seven minutes remaining in extra time, but it felt conclusive. The contrast of German celebration and Argentinian despondency echoed those thoughts, as did the haunted expressions on the Argentina fans that the Brazilian TV directors repeatedly picked out in the crowd. Argentina seemed crushed, their world falling around them, rather than desperate to lay siege in the final moments.

The deference of his team-mates towards Messi was still hindering the team even at this late, desperate stage. A couple of minutes before the end, a nicely worked move saw the ball fall to Biglia centrally on the edge of the box with an opportunity to shoot. Instead, he scuffed an uncomfortable, inaccurate pass to try to find Messi to his right, which was lofted well over their star man and went out of play. An opportunity spurned, but a vivid representation of how others were unwilling or unable to take responsibility even at that stage of the game. All hopes were pinned on Messi.

There was a final moment for him, though. Well into added time, Argentina won a free kick a good 30 yards from goal. A long way out it may have been, but it was their only hope. As fans offered their prayers, Messi lined up his shot while having to wait for the injured Bastian Schweinsteiger to be treated right in front of him. His effort ballooned way over the bar, and the day was done. The chance to win the World Cup in Brazil's iconic home was gone. As all of Brazil breathed a sigh of relief, for Argentina there was nothing but emptiness. The fullness of time would bring the consolation of having bettered Brazil, of not having the catastrophic demise the hosts had suffered, but their hopes of really being the 'Papa' in Brazil's house were gone.

'I don't know what can I say … it's a pity,' was the best a devastated Messi could muster reflecting on the defeat. 'It's a pity given all the chances we had in that game. We had the better chances and, well … we'll regret the chances we had but couldn't score for the rest of our lives.' In a moment of unnecessary agony, Messi had to suffer the ignominy of collecting the golden ball for the best player of the tournament as part of the post-match festivities.

The comparisons to Maradona were unrelenting in the aftermath, Messi narrowly failing to do what his hero had done. Even those arguments exposed the truth of how the expectation seemed to be on Messi, and Messi alone, to deliver the World Cup. In part, this is down to the Argentinian adulation of the number ten, almost deifying those who perform this playmaking role. For this to lead to an over-expectation on those same players, and a deference to them on the field, is no great leap. In Messi's case, this feeling was enhanced by his stature as one of the greatest-ever exponents of the game, and with it the sense of expectation.

Sabella, who had already declared he would step down following the final regardless of the result, was despondent but proud in the aftermath of the 2014 defeat, 'The players are bitter and sad because we had a huge dream having made it all the way to the final. We needed to be more clinical and I am sad just like the players. Beyond the pain of defeat in the final they can look themselves in the eyes and say they gave everything for Argentina.'

And this is where the ever-present question over Messi, and whether his heart was ever fully with Argentina, returned. For all the love of La Albiceleste that he frequently declared, this convenient, lazy criticism was talked about in the aftermath of defeat. As the academic Grant Farred wrote in *Entre Nous: Between the World Cup and Me*, 'Winning for Barça and not replicating that level of success for Argentina not only fed the notion that Messi was ... Catalan, first, and perhaps last and always, but it gave substance to the sense that he was Argentine only by the accident of birth.' This notion was reserved for the paranoid to my mind, but feeds the desire of Argentina, like with Brazil and their loss, to explain it away on a perceived weakness: a lack of Argentinianness. Messi was the number ten, the lauded genius, and in seeking answers to why they had lost, why he had not delivered the World Cup for them, some chose to castigate in this way.

For Messi himself, the defeat ensured the pressure on him would build yet further rather than dissipate. He had a self-confessed need to prove he was capable of winning something for Argentina, having picked up every other accolade in football. This wasn't just for the glory this would bring, but to also define his relationship with the Argentinian people. Messi would again be denied international success with Argentina following 2014, going close to winning the Copa América in both 2015 and the 2016 centenary edition, losing on penalties to Chile in the final on both occasions; frustratingly, a team who were coached by Argentinians both times. Messi missed his spot kick in the 2016 final, adding to the personal disappointment.

Such was the vitriol after the 2016 Copa América in some quarters, when Messi and Argentina lost a third final in successive years, that he quit the national team in frustration amid increased criticism and doubts, only to change his mind following a public outcry and a presidential intervention. The 2018 World Cup saw another failure, losing a spectacular match to France in the last 16 in a tournament where Argentina's sole game plan seemed further skewed towards reliance on Messi. They then lost the 2019 Copa América semi-final to Brazil in Belo Horizonte – the Argentinian upstarts put back in their place once more by Brazil.

International success may have finally arrived for Messi and Argentina in the 2021 Copa América, in Brazil no less, but that period from 2014 to 2016 was a painful one. Three finals, all lost, but none so hurtful as that of the 2014 World Cup. The pain all served to make that eventual 2021 victory both an incredible joy and massive relief for Messi, left visibly emotional at a burden finally lifted. A whole generation had never witnessed a trophy for Argentina, and it was on Messi that all hopes were pinned. He may have delivered seven years after this ultimate opportunity in 2014, but missing the global success that was at Argentina's fingertips merely served to intensify the questioning of his commitment and ultimately his Argentinianness.

Sabella wasn't immune from blame too, drawing criticism particularly for his substitutions in the final. Replacing Lavezzi with Agüero, and Higuaín – dynamic, if wasteful – with Palacio seemingly blunted the Argentinian attack. They had certainly played better in the first half and early second half, but there were few game-changing options available to him.

Higuaín would suffer the recriminatory glare too. For all the expectation on Messi, Higuaín's miss early on was the worst. His fine, instinctive finish in the quarter-final win over Belgium was seemingly forgotten in the haste to apportion blame in the wake of final defeat. His career had seen him score plenty of decisive goals for Argentina in the World Cup and Copa América, yet it is his fate to be best remembered for those he didn't score on the big occasion; his World Cup Final miss added to by other spurned opportunities in the Copa América finals that followed.

In 2015, Higuaín could have tapped in a last-gasp winner at the back post, only to miss the target. His 2016 miss was more forgivable but had similarities to 2014 in that an instinctive player had possibly too much time to think. With each lost final, and each decisive miss, the intensity of the condemnation increased, causing Higuaín to quit the national team following the 2016 final. Unlike Messi, there was no huge campaign for his return. There's nothing fair about it, and it's a real shame for a player whose ability and consistency saw him regularly selected ahead of the likes of Agüero, Tevez and Mauro Icardi, but he bore much of the blame for the 2014 World Cup loss, as he did for the subsequent lost finals too. As much as Messi had been expected to deliver, when the talisman failed to win a tournament thanks to the misses of others, the story became that Higuaín had denied Messi an international title at that time. It is such a simplified view of a variety of complex reasons why Argentina failed to win the World Cup or the Copa América, but football, like life, is rarely fair.

'People remember the goals I missed and not the ones I scored. I'm sure everyone celebrated against Belgium,' Higuaín said, in reference to his quarter-final winner. 'When you criticise someone maliciously, it hurts everyone. I saw how much my family suffered, but I gave everything for the national team. It's one thing to say that we did not achieve our objectives, but when people talk about failure, it's very hard.' Had Higuaín or Palacio or Messi scored in the 2014 final, however, this Argentina, with its tough, obdurate defence marshalled by Mascherano, may well not have failed, but delivered the grandest trophy of them all.

For Brazilians, traumatised by their own disaster, the relief was overwhelming. 'It would have rubbed a lot of salt, and chimichurri, in our wounds,' Fernando Duarte told me. 'We would never have heard the end of it had they won there.' To Argentinian eyes, victory would have validated all claims of sporting and cultural superiority, overlooking that Brazil would still have had more World Cup triumphs overall. The significance to both nations of this final had it gone Argentina's way simply can't be overstated. 'Shame about Messi,' added Duarte. 'But I would have hated to live in a world in which Argentina lifted the World Cup in the Maracanã.'

Were Argentina the best team in the 2014 World Cup? Definitely not, though they frustratingly had the ammunition to be so. But having reached the final, does their play and chances created mean that Argentina should have won it? Absolutely.

I don't want to claim that Germany were fortunate to win. Far from it. They edged a close match, were the best team of the tournament as a whole, and worthy winners. But you'd have to be ignoring the obvious to contend that Argentina didn't have the best chances of the final. Had they taken any one of these several great opportunities, perhaps it would have been Messi rather than Philipp Lahm who lifted the trophy in Rio. Given the way the match played out, it really should have been the crowning glory of a career of such exquisite brilliance.

Messi was and continues to be the finest player of his generation; one of the greatest of all time. He had the composure and the confidence to deliver, having done so at critical moments so many times before. Throughout the 2014 World Cup, when it appeared that nobody else was capable, it had been Messi who had suddenly conjured up one decisive moment after another. And yet Messi, perhaps even more so than Higuaín and Palacio, the others guilty of missing eminently scoreable chances, will be haunted by the memory of the moment when he faced Neuer all alone with World Cup immortality just a successful strike of his left boot away, but shot wide.

Epilogue

Winning is an important thing, but to have your own style, to have people copy you, to admire you, that is the greatest gift.

Johan Cruyff

I AM a football fan who is both blessed and cursed as I seem to naturally and unwittingly side with teams who are destined to either fall narrowly short, or a long way short. I seem to find a greater beauty in tales sporting tragedy than I do in those of triumph. I'm not sure why this is. After all, I would surely take all due delight if I were ever to witness my club win a trophy, or for England to win the World Cup.

The best teams losing pains me, whether they are my team or not. But the blessing is that I can take solace and indeed focus more keenly on the fact that victory is not everything. There is a beauty in defeat, a majestic poetry in dreams crushed and destiny unfulfilled. It's not that there is always a right or wrong winner, but the narrow margins of victory and defeat are too often too narrow to be the sole judge of a team's worth. Their legacy, impact and enduring memory can be worth so much more.

I think perhaps it is all Kevin Keegan's fault. He made me revel in footballing beauty and magnificence as a player and manager at Newcastle United, without the ultimate pay-off of a tangible reward at the end of it. Instead, the wide-eyed fan is left with only the intangible to cling onto. The memories of the style, swagger and graceful dynamism live longer than any memories of those who ultimately won out instead.

Perhaps, too, it is the fault of Brazil in 1982 and Denmark in 1986, who both dazzled my youthful eyes and receptive mind so wonderfully. Or perhaps it's the fault of those I never got to witness first-hand, but whose exploits and agonies so astonished me as I grew to know and understand more of the history of the World Cup: the Hungary team in 1954, or the Netherlands of 1974, the Austrians, the Brazilians, and more. Their stories all seemed to me so frustrating: the unfulfilled destiny that should by rights have been theirs. Football does not work like that, though, and it is all the better for it.

Where would the joy be if the outcome always favoured the supposed best? Where would the jeopardy be? That agonising, gut-wrenching despair we all feel in moments of high tension when it is all on the line. For me, I feel this most during a World Cup: a tournament that has always resonated with me more than the regular grind of the club game. I find a degree of purity, an appeal that grabs me on a level that the money-oriented big leagues of the club game can't quite replicate. There is an epic quality to a World Cup; national identities and aspirations, political ideals and influences, all played out on this grandest of stages. My blessing is that I can feel this when watching any great team on the World Cup stage, deriving great pleasure from teams beyond my own.

When you are a fan of football, rather than solely a supporter of one team, the game opens up so much more to you. This allows you to delight in the wondrous Brazilians of 1982, get swept up in the emotions of Italy's doomed path in 1990, and be awestruck at Bergkamp's brilliance. It allows you to hope for victory, for fulfilment for these teams, and then to feel the pain of their defeat far more than a more distant observer would.

But if writing this book has taught me anything, it is that victory is just momentary. It only lasts as long as it takes for someone else to claim the prize for themselves. Sure, it can't be taken away: that success, that moment of fulfilment is marked in the history books, the trophy is displayed, the honours list updated. But then what? Success moves on to someone else, and the moment is gone. But legacy is another matter. Legacy does not belong to the victor alone. Frequently, that legacy is all the greater for the vanquished. After all, there can be only one winner, but each tournament can provide countless tales of unfulfilled dreams and unrewarded greatness, and a legacy that outstrips that of the ultimate winner.

Some of the most loved teams played in a way that delighted those watching on, both their own fans and neutrals alike. They are remembered because they gave such joy to people, and played football with beauty and delight. Is it that such footballing beauty is incapable of claiming the biggest prize? Is a dose of pragmatism required to go all the way? Perhaps those whose beauty lasts through the generations are doomed to fail so they can live on in our hearts and minds more than in the list of champions on the trophy itself. Perhaps glory must be sacrificed on the altar of beauty. That to live on in our memories longer than many winners, the price to be paid is ultimate failure.

But then, too, the fact that these glorious teams lost is another reason we remember them so fondly. It is precisely the pain of defeat, the frustration of unfulfilled talent, of glory unclaimed that appeals to us. It is because they lost that we remember them and that they frustrate us so. Without the failure, there wouldn't be the pain, and without the pain, there wouldn't be the longing recollection. Failure and the fond memories go hand in hand.

We are drawn to sporting pain on a personal level in a way that victory can't often match. This is where the true legacy lies and where those like me gain our own fulfilment. In seeing the beauty in sporting tragedy, appreciating that there is something far greater than victory, our minds are open to the richness of the game we love. This is where you find the greatness that doesn't need victory in order to define it.

Bibliography

Books:

Araf, Jo, *Generazione Wunderteam* (Pitch Publishing, 2021)

Bailey, David, *Magical Magyars: The Rise and Fall of the World's Once Greatest Football Team* (Pitch Publishing, 2019)

Bellos, Alex, *Futebol: The Brazilian Way of Life* (Bloomsbury, 2014)

Bergkamp, Dennis, *Stillness and Speed: My Story* (Simon & Schuster, 2014)

Burns, Jimmy, *Maradona: The Hand of God* (Bloomsbury, 2010)

Cruyff, Johan, *My Turn: The Autobiography* (Macmillan, 2016)

Davies, Pete, *All Played Out: The Full Story of Italia '90* (Mandarin, 1990)

Downie, Andrew, *Doctor Socrates: Footballer, Philosopher, Legend* (Simon & Schuster, 2018)

Duarte, Fernando, *Shocking Brazil: Six Games That Shook the World Cup* (Arena Sport, 2014)

Falcão, Paulo Roberto, Brasil 82: *O Time que Perdeu a Copa e Conquistou o Mundo* (Brazil 82: The Team that Lost the Cup and Conquered the World) (Editoria AGE, 2012)

Farred, Grant, *Entre Nous: Between the World Cup and Me* (Duke University Press, 2019)

Foot, John, *Calcio: A History of Italian Football* (Harper Perennial, 2007)

Freddi, Cris, *Complete Book of the World Cup* (Harper Sport, 2006)

Glanville, Brian, *The Story of the World Cup* (Faber & Faber, 2014)

Goldblatt, David, *Futebol Nation: A Footballing History of Brazil* (Penguin, 2014)

Goldblatt, David, *The Ball is Round: A Global History of Football* (Penguin, 2007)

Hart, Simon, *World in Motion: The Inside Story of Italia '90* (De Coubertin Books, 2018)

Horsfield, Stuart, *1982 Brazil: The Glorious Failure* (Pitch Publishing, 2020)

Kuhn, Gabriel, *Soccer Vs. the State: Tackling Football and Radical Politics* (PM Press, 2011)

MacDonald, Rob & Bushby, Adam, *From the Jaws of Victory: A History of Football's Nearly Men* (Halcyon Publishing, 2020)

Maradona, Diego, *El Diego: The Autobiography* (Yellow Jersey, 2005)

Mason, Tony, *Passion of the People?: Football in South America* (Verso, 1995)

Mølby, Jan, *Jan the Man: From Anfield to Vetch Field* (Gollancz, 2000)

Perdigão, Paulo, *Anatomia de uma Derrota: 16 de julho de 1950 – Brasil x Uruguai* (Anatomy of a Defeat) (L&PM Editores, 2014)

Perryman, Mark, *1966 and Not All That* (Repeater, 2016)

Puskás, Ferenc & Taylor, Rogan, *Puskás on Puskás: The Life and Times of a Footballing Legend* (Robson Books, 1998)

Reid, Michael, *Brazil: The Troubled Rise of a Global Power* (Yale University Press, 2015)

Smyth, Rob, Eriksen, Lars & Gibbons, Mike, *Danish Dynamite: The Story of Football's Greatest Cult Team* (Bloomsbury, 2014)

Syed, Matthew, *The Greatest: The Quest for Sporting Perfection* (John Murray, 2017)

Thacker, Gary, *Beautiful Bridesmaids Dressed in Oranje: The Unfulfilled Glory of Dutch Football* (Pitch Publishing, 2021)

Wilson, Jonathan, *Angels with Dirty Faces: The Footballing History of Argentina* (Orion, 2016)

Wilson, Jonathan, *Behind the Curtain: Football in Eastern Europe* (Orion, 2006)

Wilson, Jonathan, *Inverting the Pyramid: The History of Football Tactics* (Weidenfeld & Nicolson, 2013)

Wilson, Jonathan, *The Names Heard Long Ago: How the Golden Age of Hungarian Football Shaped the Modern Game* (Bold Type Books, 2019)

Winner, David, *Brilliant Orange* (Bloomsbury, 2000)

Publications:

A Noite
Bleacher Report
Daily Herald
Daily Mail
Daily Record
Daily Telegraph

El Diario
El Grafico
ESPN
FIFA.com
FourFourTwo
Game of the People
Goal
In Bed With Maradona
Irish Times
Jornal dos Sports
La Gazzetta dello Sport
La Prensa's comment noted
Manchester Guardian
Mundial Magazine
New York Times
Neues Wiener Journal
O Globo
O Mundo
Olympics.com
Pariser Tagezeitung
Rodaviva
SB Nation
The 42
The Blizzard
The Guardian
The Observer
The Times
These Football Times
Welt am Montag
World Soccer

Documentaries:

Soccer Shoot-Out: The Official Film of 1990 FIFA World Cup Italy

The Last Yugoslavian Football Team

Also available at all good book stores

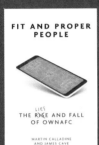

9781801500470

9781801501002

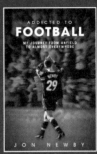

9781801500739

9781801500876

9781801500906

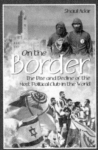

9781801500913

9781801500920

9781801500951

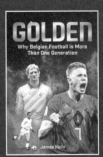

9781801501057